Introduction

T his book is the companion volume to The History Channel's documentary series *10 Days That Unexpectedly Changed America*. The History Channel selected the dates after a long, deliberative process that included an all-day meeting with a group of distinguished historians who suggested dozens of possible days. Viewers also made suggestions. Over the next few months, a small group of historians and producers discussed, debated, and sometimes fought over which days should be on the final list. There was one issue on which we all did agree: given the difficulty of gaining proper historical perspective on the recent past, we chose not to include any event that occurred after 1965.

Obviously any list is subjective and no two people will agree on the same days. We deliberately sought out surprising dates that would provoke discussion and debate. That meant overlooking many obvious choices—the signing of the Constitution, the first shots of the Civil War fired upon Fort Sumter, and the attack on Pearl Harbor—in favor of days whose importance and impact have been undervalued. That impact could be as real and dramatic as the bloody Civil War battle of Antietam, or as subtle and symbolic as Elvis Presley's appearance on *The Ed Sullivan Show*.

The range of topics chosen also covers the span of our history from settlement to the recent past, and reveals the great diversity of our national experience. Reflecting changes in recent historical scholarship, the days tell the story of our past from the bottom up

1

and from the top down. They tell the story of rural farmers, gold-seeking forty-niners, immigrant workers, and disenfranchised African Americans all seeking their pieces of the American dream. But it also tells the story of noble statesmen, powerful presidents, decisive generals, and brilliant scientists who almost single-handedly changed the course of history.

After choosing the days, The History Channel commissioned ten award-winning filmmakers to produce the documentaries and asked me to write the companion book. I worked independently of the filmmakers: we did not share notes or discuss narratives. As a result, the book examines the same days but often uses different facts to make its case. While each of the documentaries focus exclusively on one day, the book develops themes that tie the days together.

Taken together, the days shed light on what it means to be an American. In most nations, national identity is determined by either birth or geography. As the famous nineteenth-century French observer Alexis de Tocqueville noted, however, Americans were unique because "they have arrived at a state of democracy without having to endure a democratic revolution; and they are born equal, instead of becoming so." Since they were "born equal," Americans shared a distinctive ideology that revolved around a commitment to the ideals of individual freedom, equality, and democracy. "It has been our fate as a nation not to have ideologies but to be one," observed the historian Richard Hofstadter.

That ideology has many sources, but our first day, which tells the story of the English attack on the Pequot stronghold of Fort Mystic on May 26, 1637, reveals its Puritan origins. The Pequot war guaranteed the success of the Puritan experiment in the New World. Over time, the Puritans would play a major role—perhaps the central role—in shaping what would later evolve into a unique

American political culture. According to the social scientist Samuel Huntington, the Puritans were "the original source . . . of the mortal passion that has powered the engines of political change in America." Puritanism, he argued, "bequeathed to the American people the belief that they were engaged in a righteous effort to ensure the triumph of good over evil." Puritan moral absolutism provided American politics with what Hofstadter called "fits of moral crusading." "There have been few more persistent themes in American politics," wrote the political scientist Grant Mc-Connell, "than that of outraged virtue."

In the eighteenth century, "outraged virtue" inspired the colonists to revolt against the injustices of the British empire and to articulate a set of "shared ideals," which found full expression in the Declaration of Independence: "We hold these truths to be self-evident, that all men are created equal, that they are endowed by their Creator with certain unalienable Rights, that among these are Life, Liberty, and the pursuit of Happiness." In 1944, Gunnar Myrdal referred to this constellation of ideals as "the American Creed" in his book *An American Dilemma*. He pointed out that despite the nation's enormous diversity, Americans had "something in common: a social ethos, a political creed," which he defined as "the essential dignity of the individual human being, of the fundamental equality of all men, and of certain inalienable rights to freedom, justice, and a fair opportunity."

The American revolutionary experience gave birth to the American Creed, but it left many questions unanswered. Who would share in the benefits of democracy? What was the proper balance between individual liberty and social order? How do you reconcile conflicts within the creed between, for example, the belief in individualism and the desire for equality? How do you protect democracy from foreign threats without undermining the ideals of democracy at home? Over the next two centuries, Americans would struggle to answer those questions. The fights, many of them documented here, took place in the streets and in courthouses, on bloody battlefields and in the halls of Congress. Each of the battles helped clarify the meaning of the American Creed and define what it means to be an American.

The commitment to these vague but deeply held ideals has been the source of much of the social conflict in America. Most political reform movements in America have been inspired by the contradiction between the ideals of freedom and equality and the reality of everyday life. That tension was built into the nation's founding documents, finding full expression in the gap between the soaring ideals of the Declaration of Independence and the harsh reality of power politics enshrined in the Constitution. In the most striking, and most painful, contradiction, Thomas Jefferson, who penned the words "all men are created equal," also owned slaves, and the Constitution embedded slavery into the foundation of the new republic.

Each of our days provides a snapshot of the nation as it attempts to address some of the tensions at the heart of the American democratic experiment. These days reveal that our national identity is not set in stone; it is full of internal tensions and contradictions and has evolved over time as the nation struggled, often against its will, to reconcile its soaring idealism with practical necessity. America, in other words, is a work in progress.

In addition to addressing the tension between American ideals and practice, the days underscore the importance of contingency in history—the idea that key moments are often the product of random events, not purposeful action. Many of the essays ask how American history might have changed had events turned out differently. Would the founders have adopted a different constitution had Daniel Shays not led his ragtag army in rebellion against Massachusetts authorities? How would American history have unfolded if Lee's Special Orders No. 191 had not been found and given to General McClellan in the days before Antietam?

Finally, the book places people at the center of the story of America's past. While recognizing that history is often the product of large impersonal forces and that change can be painstakingly slow, the stories told here show how individuals, sometimes by design but often by accident, can change the course of history.

HISTORY™

10 DAYS
THAT UNEXPECTEDLY
CHANGED
AMERICA

THE HISTORY CHANNEL® PRESENTS

HISTORY™

10 DAYS
THAT UNEXPECTEDLY
CHANGED
AMERICA

Steven M. Gillon

THREE RIVERS PRESS
NEW YORK

All rights reserved.
Published in the United States by Three Rivers Press, an imprint of the
Crown Publishing Group, a division of Random House, Inc., New York.
www.crownpublishing.com

Three Rivers Press and the Tugboat design are registered trademarks of
Random House, Inc., New York.

THE HISTORY CHANNEL and the "H" logo are registered trademarks
of A&E Television Networks. All rights reserved.

Library of Congress Cataloging-in-Publication Data

Gillon, Steven M.
    Ten days that unexpectedly changed America/Steven M. Gillon.—1st ed.
    1. United States—History—Anecdotes. I. Title.
    E178.6G55 2006
    973—dc22   2005037101

ISBN-13: 978-0-307-33934-8
ISBN-10: 0-307-33934-3

Printed in the United States of America

Design by Maria Elias

10 9 8 7

First Edition

This book is dedicated to Nick Davatzes, CEO Emeritus, AETN.

Contents

1

May 26, 1637
Massacre at Mystic

O n the moonlit night of May 26, 1637, Puritans from Massachusetts Bay Colony attacked a large Pequot village at a
place called Missituck, located near the Mystic River in Connecticut. The assault began on May 25 with an all-day march through
solidly held Pequot territory. As dusk approached, the seventy
English, seventy Mohegans, and five hundred Narragansetts warriors led by Major John Mason and Captain John Underhill
reached the outskirts of the Mystic settlement, where they decided
to rest for a few hours. By 2 A.M. on the morning of the twenty-
sixth, the English were poised to put an end to the war that had
been raging between them and the Pequot for more than a year.

With the aid of clear skies and a brightly lit moon they began
their final assault. Mason and Underhill divided their forces into
northern and southern contingents and attacked through the two
entrances to the village. According to their own accounts, Mason
led his men through the northeast gate when he "heard a Dog
bark, and an Indian crying *Owanux! Owanux!* Which is Englsh-
men! Englishmen!" After removing piles of tree branches that

blocked their approach, Captain Underhill led his men through the other entrance with "our swords in our right hand, our carbines and muskets in our left hand." The Pequots, initially startled by the attack, quickly regrouped and pelted the invaders with arrows. Two Englishmen were killed and twenty others wounded. Some were shot "through the shoulder, some in the face, some in the legs."

Instead of engaging the Englishmen, many of the Pequots, especially women and children, stayed huddled in their wigwams. Frustrated that his enemy refused to fight by traditional European rules of engagement, Mason decided to burn the village. He lit a torch, setting fire to the wigwams. At the same time, Captain Underhill "set fire on the south end with a train of powder. The fires of both meeting in the center of the fort, blazed most terribly, and burnt all in the space of half an hour." Dozens of men, women, and children were burned alive. Mason observed that the Pequots were "most dreadfully amazed . . . indeed, such a dreadful Terror did the Almighty let fall upon their Spirits, that they would fly from us and run into the very Flames, where many of them perished." Another Englishman who saw the slaughter wrote: "The fire burnt their very bowstrings . . . down fell men, women and children . . . great and doleful was the bloody sight." After setting the fires, Mason ordered his men to "fall off and surround the Fort." From this vantage point, they slaughtered anyone trying to flee the flames. The carnage was so frightening that Uncas, a Mohegan sachem (chief) allied with the English, cried, "No more! You kill too many!"

The light of a late spring morning brought into full focus the carnage that had been perpetrated the previous night. The Pequot were reeling from the most gruesome act of ethnic cleansing perpetrated by European colonizers on American soil. Fort Mystic lay in smoldering ruins. Dwellings that once housed Pequot families were reduced to hot piles of ash, and the once formidable wooden palisade that surrounded Mystic was burning. Hundreds of Pequots were either dead or dying—mostly women, children, and elderly members of the tribe. The stench of burning human flesh filled the morning air. "It was a fearful sight to see them," observed William Bradford, who came to America on the *Mayflower* in 1620 and served as governor of Plymouth Colony, "thus frying in the fire and the streams of blood quenching the same, and horrible was the stink and scent thereof; but the victory seemed a sweet sacrifice, and they gave the praise therof to God, who had wrought so wonderfully for them, thus to enclose their enemies in their hands and give them so speedy a victory over so proud and insulting an enemy."

Major Mason considered his actions that day to be righteous, and he went to his grave believing that the violence at Mystic pleased the English God in true Puritan form. "Sometimes," he wrote, "the scripture declareth that women and children must perish with their parents . . . We had sufficient light from the word of God for our proceedings." Mason, like most of the English commentators of the era, framed the conflict in terms of savagery and civilization; the "civilized" Protestants of the English empire were asserting their natural authority over "savage," pagan, and dark-skinned Indians. As the last fires at Mystic burned out, news of the tragedy spread throughout New England. A new and terrible era had begun.

* * *

The battle at Mystic had its roots in the initial contact in the early seventeenth century between English settlers and native peoples living in New England. The Pilgrims, who arrived in 1620, had the good fortune of encountering Squanto, a Wampanoag who helped the Pilgrims adjust to their new world. Within a few years, however, relations between the Pilgrims and local tribes soured. No matter how friendly the initial contact, it could not alter the English view of natives as untrustworthy savages. Indians, preached Anglican bishop John Jewell, were "a wild and naked people" who lived "without any civil government, offering up men's bodies in sacrifice, drinking men's blood . . . sacrificing boys and girls to certain familiar devils." Over the next few years the settlers stole native crops and acquired their land. In 1622, a militia captain killed eight friendly Indians, impaling the head of the sachem on top of the fort at Plymouth as a clear signal of their power. The Indians had a word for the white settlers: *wotowquenange*, which meant stabbers or cutthroats.

Both sides were already deeply suspicious of each other by the time Jonathan Winthrop and the six hundred Puritan settlers arrived on the shores of Massachusetts in June 1630. Unlike the mostly male crews of fortune seekers and laborers that landed in Virginia more than a decade earlier, the Puritans who founded the Plymouth Colony came as families—husbands, wives, children, and servants—seeking to locate permanently. They came to America determined to create a "Citty on the Hill," a utopia where individuals would work in common struggle to serve God's will. Winthrop wanted to escape a decadent England, with its Catholic queen, beggars, horse thieves, and "wandering ghosts in the shape of men." The Puritan mission was to tame the wilderness so their commonwealth would "shine like a beacon" back to immoral England.

The Puritan families wanted land and access to all of the bounties that the New World had to offer—a goal that put them in competition with the Indians for local natural resources. Most

Puritans viewed Indians as dangerous, temporary obstacles to permanent English settlement in New England, not potential partners in the development of a new society. "The principall ende of this plantacion," their charter stated, was to "wynn and incite the natives of [the] country, to the knowledg and obedience of the onlie true God and Savior of mankinde, and the Christian fayth."

The Puritans came to America prepared to use force to achieve their ends. The Massachusetts Charter instructed settlers "to encounter, expulse, repel, and resist by force of arms" any effort to destroy the settlement. The settlers who arrived in Massachusetts aboard the *Arabella* were told to "neglect not walls, and bulwarks, and fortifications for your own defence." They brought with them five artillery pieces, skilled artisans who could make weapons, and a handful of professional soldiers. Shortly after arriving they set up a militia company. All males between the ages of sixteen and sixty were expected to serve.

Within the first three years as many as three thousand English had settled in the colony. By 1638, the population had swelled to eleven thousand. As the colony grew, the Puritans laid claim to land owned by the Indians. As God's "chosen people," the Puritans felt entitled to the land occupied by native tribes, often using Scripture to justify the outright seizure of territory. The new land was an untamed wilderness and their job was to subdue it for the glory of their God. The Puritans also offered secular justifications for taking possession of the land. Winthrop created a legal concept called *vacuum domicilium*, which proposed that Indians had defendable rights only to lands that were under cultivation. "As for the Natives in New England, they inclose noe Land, neither have any setled habytation, nor any tame Cattle to improve the Land by," Winthrop reasoned. If they left Indians land "sufficient for their use, we may lawfully take the rest, there being more than enough for them and us."

The Puritans' most powerful weapons in seizing Indian land were neither laws nor guns, but microbes. Over the centuries, Europeans had been exposed to and, through a process of evolution, developed immunity to a host of viruses. Indians, isolated on a distant continent, had never been exposed to the deadly microbes and therefore had no immunity. Smallpox was the biggest killer, but syphilis and various respiratory diseases added to the death toll. Tens of thousands of Indians died in the first year after the arrival of the English. By some estimates, disease killed 75 percent of the tribes in southern New England in less than two years. An Englishman wrote that the Indians had "died on heapes, as they lay in their houses, and the living that were able to shift for themselves wouyle runne away and let them dy, and let there Carkases ly above the ground without buriall."

As more Puritans disembarked in America, their settlements expanded farther west and south, eventually bringing them into contact with the Pequot. There were roughly thirteen thousand Pequots occupying the two thousand square miles of territory between the Niantic River in Connecticut and the Wecapaug River in Rhode Island. Little is known about the Pequot before their contact with Europeans. One historian described them as the "most numerous, the most warlike, the fiercest and the bravest of all aboriginal clans of Connecticut." Like other native tribes in southern New England, they depended on farming, hunting, and fishing for survival. The main difference between them and other nearby tribes, such as the Narragansett, Nipmuc, and Mattabesic, was that the Pequot built fortified villages. By 1637 they had constructed two large fortified hilltop villages—at Weinshauks and Mystic. In addition to these forts, they built smaller villages nearby containing as many as thirty wigwams, which were surrounded by a few hundred acres of cultivated land.

Highly organized with a powerful grand sachem and tribal council, the Pequot managed to establish military dominance over the other tribes in New England. In an effort to monopolize trade with early Dutch explorers, the Pequot subjugated nearby tribes. By the 1630s, the Pequot were the dominant political and military force in the area. Not only had they established extensive trading networks throughout the region, but they also occupied some of the region's most fertile soil.

Just as the English were planning to expand into Pequot territory, the tribe was decimated by disease. By 1634, the tribe that had numbered thirteen thousand a few years earlier now had only three thousand. John White, a planter in New England, wrote that "the Contagion hath scarce left alive one person of an hundred." Whole Indian tribes were decimated—too sick to hunt, fetch wood for fire, or take care of one another. Their bodies were full of bursting pox boils; "their skin cleaving by reason thereof to the mats they lie on. When they turn them, a whole side will flay off at once, and they will be all of a gore blood, most fearful to behold." The Puritans believed that the epidemics were gifts from God. "If God were not pleased with our inheriting these parts," Puritan Jonathan Winthrop wondered, "why did he drive out the natives before us? And why doth he still make room for us, by diminishing them as we increase?"

The once powerful Pequot found themselves under assault from all directions. Not only were they reeling from disease, they faced new economic competition. The Pequot occupied land that was rich in wampum—small sea shells drilled and strung together into beads. Until the arrival of the Europeans, wampum had served as a medium of exchange and communication for many tribes. They used it to create the insignia of sachems, command the service of shamans, console the bereaved, celebrate marriages, end blood feuds, and seal treaties. The Dutch, and later the English, however, recognized the economic value of wampum and started using it as a form of currency. Initially, the Pequot benefited from a lucrative trading system that involved exchanging wampum and furs for European manufactured goods. Eventually, however, the English decided to make their own wampum. Using steel drills, they produced large quantities of wampum, driving down its value and undermining the source of the Pequot's economic power.

The Pequot were divided over how to respond to the new economic threat posed by the English. The sachem Sassacus, deeply distrustful of the English, called for building an alliance with the Dutch to try to repel the English. The sub-sachem Uncas, who had married Sassacus's daughter, opposed these efforts. Believing it was futile to resist the more numerous and well-armed English, he advocated cooperation. (Uncas would be forever remembered as the fictionalized character in James Fenimore Cooper's *The Last of the Mohicans.*) The debate between these two powerful men ripped the tribe apart at a critical moment. After a series of heated debates, the tribal council sided with Sassacus and forced Uncas to leave the village. An angry Uncas formed a separate tribe, the Mohegan, and joined forces with the English in an effort to destroy his former tribe. Decimated by disease and torn apart by rival factions, the Pequot had never been more vulnerable.

The English moved quickly to take advantage of the opportunity. The immediate cause of the horrific attack on Mystic was revenge for the deaths of two Englishmen. In 1634, Captain John Stone, an English merchant, and his crew were found dead on their ship on the Connecticut River. Stone fell far short of the

God-fearing ideal for an Englishman of the times. He was a notorious drunk, cheat, and liar. At the time of his death he was in
trouble for stealing a ship full of Dutch trade goods from the
Dutch governor of New York after a night of hard drinking.
(Stone got the governor drunk as a diversionary tactic.) Informants from the Narragansett told colonial authorities that the Pequot ruthlessly murdered Stone and his men in their sleep. The
Pequot told a different story. They claimed that Stone had taken
two Indians captive. When Stone refused to release them, they
took the ship by force. "This was related with such confidence and
gravity," Winthrop said, "as having no means to contradict it, we
inclined to believe it."

Although they believed the Pequot version of events, colonial
authorities faced a dilemma. They could not let the murder of
Englishmen go unpunished, but they were not exactly heart-
broken by the death of the unscrupulous Captain Stone. Never-
theless, they needed to punish somebody. It was important, the
English believed, to set an example: God's people needed to deal
sternly with the savages. In 1634 the English demanded that the
Pequot provide them with more beaver pelts and wampum
strands, as well as swift delivery of the "murderers" of Captain
Stone. The Pequot opted for large land cessions to meet the economic obligations of the treaty (ceding most of Connecticut to
the English), but they would not deliver Stone's "murderers" to
colonial authorities.

In the summer of 1636, Massachusetts authorities were tired of
waiting. On July 4, they commissioned Jonathan Winthrop to deliver a final ultimatum to the Pequot: turn over those responsible
for Stone's death to the proper authorities or suffer the wrath of
English military forces. If they failed to comply, the English
would "revenge the bolld of our countrymen as occasion shall

serve." The ultimatum became moot when, on July 20, the mutilated body of John Oldham, another English merchant trading in
Pequot country, was found aboard his ransacked ship. John Underhill, later a participant in the slaughter at Mystic, wrote that it
was the "Block Islanders" who "pretended to seek trade with John
Oldham, and once aboard his ship killed him, and stole all of his
goods." The tragic irony, however, is that the "Block Islanders"
were not even Pequot—they were a subtribe of the Narragansett.
Such details did not bother the English.

The English commissioned Captain John Endicott to seek revenge for the murders of Stone and Underhill. In August 1636 he
set sail from Boston with about ninety men. Endicott was the
epitome of all things Puritan: his long yet trimmed beard, his
curled mustache, his square face, and his deep-set eyes bestowed
upon him an aura of sober piety. A leader in New England since
his arrival at Salem in 1628, Endicott was an imposing figure of
authority. As former governor, and in 1636 the assistant governor to Jonathan Winthrop, he had spent his years in the colony
making sure that the Puritan ideals became reality. Now his goal
was to punish the Indians. For his first campaign he added to his
black robes and broad white collar the body armor of an English
military captain and set out to settle the score with the Block
Islanders.

Unfortunately for Endicott, the Block Islanders anticipated his
attack. Just before dusk on August 22, 1636, Endicott's small army
landed in three ships on the coast of Block Island. According to
Underhill, "fifty or sixty able fighting men, men straight as arrows,
very tall, and of active bodies . . . their arrows notched" waited for
the landing party. After unleashing a heavy barrage of arrows, the
natives disappeared into the darkness. His troops spent the next

two days "burning and spoyling the Iland." But when the attack was over, only one Indian and a number of the tribe's dogs lay dead. Dismayed by the lack of bloodshed, Endicott and his men fled to Connecticut in search of Pequot to punish. Once again, the Indians slipped away, although the English managed to kill one man, destroy a few wigwams, and steal some corn. Afterward, Endicott decided to allow his men a few days of rest at nearby Fort Saybrook. The residents were not thrilled to see him, realizing the Indians would later punish them for providing refuge. "You come here to raise these wasps around my ears, and then you will take wing and flee away," cried the fort commander.

After four restless days at Fort Saybrook, Endicott and his men sailed to the Pequot River. Pequot and Western Niantic were apparently unaware of Endicott's mission, despite his previous skirmishes. According to Underhill, "The Indians spying us came running in multitudes along the water side crying, 'what cheer, Englishmen, what cheer, what do you come for?' to Pequot river." The next day a Pequot elder boarded one of the ships and asked the English for the purpose of their visit. An officer explained that "the governors of the Bay sent us to demand the heads of those persons that had slain Captain Norton and Captain Stone and the rest of their company." A few hours later, Endicott attacked the village, but once again, the Indians had already fled into the woods. "Thus," an officer said, "we spent the day burning and spoiling the country." Endicott then returned to Boston.

Just as the Fort Saybrook commander had feared, the "wasps" began to sting. By April 1637, eight months after the Endicott expedition, the Pequot had killed thirty colonists in Connecticut— about 5 percent of the English population. They took numerous female captives, burned storehouses, and slaughtered livestock.

Many of the victims were tortured and dismembered. At Saybrook, the natives seized a captain, "tied him to a stake, flayed his skin off, put hot embers between the flesh and skin, cut off his fingers and toes, and made hatbands of them."

The Puritans then declared war against the Pequot, mobilized their fighting units, and prepared for battle. Both sides engaged in a desperate struggle to win over the Narragansett, who could tip the balance of power in the region. The Pequot tried to convince them that, despite their past differences, they now shared a common goal of removing the British from the continent. For their part, the Puritans sent Roger Williams, a dissident preacher banished to Rhode Island, on a dangerous mission to meet the Narragansett tribe's chief. He sailed from Providence "all alone, in a poor canoe, and . . . through a stormy wind, with great seas." It was worth the effort: The Narragansett agreed to sever all ties with the Pequot and to aid the British. In return, the Puritans promised "perpetual peace."

The English raised an army of ninety men under Major John Mason, a veteran of European wars whom one contemporary described as "full of Martial Bravery and Vigour." In the spring of 1637, Mason set out for Saybrook to meet up with the Massachusetts militia and nearly six hundred Indian allies—five hundred Narragansetts and roughly seventy Mohegans. He was instructed "not to do this work of the Lord's revenge slackly." He wanted to send a clear signal that he planned to impose harsh punishment on the local Indians. He decided to set an example. On the journey to Mystic, Mason's Mohegan allies discovered a lone Pequot male. They took him prisoner and then tortured him. He was drawn and quartered, and as he lay dismembered, Captain Underhill (who joined Mason upon his arrival at Saybrook) delivered the final blow: a musket shot to the head.

* * *

The battle at Mystic lasted less than an hour but it cast a long shadow over future relations between Indians and English settlers. For the first time, the English Puritans realized they held the power to dominate the people they saw as godless savages, showing little reluctance in using overwhelming force to achieve their ends. Almost overnight, the balance of power in America shifted from the unorganized natives to the English colonists. The destruction of the Pequot removed a major obstacle to Puritan expansion and English settlement in America. It also destroyed any hope, in the words of one historian, that Indians and whites "could live with themselves, each other, and the land." In areas where the balance of power between natives and Europeans was more evenly distributed, the two sides were forced to develop a shared culture. This was the pattern that developed, for example, in the Great Lakes region, where neither the French nor the Indians had enough power to enforce their will on the other. But the pattern of brutal repression established in New England became the model for how whites would treat natives across the country. The Pequot War set up the tragic irony of American history: a nation founded on the highest ideals of individual liberty and freedom was built on slaughter and destruction of epic proportions.

After the destruction of Mystic, the Pequot were on the run and in hiding. Nearly two hundred surrendered to the Narragansett, hoping for better treatment than they would receive from the English. Over the next few months, the Englishmen used their superior firepower to massacre many of the remaining Pequot, eventually wiping out two-thirds of the tribe. Following orders to "utterly root them out," the Puritans beheaded the sachems they had captured and committed numerous other atrocities. A witness described how the English tortured one prisoner: "They tied one of his legs to a post, and twenty men, with a rope tied to the other, pulled him in pieces." The English beheaded one Pequot sachem who refused to cooperate. As a warning, they placed his head in a tree. (The site near Guilford Harbor is still known as Sachem Head.) The brutality was calculated not just to subdue the Pequot but to send a signal to other Indian tribes.

But the English still sought one final Pequot prize. They were determined to find the sachem Sassacus, who was traveling with about 400 of his followers. Major Mason followed in pursuit with about 160 men, including Uncas and his scouts, finally catching up with Sassacus in a village near Fairfield, Connecticut. After negotiating for the release of 200 women and children, Sassacus managed to slip away. Traveling west with about 80 warriors, he turned to his old enemies, the Mohawk, for help. He hoped to plead his case to the tribal council, but he and his warriors were killed before they had a chance. The Mohawk cut off Sassacus's head and sent it to the English as a token of friendship.

The war between the English and the Pequot came to an official end in September 1638 when the remaining tribal leaders signed the Treaty of Hartford, which revoked legal recognition of the Pequot nation. The Puritan authorities went so far as to forbid the use of the Pequot name. According to Major Mason, the step was necessary "to cut off the remembrance of them from the earth." The New Englanders then sold many of their Pequot captives into slavery to spend the rest of their days working in the sugar plantations of Barbados. The Pequot tribe, or so it seemed by the fall of 1638, was destroyed, and peace was restored to New England. But New England's troubles, and the story of the Pequot people, were far from over.

The Pequot War set in motion a process of destruction that would culminate with one of the bloodiest wars in American history: King Philip's War. This war, an extension of the Pequot War, ended all violent resistance by Indians to English colonization in New England. With the Pequot vanquished, the Puritans continued their expansion in North America south and west, their numbers growing to nearly fifty thousand by 1675. As they expanded their influence they clashed with other tribes, including some who had sided with the English in the Pequot War. That year, Metacom, a Wampanoag sachem known to the English as King Philip, spelled out his tribe's grievances with the Puritans in a meeting with the well-intentioned John Easton, the governor of Rhode Island. Fortunately for historians, Easton took detailed notes of the meeting.

Metacom was the grandson of Massasoit, the sachem of the Wampanoag who aided the settlers at Plymouth and who fought with them against other tribes. Massasoit believed that natives and English could coexist, but over time Metacom realized the English wanted domination, not cooperation. He watched the condition of his people deteriorate as they suffered one humiliation after another. The Wampanoag "had bine the first in doing good to the English and the English the first in doing rong," Easton quoted Metacom as saying.

Metacom complained that the English used phony contracts to grab large areas of land. In some cases, the chiefs "being given to drunknes, the English made them drunk and then cheted them in bargens." In other cases, they simply allowed cows and pigs to roam over the land, destroying traditional Indian hunting lands. The Wampanoag had assumed that "when the English [bought] land of them that they wold have kept ther Catell upone there owne land." Metacom also objected to Puritan missionary efforts to convert Indians to Christianity by setting up "praying towns" where natives would adopt an English way of life and pray to the Puritan god. The most famous missionary of this time was John Eliot, a plump man who first preached the Christian message to the Indians in 1646—in their own Algonquian language. Eliot took on the task of translating and publishing the Bible in the Algonquian language. He also wrote a tract titled *Indian Dialogs*—a step-by-step primer on how to get one's fellow tribesmen to reject their Indian identities and become "civilized." Most New England tribes resisted the missionary work. Less than 10 percent of the total Indian population of New England moved to praying towns, and only a few dozen natives were baptized.

The incident that brought the two parties back to the brink of war occurred when three of Metacom's followers were accused, tried, and convicted—and then summarily executed—for the mysterious murder of a "Praying Indian" named John Sassamon. In January 1675 Sassamon was found dead, his neck broken, beneath the ice of a local pond. Sassamon was no ordinary Indian. When his parents died of smallpox, he was raised by adoptive English parents and fought for the English in the Pequot War. He learned English from John Eliot and he later helped establish the praying town at Natick. Sassamon made such a strong impression that Eliot sent him to Harvard. When he returned he served briefly as King Philip's scribe and interpreter until the sachem discovered that he was using his translating skills to gain land for himself. Sassamon fled, living briefly in a praying town before taking a plot of land near Assawompset Pond. Massachusetts leaders immediately assumed that he died at the hands of Indians doing the bidding of the increasingly insubordinate and uncontrollable Metacom.

After presenting his long list of grievances, Philip refused Easton's invitation to lay down his arms. A few days later Wampanoag warriors looted the town of Swansea in Connecticut. King Philip's War had begun. Over the next few weeks, Philip's forces set English towns on fire all along the Massachusetts and Connecticut frontier. By the summer, the other tribes in New England—primarily the Narragansett, Pocomtuck, and Pocasset—joined the Wampanoag effort in a final effort to preserve their culture and push the Puritans into the sea. By the winter of 1676, Indian warriors had attacked and burned the towns of Lancaster, Medfield, Weymouth, and Groton. The colonies were left reeling. Believing that Indian successes were a punishment from God, Puritans across New England engaged in a ritual of fasting, prayer, and days of humiliation, seeking forgiveness. By spring, it seemed as if Metacom would soon march into the heart of Boston.

The English directed their first successful offensive of the war not against the Wampanoag but the Narragansett—their former allies in the Pequot War. Under the leadership of Josiah Winslow, governor of Plymouth, the Puritan army planned to launch a Mystic-like raid on the Narragansett. In a scene strikingly familiar, the English surrounded the Narragansett's fortified village located on a small island in the "Great Swamp" just east of the Chipuxet River on December 19, 1675. They attacked before dusk, just as the Indians were eating. They forced their way through a gap in the fortress, torched wigwams and shot fleeing natives. Others were trapped in the inferno. "[T]hey and their food fried together," one English observer remarked. By the time it was over, more than three hundred Narragansett warriors and an equal number of women and children lay dead, but the English also paid a heavy price. More than eighty soldiers were killed or wounded.

The English brutality enraged other tribes. In February and March Indian armies attacked the town of Medfield, just twenty miles outside Boston. Over the next few months, fighting raged up and down the coast, from Maine to the upper Connecticut coast. Indians managed to raid Providence, Rhode Island, burning to the ground the home of that state's founder and former governor, Roger Williams, now in his seventies. In Lancaster, thirty miles west of Boston, Indians massacred all of the residents and took the wife of a local preacher captive; she lived to write an account of her ordeal, describing how Indians overran their cabins, dragged her friends outside, including a woman and a child, and hacked them to death. "Thus were we butchered by these merciless heathen, standing amazed, with the blood running down to our heels. . . . Oh the doleful sight."

It was only a matter of time, however, before the English quelled the rebellion and solidified their control over New England. On the night of August 12, 1676, the English and their Indian allies hunted down Metacom in his home village in Rhode Island. While he slept, a small company of soldiers surrounded his hut and opened fire. Metacom was shot and killed as he tried to retreat. The English captain who described his prize as "a doleful, great, naked, dirty, beast" ordered the body decapitated and quartered, the various pieces hung from trees. His head was returned to Plymouth where, during Thanksgiving celebrations in 1676, it was paraded through the towns as evidence of God's renewed favor for his chosen people.

King Philip's War devastated New England—nearly 5 percent of its European population died. Most of the inland Puritan towns lay in ruins. It would take forty years for the English to recover. But nearly 30 percent of the Indians of the region perished in the conflict. King Philip's War represented the last gasp of the Indian tribes of coastal New England. Puritan domination of New England was now complete. There would be no assimilation of Indian culture.

* * *

The Puritan victory over the Indians, which started with the raid at Mystic and ended with King Philip's War, set the pattern for European and Indian relations for the next two centuries. The war became part of the mythology of the American frontier as it advanced west: the triumph of light over darkness, civilization over savagery. By demonizing the Indians, and viewing the conflict as between the devil and God, the Puritans provided the nation with language it could use to justify wholesale destruction of native cultures. "The Devil decoyed those miserable savages [to New England] in hopes that the Gospel of the Lord Jesus Christ would never come here to destroy or disturb His *absolute empire* over them," observed Congregational minister and author Cotton Mather in 1702. The settlers, Edward Johnson proclaimed in 1654, had turned "this Wilderness" into "a mart" that attracted traders from throughout Europe. "Thus," he declared, "hath the Lord been pleased to turn one of the most hideous, boundless, and unknown Wildernesses in the world in an instant . . . to a well-ordered Commonwealth."

This image of transforming wilderness into civilization would emerge as a central ingredient in the notion of Manifest Destiny, repeated thousands of times as the settlers made their way across the continent. King Philip's War became, in the words of the historian Richard Slotkin, "an archetype of all the wars which followed." For the next two centuries, Americans drew sharp distinctions between themselves and native peoples, dismissing Indians as backward, uncivilized savages who needed to be conquered. From the Great Lakes to the Mississippi Delta, and eventually to the Pacific Ocean and beyond, all Native American people—as individuals, as families, as nations—confronted waves of immigrants who sought to divest them of land rights and eradicate their cultural heritage.

The pattern set in motion in the seventeenth century culminated nearly two hundred years later in May 1830, when Congress passed the Indian Removal Act, which forcibly transferred the tribes in six southern states to territory west of the Mississippi. "It gives me great pleasure to announce to Congress that the benevolent policy of the government, steadily pursued for nearly thirty years, in relation with the removal of the Indians beyond the white settlements is approaching to a happy consummation," declared President Andrew Jackson. In reality, the policy was anything but "benevolent." Over the next decade, the government forced more than seventy thousand Indians to abandon their homes to make room for white settlers, sending them on a harsh journey—the Trail of Tears—to unoccupied territory that would become the state of Oklahoma. "It is impossible to conceive the frightful sufferings that attend these forced migrations," observed Alexis de Tocqueville. "They are undertaken by a people already exhausted and reduced; and the countries to which the new-comers betake themselves are inhabited by other tribes, which receive them with jealous hostility. Hunger is in the rear, war awaits them, and misery besets them on all sides." The government promised they could occupy the new land for "as long as grass shall grow and rivers run." As was often the case, the government broke that promise when it was no longer convenient and forced them to move again in 1906.

While the Native American experience has been one of tragedy, it has also been a story of cultural renewal and triumph. In 1666, the English gave the Pequot a three-thousand-acre parcel of unspoiled woodland called Mashantucket. Through a vicious cycle of poverty, emigration, and loss of territory, no more than fifty Pequots were still on the reservation by 1921. Until the early seventies, three women, Elizabeth George and her half sisters, Martha Langevin and Alice Brend, lived on the 213.9-acre tract and served as leaders of the tribe. After the death of Elizabeth George in 1973, the Mashantucket Pequot reorganized under the leadership of her grandson, Richard Hayward, who worked to bring people back to the reservation, to recover stolen land, and to gain federal recognition.

Determined to keep the tribe alive, he and other tribal leaders petitioned the government for federal recognition in 1983, a move that conferred legal status, rights, and privileges and exempted them from many state and federal laws. On October 18, 1983, President Reagan signed a bill extending federal recognition to what was now known as the Mashantucket Pequot Tribe of Connecticut. The bill also returned to the tribe an additional fourteen hundred acres of land that had been illegally seized. Appropriately, the *New York Times* headline read: "Pequot Indians Prevail in Battle Begun in 1637."

Ironically, the Pequot used the sovereign status implied in their treaty, which the victorious Puritans had forced them to sign, in order to circumvent the Puritan traditions and laws that restricted gambling in Connecticut. On July 5, 1986, the Pequot opened their first bingo operation, which quickly expanded into six profitable casinos, the world's largest bingo facility, three resort hotels, theaters, salons/spas, gift shops, and golf courses. By 2004, Foxwoods Resort Casino was making an estimated $1.3 billion annually and was widely acknowledged as the world's most profitable gambling operation. The U.S. Census Bureau reported that in the year 2000, the Pequot population had risen to 590 individuals—most of whom have returned to the reservation or nearby areas. As of 1992, the Mashantucket Pequot were the wealthiest Native American tribe in the country.

The massacre unleashed by Major Mason on Fort Mystic that spring night in 1637—the "utter destruction" of which he so gleefully wrote—was never completed. The destruction of the Pequot and other native civilizations in North America cleared the way for the towns and villages that would soon emerge as the backbone of America's democratic experiment. The Pequot experience reminds us of our nation's tragic and violent origins. But it also highlights the redemptive quality of American democracy: its ability to adapt, to change, and, occasionally, to right past wrongs. In the end, the Pequot used democratic values and the legal institutions created to support them to reestablish their ancient claim to the land stolen from them by generations of European settlers. As one observer noted: "After a 350-year truce, the Mashantucket may actually have won the Pequot War."

For Further Reading

For an excellent general history of the period, see Gary Nash's very readable and provocative *Red, White & Black: The Peoples of Early North America* (1992). Anyone interested in pursuing further reading on the subject of the Pequot War or Pequot cultural reinvention must start with the collection of essays edited by Laurence M. Hauptman and James D. Wherry titled *The Pequots in Southern New England: The Fall and Rise of an American Indian Nation* (1990). Alfred A. Cave's *The Pequot War* (1996) is the most recent book-length treatment of the war. Ian K. Steele's *Warpaths: Invasions of North America* (1994) offers the reader a very concise outline of events, from Captain Stone to the Treaty of Hartford, and even continues on with King Philip's War in the 1670s. Also useful are Neal Salisbury's *Manitou and Providence: Indians, Euro-*

peans, and the Making of New England, 1500–1643 (1982) and Alden T. Vaughan's article "Pequots and Puritans: The Causes of the War of 1637," in Alden T. Vaughan and Francis J. Bremer, eds., *Puritan New England: Essays on Religion, Society, and Culture* (1977). Richard Drinnon's *Facing West: The Metaphysics of Indian-Hating & Empire-Building* (1980) contains an excellent biographical sketch of John Endicott.

There are numerous primary sources pertaining to the Pequot War. Some have been published and modernized for easier reading. Major John Mason's *A Brief History of the Pequot War*, John Underhill's *News from America*, and William Bradford's *History of Plymouth Plantation* have all been widely reproduced in the last few decades. Henry W. Bowden and James P. Ronda edited the last published edition of John Eliot's Indian dialogues, simply titled *John Eliot's Indian Dialogues: A Study in Cultural Interaction* (1980). Many of the historians who have dealt with the Pequot War have also written on the subject of King Philip's War. The most in-depth analysis of King Philip's War comes from Jill Lepore, author of *The Name of War: King Philip's War and the Origins of American Identity* (1998).

January 25, 1787

Shays' Rebellion:
The First American Civil War

Perhaps no document did more to shape the course of American history than the Constitution, which the convention delegates signed on September 17, 1787. The Constitution, and the Bill of Rights that followed in 1791, enshrined the principles of the American Revolution into law and created the framework that would govern our nation into the twenty-first century.

Every schoolchild knows about the heroic efforts of the founding fathers to turn their revolutionary ideals into practical government policy. But how many people, much less young students, have ever heard of Daniel Shays or the rebellion that bears his name? It is very likely that had Daniel Shays not taken up arms against his own government, the founders would not have abolished the truly dysfunctional Articles of Confederation and written a new constitution. There had been other attempts to abolish the articles and create a more powerful, central government. Each had failed. Shays' rebellion tipped the balance in favor of reform.

Daniel Shays is a shadowy figure. Since he never posed for a portrait, and none of his contemporaries ever described him, modern historians have no idea what he looked like. We do know that he was born in eastern Massachusetts, where he worked as a farm laborer before enlisting in the Revolutionary War. He rose quickly through the ranks to become a sergeant, fighting in some of the bloodiest battles of the war, such as Lexington, Bunker Hill, and Saratoga. He earned the respect of his men for his courage in battle. "I served in the company of Shays," recalled one soldier. "I knew him to be a brave and good soldier."

After the war, Shays returned home to Pelham in western Massachusetts, where he bought a small farm. He hoped to put his military past behind him, raise his family, and live out his life in the quiet countryside. He had risked his life to fight for the ideals of the American Revolution: to free the colonies from the burden of an oppressive government and to allow local communities, and their democratically elected representatives, to govern their citizens. But it soon became apparent to him, and many other veterans, that a new form of homegrown tyranny was quickly replacing the old British one. The problem was familiar: a distant government was imposing heavy taxes on its citizens, forcing many of them into debt—only this time it was not the British Crown but the elected state legislature in Boston.

The home to which Daniel Shays and thousands of other veterans returned after the Revolutionary War was very different from the one they had left—and not in ways they had expected. In western Massachusetts where Shays lived, survival depended on the barter of goods and services. A housewife might trade a female neighbor a bucket of peas for some sewing projects. A midwife would accept a sack of potatoes as payment for a home visit. A parson accepted a few chickens for his services. Barter was also used to acquire goods that were not produced locally at this time. The cycle worked like this: a farmer in western Massachusetts would turn over part of his wheat crop to pay his bill at the local dry goods shop. The shopkeeper would send the wheat, along with the crops collected from other farmers, to Boston to satisfy his own creditors. A Boston merchant would ship the wheat to Barbados or Jamaica, and send the proceeds from its sale to London to pay off debts to the London trading house that had sent the merchant the manufactured goods that he had distributed to small-town shopowners on credit. No currency changed hands; it all took place on paper in London.

That system came crashing down after the signing of the Treaty of Paris in 1783. Until the end of the war, the colonies belonged to the British empire and enjoyed all the rights of trade with other nations under British rule. Now that they were an independent nation, however, the colonies were considered a foreign country and lost many of their trading privileges, including access to Britain's Caribbean markets. Suddenly, British creditors demanded hard cash from American merchants. Faced with an end to the lucrative West Indies trade and confronting an economic downturn, many merchants needed to raise large sums of money to stay afloat. The large merchant houses pressured their debtors for payment; those debtors in turn put pressure on small businesses that owed them money.

The result was a chain reaction of defaults by farmers and small businessmen. Many farmers were forced to auction off their homes, furniture, grain, and livestock to cover their debts. They grew increasingly angry and frustrated as they helplessly watched local courts threaten family members with prison terms if they failed to pay their debts. By some estimates, as many as one in three families in Worcester County were forced into debt court. In early 1784 Daniel Shays was hauled into court by a merchant for a twelve-pound debt. A few months later, a retailer from Brookfield prosecuted Shays for three pounds.

At the same time they were being squeezed by merchants to pay their commercial debts, state legislators in Boston were raising taxes to pay off the state's war debt. Under the nation's first constitution, the Articles of Confederation (1781–1789), the central government lacked the power to regulate trade or to collect taxes. Each state was responsible for developing its own plan for paying back the staggering Revolutionary War debt. During the revolution, Massachusetts issued bonds to its troops instead of money. Speculators bought the notes from the hungry troopers at a fraction of their value. The state now owed its debt to a handful of powerful men who lived in Boston. Nearly all of these men either served in the legislature or had relatives who did.

After the victory at Yorktown and the end of the war, the Massachusetts legislature had to develop a strategy for paying back its debt. It could have followed the example of Rhode Island and simply printed more paper money, allowing people to pay their taxes and their debts with inflated currency—a position favored by farmers but opposed by merchants. Or Massachusetts lawmakers could have decided to lessen the burden by extending the length of payment over a number of years. Instead, the legislature chose to redeem at face value the notes that speculators had cheaply purchased from veterans and to settle the state's debt quickly—an approach that benefited Boston's wealthy speculators and hurt veterans and farmers. Poor farmers living in the western part of the state saw their tax burden increase by five or six times at the same time that the bonds, which they had earned for their wartime service but sold to wealthy speculators in desperation, began reaping generous profits. For many, the taxes were more burdensome than they had been under the British. In a cruel twist of fate, the heroes of the revolution were going broke paying their own salaries.

Initially, farmers tried to address their grievances by working through the legislature. After all, many were former Revolutionary War veterans who had risked their lives to establish democratically elected institutions for exactly this purpose. They petitioned the legislature to print paper money, lower taxes, and enact democratic reforms that would make both the legislature and the courts more responsive to their needs. Instead, they got the Massachusetts Constitution of 1780, which retained property qualifications for voting, offered judges tenure for good behavior, and gave the governor broad administrative powers. Year after year, the legislature adjourned without considering the request of farmers to lower taxes or print paper money.

In 1782, a preacher named Samuel Ely became the first to organize farmers in western Massachusetts. His target was the courthouse—the most obvious symbol of state authority in the area. He not only tried to shut down the local court, he also leveled a verbal broadside against the entire state government. Authorities arrested him and charged him with sedition for having stated that "the constitution is broke already, the governor has too much salary, the judges of the superior court have too much salary." He also warned that "the general Court should not sit. We will pay no more respect to them than to puppies." A supportive mob helped break Ely out of prison and he fled to Vermont.

As economic conditions worsened, frustration increased. Shortly after the end of the war a steep depression combined with rising inflation to cripple the young economy. As the prices for their crops dropped, farmers saw their wages plummet to less than forty cents per day, even as their taxes were increasing. Between 1780 and 1782, the Court of Common Pleas of Hampshire County in Massachusetts saw a 262 percent increase in the number of debt cases. More than 30 percent of adult males were unable to pay their debts. The situation was even worse in Worcester, where debtors made up 80 percent of those in the local jail—a dirty three-story building right out of a Dickens novel. In one year alone, 1785, the court processed four thousand suits for debt.

By the summer of 1786, patience was running thin. Farmers decided it was time to escalate their demands. They called for a countywide convention, to be held at the Hartford home of Colonel Seth Murray on August 22. Fifty towns were represented. The convention adopted twenty-one articles that, taken together, called for radical changes that would make the state government more responsive to their needs. The insurgents believed the leaders in Boston had betrayed the principles of the American Revolution. In a republican government, noted William Whiting, the people had the right to oppose tyranny. "Whenever any encroachments are made either upon the liberties or properties of the people, if redress cannot be had without, it is virtue in them to disturb government." The protesting farmers believed they were fighting to uphold the noble ideals of the revolution—ideals that had been subverted by a powerful elite in Boston. "I earnestly stepped forth in defense of this country [in 1776], and liberty is still the object I have in view," a rebel wrote in a local paper.

The Massachusetts insurgents were not out to destroy the government—despite the claims of their critics. Instead, their goal was to restore a moral economy where judges and other state officials would stop taking advantage of their positions of power in Boston and return authority to the town councils. They called themselves Regulators, a term taken from the volunteer bands that patrolled the Carolina backcountry during the 1760s. In North

Carolina, the Regulators were simple men who joined together to fight off corrupt sheriffs, lawyers, and colonial officials who supported land speculators and foreclosed on the property of poor people who could not pay their debts. Since they viewed themselves as true patriots, the northern Regulators adopted many of the symbols of the revolution. They modeled their meetings after the Committees of Public Safety set up by the patriots during the tense days before the revolution. They wore a sprig of evergreen as their badge. The evergreen was a symbol of liberty on Massachusetts flags and coins. It was the same symbol that George Washington's men wore during the Revolutionary War.

To underscore the seriousness of their demands, 1,500 farmers, many of them Revolutionary War veterans, marched in military formation with fifes and drums on the Northampton courthouse on August 31, 1786. The judges who sat in this courthouse frequently ruled against farmers who could not pay their taxes or jailed them for debts owed to merchants. When these judges, escorted by the sheriff, tried to enter the building, the farmers blocked their entrance.

The demonstration ignited a wildfire of protest. A few days later, a group of one hundred protesters armed with bayonets blocked justices from entering the courthouse in Worcester. The Regulators listened for two hours as Judge Artemus Ward, a Revolutionary War veteran himself, tried to convince them to desist. He failed and they forced the court to close. Hoping to put an end to the insurrection, Governor James Bowdoin called out the militia, but most either refused the call to action or sided with the rebels. The general in charge reported that despite "the most pressing orders," the vast majority of militiamen were reluctant "to turn out for support of the government." In Concord, hundreds of rebels prevented the local courthouse from opening. In Great Barrington, on the evening before the opening of the Berkshire County Court, a group of armed insurgents surrounded the courthouse. The following morning the militia, under the command of General John Paterson, marched into town with more than a thousand men. Within a few hours, however, more than eight hundred of his men had sided with the rebels, who demanded that the judges sign an agreement not to hold court "until the Constitution of the Government shall be revised or a new one made."

By the end of the year, the uprising involved more than nine thousand insurgents in every New England state except Rhode Island. "You would be astonished to know with what amazing rapidity the spirit of the insurgents propagates," noted Joseph Hawley. "Many are infected with it of whom you would never have the least suspicion." Hawley did not know who was fanning the flame, but "the fire is now become such a flame as I cannot describe it to you. The General Court have not had any affair of greater magnitude before them since the revolution."

Opponents, many of them also Revolutionary War veterans, viewed the protesters as a threat to the survival of the young republic. "Rebellion against a king may be pardoned, or lightly punished," observed Samuel Adams, "but the man who dares to rebel against the laws of a republic ought to suffer death." Men who had questioned whether democracy could succeed felt they were watching their worst fears being realized—a democratic "mob" destroying orderly government. One conservative said the rebels consisted of people "who wished to carry popular measures to such extremes as to shew their absurdity, and demonstrate the necessity of lessening the democratick principles of the constitution." They believed the central question facing the young republic was how to balance the demands of democracy with the need to preserve social order. "[I fear] evil minded persons, leaders of the insurgents . . . [waging war] against the Commonwealth, to bring the whole government and all the good people of this state, if not continent, under absolute command and subjugation to one or two ignorant, unprincipled, bankrupt, desperate individuals."

At issue were two very different views of the legacy of the American Revolution and the true nature of democratic government. For many farmers, the revolution represented a triumph of liberty over power. Individual citizens banded together in their local communities to repel a distant and oppressive foreign power that was unresponsive to their needs. They were inherently distrustful of centralized power, whether it was in London or Boston, and embraced a small-town version of democracy. The administration of government, they believed, should be kept close to home and reflect the needs and desire of "the people." Those who opposed the rebellion had a very different view of the revolution. They never intended to create a democracy; instead they wanted to replace a self-perpetrating aristocracy with a democratically elected meritocracy. In their minds, the ideal system would produce a delicate balance where the best men would naturally rise to the top of the political hierarchy.

Soon after the disturbances at Northampton, the Massachusetts legislature used the carrot-and-stick approach to bring about an end to the rebellion. The carrot included extending the deadline for paying taxes from New Year's Day to April 1, 1787. Plans were announced to sell a large chunk of land in Maine (then a district of Massachusetts) to alleviate part of the burden on taxpayers by providing some ready funds to retire the state's debt. An act was also passed that granted immunity to any insurgents who took an oath of allegiance to the state by the end of 1786. The stick included a proclamation that "whosoever officer or soldier shall abandon any post committed to his charge, or shall speak words inducing others to do the like in time of engagement, shall suffer death." In addition, the new legislation expanded police powers, permitting sheriffs and other officers of the state to fire upon groups of twelve or more armed men who refused to disperse upon command. It declared that rioters "shall forfeit all their lands, tenements, goods and chattels to the Commonwealth . . . and shall be whipped 39 stripes on the naked back, at the public whipping post and suffer imprisonment for a term not exceeding 12 months."

Flexing his new powers, Governor Bowdoin issued warrants for five rebels who had been especially troublesome and sent three hundred light horsemen into western towns searching for them. They captured three of the rebels, but rumors spread that the soldiers also "put out the eye of a woman, and stabbed and cut off the breast of another, and mangled an infant in the cradle." More than thirty towns officially protested the governor's actions, likening them to "British tyranny," claiming they were "dangerous, if not absolutely destructive to a Republican government."

Instead of quelling the rebellion, the aggressive actions only increased the anger of the farmers. On September 20, 1786, Daniel Shays made his first appearance in the annals of the insurrection when he led a group of six hundred men in a successful assault on the courthouse in Springfield, Massachusetts. Wearing his old buff and blue uniform left over from the war, Shays moved against the state supreme court at Springfield, attacking before the judges could consider treason indictments against the arrested rebels. The attack caught the governor off guard. Neither he nor the local sheriff had any advance warning of the assault, which made them believe the insurrection was both better organized and more dangerous than they had previously thought. If the rebels could organize a surprise attack on Springfield, then could Boston be next?

The legislature had thus far been reluctant to declare martial law, but now the governor decided to take matters into his own hands. With the legislature out of session, Governor Bowdoin turned to a group of Boston bankers to fund the creation of a 4,400-soldier mercenary army under the command of General Benjamin Lincoln, a man with a checkered military past. Although he fought bravely at the Battle of Saratoga, Lincoln had surrendered his army at Charlestown and was held in a British prison until he was eventually exchanged for a British general. Now weighing more than three hundred pounds, he was, according to one historian, "almost as wide as he was tall." Only a handful of Lincoln's men had any combat experience. Around the same time, a panicked Continental Congress authorized the mobilization of 1,200 troops and placed them under the authority of General William Shepard.

By raising an army, the governor tapped in to a deep fear of standing armies that went back to the days of the British occupation. The action further radicalized farmers living in small towns in western Massachusetts. Shays saw the number of insurgents under his command swell to more than a thousand men. On December 7, Shays issued a proclamation protesting the untrammeled power of the state's officials. Leading the list however, was "the present expensive mode of collecting debts, which, by reason of the scarcity of cash, will of necessity fill our gaols with unhappy debtors, and thereby a reputable body of people rendered incapable of being serviceable to either themselves or the community."

On December 26, Shays made plans to march on the federal arsenal in Springfield. Built during the Revolutionary War to supply troops, this building housed seven thousand new muskets and more than two hundred tons of shot and shells. Capturing the arsenal would provide the rebels with a major strategic advantage and enough armaments to continue fighting. Word of the impending assault reached Boston on New Year's Day, 1787. Anticipating the attack, General Shepard led his troops through a blinding snowstorm to arrive in Springfield before Shays' men could seize the facility.

To counter, Shays divided his troops into three groups and surrounded the arsenal. The largest body, under his control, which numbered 1,100 men, approached by Boston Road. On the other side of town, Luke Day, another former Continental Army officer, stood ready with 400 Regulators. To the north, Eli Parsons waited with 400 Regulators from Berkshire. When he learned that General Lincoln and his 4,400 men were moving to join forces with Shepard, Shays decided to move up the timetable for his assault. Shays sent a message to Luke Day, saying that he should attack the arsenal on January 25. Day replied that his men would not be ready for the assault until January 26 at the earliest. As is often the case in warfare, however, luck and circumstance foil the best-laid military plans. Shepard's men intercepted Day's note to Shays. At 4 P.M. on January 25, Shays began his assault marching up Boston Road toward the arsenal, unaware that he was missing a large group of his troops.

When Shays came within 250 yards of the arsenal, General Shepard sent out officers to ask him what he wanted. Shays said that "a battle was all he wanted" and then shouted to his men, "March, God Damn you, march." When the rebels reached 100 yards (within musket range), Shepard opened up with his cannons, twice firing over their heads. This only quickened the advance of the Regulators. Finally, at point-blank range, Shepard fired his cannons directly into the center of the insurgent column. "A cry of murder arose from the rear of the insurgents," noted an observer. The farmer-soldiers under Shays' command never thought that their fellow veterans would fire on them directly. Four men died and many others suffered wounds. Panic gripped the rebels. Shays attempted to rally his men, but they broke ranks and retreated to Ludlow, ten miles away. Shepard wrote later that evening to Governor Bowdoin, "Had I been disposed to destroy them, I might have charged on their rear and flanks with my infantry and two field pieces, and could have killed the greater part of his whole army within twenty minutes."

Once the rebel attempt to seize the arsenal failed, it was only a matter of time before the rebellion was defeated. On February 3, government troops marched through subzero temperatures and a snowstorm to surprise the rebels as they camped at Petersham. The rebels scattered into the woods. Daniel Shays escaped to Vermont. Shays' Rebellion was over, although the governor declared that the state of insurrection continued. A special court indicted more than two hundred rebels and prosecuted them in formal trials. In April 1787, five of Shays' men were charged with treason and were condemned to hang.

The Shaysites lost the rebellion, but they won the peace in Massachusetts. In May, voters dismissed the aristocratic "merchant party" that had dominated the legislature. The new legislature slashed taxes as much as 90 percent for some of the western districts. The legislature also placed a moratorium on debt collection. The state's hardline governor lost his race to the popular John Hancock, famous signatory of the Declaration of Independence, who took a softer view of the farmers' rebellion. On the morning of June 21, 1787, the day the five rebels were sentenced to march to the gallows, Hancock dramatically granted them a reprieve to show the power and mercy of his new government.

Shays' Rebellion exposed the fragility of the new American democracy, but it also highlighted its possibilities. It provided other struggling "common people" with the confidence to act on their own grievances, and to do it outside the established channels. Shays' Rebellion ignited a wave of resistance to debt collection and taxes from New England to South Carolina. In the summer of 1786, a "tumultuous assemblage of the people" shut down a county courthouse in Maryland. In South Carolina, angry farmers attacked the Camden Courthouse and dismissed the judges. A panicked justice warned that not even "five thousand troops, the best in America or Europe, could enforce obedience to the Common Pleas." In Maryland and Virginia, organized protesters prevented the auction of cattle and property seized for debt. "The only thing at this critical moment that can rescue the states from civil disorder," wrote Pierce Butler, is a "strong national government."

By exposing the weaknesses of the federal government as it existed under the Articles of Confederation, Shays' Rebellion also provided ammunition to the handful of nationalists pushing for a new constitutional convention. Under the articles, each state had retained its sovereignty. Despite growing fear that Shays and his men were going to march on Boston and imperil the fragile new republic, the U.S. Congress had no power to compel other states to provide money and soldiers to put down the insurrection. It could only "request" support from the states. But this was only one of a myriad of problems plaguing the federal government. Congress had no funds, since it had no taxation powers. Each state acted as if it were an independent nation. Many states were battling over the same trade and import duties. New Jersey had gone as far as to set up its own customs service. Democracy had so far produced legislatures filled with narrow-minded men deeply protective of their local interests but blind to the national interest.

Leading the call for a new national convention was Virginia's

James Madison. A small man, "no bigger than a snowflake," as someone wrote of him, Madison was an unlikely political leader. Timid and self-conscious in public, he preferred to work behind the scenes. In 1785, deeply worried about the fate of the young republic, he retreated to his family home and began an intensive study of failed confederacies. He concluded from his study of history that nations needed a strong central government to survive. In America, he determined, the states wielded too much power, which in the end could only produce chaos and failure. If left unchanged, America would remain a collection of small, feuding fiefdoms, unable to fulfill the high ideals of the founders and vulnerable to foreign powers. For Madison, Shays' Rebellion highlighted all the problems with the Articles of Confederation and underscored the need to create a new government. "The rebellion in Massachusetts is a warning," he declared.

Shays' Rebellion also exposed the tension facing the new government. As Madison would later write in number 51 of *The Federalist:* "In framing a government which is to be administered by men over men the great difficulty is this: you must first enable the government to control the governed, and in the next place oblige it to control itself." By 1787 the weakness of the central government was apparent to everybody. So was the cause: "the democratic parts of our constitutions," as Virginia's Edmund Randolph put it, meaning the state legislatures. The legislatures were parochial. Worse, they bent too quickly to popular will. Instead of controlling the governed, they were controlled by them. And these state legislatures held the balance of power under the Confederation. Said Elbridge Gerry of Massachusetts, until then a local-government man, "The evils we experience flow from the excess of democracy."

Virginia's governor, Patrick Henry, invited the other states to a general convention, to be held in September 1786 at Annapolis, to resolve trade issues and other problems with the articles. When the convention opened on September 11, only five states had sent delegates—New York, New Jersey, Pennsylvania, Delaware, and Virginia. They met on the same day that Shays' Regulators had shut down a courthouse just eighteen miles outside Boston. Most contemporaries believed that Massachusetts had created one of the most balanced constitutions. If rebellion could come to Massachusetts, what about the other states? From Paris, Thomas Jefferson dismissed the rebellion and its meaning. "[A] little rebellion now and then is a good thing," he wrote to Madison in 1787, "and as necessary in the political world as storms in the physical." Madison felt that his fellow Virginian had been out of the country too long to appreciate the seriousness of the situation. Alexander Hamilton was convinced that the "futile and senseless Confederation" should be replaced by a strong national government that controlled "all but the mere municipal laws of each state." Before leaving town, Hamilton helped draft a new resolution calling for a "general meeting, of the States, in a future Convention, for the same, and such other purposes, as the situation of public affairs, may be found to require."

Madison hoped to use news from Massachusetts to build support for the Constitutional Convention and for his pleas for a stronger government. His hopes hinged on George Washington. After the war, Washington had retired to Mount Vernon, his 6,700-acre farm along the Potomac. By 1787 he had become a mythic figure in the eyes of his countrymen. Madison knew that if Washington would lend his prestige to a Constitutional Convention, his hopes may be realized. At first, Washington resisted. He had announced his retirement from public life. How could he go back on his word? He had also just declined another invitation to go to Philadelphia around the same time to attend a meeting of Revolutionary War officers. How would it look if he now accepted this invitation from Madison? His real concern, however, was that the convention would fail.

Madison appealed to Washington's deep sense of patriotism by feeding him news about Shays' Rebellion, reminding him in the process what a threat it posed to the republic that he had risked his life to create. It is unlikely that the Constitutional Convention would have been successful if Washington had not attended, and it was Daniel Shays who convinced the general to end his retirement and return to public life. "The situation of the general government, if it can be called a government, is shaken to its foundation, and liable to be overturned by every blast," Madison wrote to Jefferson in France. "In a word, it is at an end; and, unless a remedy is soon applied, anarchy and confusion will inevitably ensue."

By March 1787, Washington's position on the new convention was clearly changing. While he had previously felt that his reputation would be damaged if he attended and the session failed to draft a new constitution, now he was worried about how history would view his actions if he failed to attend the meeting. "A thought . . . has lately run through my mind," he wrote. "It is, whether my non-attendance in this Convention will not be considered as dereliction to Republicanism, nay more, whether other motives may not (however injuriously) be ascribed to me for not exerting myself on this occasion?"

In a letter to Madison dated November 5, 1786, Washington articulated his fears about the rebellion:

Let us look to our National character, and to things beyond the present period. No Morn ever dawned more favourable than ours did—and no day was ever more clouded than the present! Wisdom, & good examples are necessary at this time to rescue the political machine from the impending storm. . . . How melancholy is the reflection in that so short a space we should have made such large strides to the predictions of our transatlantic foes!—"Leave them to themselves & their government will soon dissolve." . . . What stronger evidence can be given to the want of energy in our government than these disorders? If there is not power in it to check them, what security has a man for life, liberty, or property?

A few weeks after news of Shays' defeat at Petersham reached Philadelphia, Congress agreed to a convention to amend the Articles of Confederation. Three months later, the convention met in the nation's capital. Washington's arrival in Philadelphia on Sunday, May 13, was greeted with the chiming bells of Christ Church, cannon fire, and the cheers of a large crowd. Six years after the end of the American Revolution in Yorktown, Washington was still the most celebrated American.

The Constitutional Convention was scheduled to begin on May 14, 1787, but did not achieve a quorum of delegations from more than half the states until May 25. (In the end, there were twelve delegations. Rhode Island, dominated by radicals, suspected a plot and boycotted the convention. "Rogue's Island," some of the delegates called the state.) The delegates immediately elected Washington president of the convention when deliberations began on May 25, 1787. The aging general seldom participated in the debates, but his solemn dignity put the participants on their best behavior.

The delegates met in the same room at the Philadelphia statehouse where the Declaration of Independence had been signed.

After adopting the rules, including one to keep the proceedings secret, James Madison, the leader of the Federalist forces calling for a strong national government, outlined his agenda. Dubbed the "Virginia Resolves," the plan called for creating three branches of government: an executive, judiciary, and legislature divided into two houses. After four weeks of debate, the diminutive William Patterson of New Jersey rose to present an alternative plan—the Anti-Federalist proposal, which only modestly revised the Articles of Confederation and favored state sovereignty over federal power.

Although he was not in the room, Daniel Shays cast a long shadow over the proceedings and the debates between Federalists and Anti-Federalists at the convention. Ironically, a revolution created to limit the power of distant authority may have resulted in an even stronger federal government. According to Revolutionary War hero Henry Knox, the uprising "wrought prodigious changes in the minds of men in that state respecting the powers of government—everybody says they must be strengthened and that unless this shall be effected, there is no security for liberty and property." Fear of government had shaped the creation of the Articles of Confederation; fear of democracy defined the discussion over the new constitution. A Virginia delegate spoke of the need to restrain "the turbulence and follies of democracy," while a New York representative complained about the dangers of the "popular phrenzy."

Few went as far as Alexander Hamilton, who claimed that all "communities divide themselves into the few and the many," and it was essential that the few—meaning the rich and powerful— have "a distinct permanent share in the government." Most of the delegates did not want to retreat from the spirit of the revolution, which clearly placed sovereignty in the hands of the people, but they were also eager to place more limits on democracy and invest more power in government. Most of the delegates found attractive Madison's idea that both power and liberty could be balanced by creating an extended republic with large electoral districts that would allow the election of "men who possess the most attractive merit," while preventing the formation of an "unjust and interested majority."

Shays' uprising allowed the socially conservative Federalists (usually the wealthy and well educated) to seize the middle ground of the debate, pushing the Anti-Federalists into arguing that the proposed Constitution was too much too soon. Federalists merely had to make allusions to "insurrections" or "brigands" to conjure the image of Shays. They rarely had to mention him by name. Madison referred to him obliquely while criticizing the Anti-Federalists. "The insurrections in Massachusetts admonished all of the States of the danger to which they were exposed," he argued. The Anti-Federalists found themselves in the awkward position of opposing a plan that might "insure domestic Tranquility," which made them sound uncomfortably like Shays' rebels. "Every state has its Shays, who, either with their pens—or tongues—or offices—are endeavoring to effect what Shays attempted in vain with his sword," proclaimed the *Pennsylvania Gazette*. The paper went on to say that all Federalists "should be distinguished hereafter by the name of Washingtonians, and the Antifederalists, by the name Shayites, in every part of the United States."

The Federalists dominated the debate about the structure of the new government. A compromise framework closely resembling Madison's original proposal carried by a vote of seven to three on June 19, 1787. They divided the structure of the new federal government into three branches. The people would elect only the House. The Senate would act as a check on the rambunctious lower assembly because senators would be chosen by the state assemblies, which would be less swayed by demagogues. The senators' six-year terms and rotating elections would ensure that they would not find themselves turned out of office immediately if they supported unpopular measures. The judges of the Supreme Court sat for life and thereby created another barrier to radical shifts in the popular will. The president was elected indirectly, by an electoral college. Thus, Shays' influence can be seen in the conservative structure of the federal government—it did not deny people a voice in the government; rather, it channeled and broke up power in such a way that if the people wanted change, it would take years of state and national elections to bring it about. During that time, public opinion might change and reverse what would have been a rash course of action.

The document also equipped the federal government with the means to put down revolts and defend the country, as well as resolve nagging issues like interstate trade and the value of money (Article I, Sec 8.5). According to Article I, Sec 8.15 of the Constitution, the federal government had the power "to provide for calling forth the Militia to execute the Laws of the Union, suppress Insurrection, and repel Invasions." Article I also addressed the problem of debt moratorium, prohibiting the states from passing "laws impairing the Obligations of Contracts" (Sec 10.1). The same section prohibited the states from making "any Thing but gold and silver Coin a Tender in Payment of Debts." The hope for cheap, state-issued paper money died with those words. Article IV, Sec 2.2 provided for the extradition of fugitives to the state where they committed their crime. Section 4 of the same article promised the states protection against domestic violence. It created a federally controlled military that could cross state lines to put down rebellions and chase fugitives.

In September, the debate moved from Philadelphia to the thirteen states for ratification. Throughout the state conventions, critics of the new Constitution complained that Shays had provided a pretext, an excuse that supporters had used to fend off criticism of the Constitution. "The most trifling events have been Magnified," an angry Uriah Forrest wrote to Jefferson of this tactic, "into Monstrous outrages." Realistically, however, Anti-Federalists looked on Shays' insurrection with resignation, describing it as a hurdle they had never managed to surmount. Centinel, the pseudonym used by the author of a series of Anti-Federalist essays published in the Philadelphia *Independent Gazetteer*, wrote in the last of his letters that the Constitution had been viewed "through the medium of a SHAYS," and as a result, supporters of the existing system had "lost her ablest advocates." Shays had placed the Anti-Federalists in a politically untenable position. They were trapped between rebellion and counterrevolution, opposed to both Shays and his Federalist adversaries. The Anti-Federalists tried, but failed, to create a tenuous middle ground "between these two parties."

Nine states would have to agree for the new Constitution to become law. Delaware was the first state to ratify the new Constitution. Pennsylvania, New Jersey, and Georgia followed. Attention shifted to Massachusetts, where 350 delegates gathered at the Brattle Street Church in Boston on January 8, 1788. The delegates from rural western Massachusetts, 29 of whom had once ridden with Daniel Shays, opposed the Constitution. Farmer and war veteran Amos Singletary charged that under the new Constitution, "they will swallow up all us little folks, like the great

Leviathan . . . just as the whale swallowed up *Jonah*." As expected, the inland market towns and the eastern ports rallied in support of the document. Passage was uncertain until the Federalists promised to include a Bill of Rights as part of the Constitution. The move helped sway a handful of undecided delegates. On February 8, 1788, just a few days past the anniversary of the battle at Petersham, Massachusetts ratified the Constitution by a margin of nineteen votes. Soon after the Constitution was ratified, the editor of the *Massachusetts Centinel* observed that the "late insurrections in the Commonwealth . . . must be considered as the cause of bringing into existence, at a much earlier period than would otherwise have been, the [federal] government."

* * *

After the rebellion, Shays fled to Vermont. After requesting and receiving a pardon, he moved to Sparta, New York, where he died on September 29, 1825. In the years since his death, Shays has become a symbol of protest—of an enduring American faith in individual rights and local democracy. He exposed the tension at the heart of the new American experiment in democracy. How does a nation founded on the idea that liberty and power are antithetical create institutions of government that guarantee order and protect individual rights? The first American government—the Articles of Confederation—tried to strike the balance in favor of small-town democracy and states' rights. The challenge from Shays' insurgents, however, emboldened nationalists who called for a stronger national government. They succeeded in creating a new Constitution with expanded federal power, but they never resolved the tension exposed by Shays' rebels. If anything, the new Constitution widened the gap between the ideals of the revolution, which found expression in the claim of the Declaration of

Independence that "all men are created equal," and the realities of power enshrined in the Constitution that institutionalized slavery and limited direct democracy.

The gap between American ideals of democracy and the realities of power have emerged as an enduring tension in American history. From time to time, Shays' name has been invoked to justify a multitude of political causes. During the Civil War, southerners invoked Shays to support their insurrection, claiming a common heritage of states' rights. Like slave owners, Shays' rebels "assumed the right, each for himself, to judge of the propriety of any law passed by his State Legislature, and to obey or defy it according to his own pleasure." Later in the nineteenth century another generation of farmers in the South and West raised the banner of agrarian resistance to distant rule from the East.

This populist tradition persisted into the twentieth century, even as the size and scope of federal power expanded. It found expression on the left in figures like Louisiana's Huey Long, the 1930s radical who called for redistribution of wealth, and, on the right, in the antics of demagogues like Joseph McCarthy, who attacked the Washington elite for harboring Communists in the 1940s and 1950s. What they shared with Daniel Shays was a faith in the "common man" and disdain for the elite and powerful. In 1987, President Ronald Reagan compared modern-day tax reformers to Shays' rebels, claiming they shared a common heritage of skepticism of federal authority and respect for individual rights. Congress declared the week of January 18 as Shays' Rebellion Week and Sunday, January 25, 1987, the two-hundredth anniversary of the assault on the Springfield arsenal, as Shays' Rebellion Day. The legacy of Daniel Shays had come full circle: from reluctant leader of a colonial rebellion to celebrated hero of the Washington establishment.

For Further Reading

David P. Szatmary, *Shays' Rebellion* (1980) and Leonard L. Richards, *Shays's Rebellion* (2002) are the two most complete monographs on the causes and consequences of the rebellion. The rebellion has also been the subject of a number of excellent scholarly articles. For an insightful collection of essays, see *In Debt to Shays: The Bicentennial of an Agrarian Rebellion* (1993), edited by Robert A. Gross. Also valuable on the origins of the revolt are Jonathan Smith, "The Depression of 1785 and Daniel Shays' Rebellion" in *William and Mary Quarterly* 3, no. 1 (1948): 77–94; and John L. Brooke, "To the Quiet of the People: Revolutionary Settlements and Civil Unrest in Western Massachusetts, 1774–1789" in *William and Mary Quarterly* 46, no. 3 (1989): 425–462.

For general context on the revolution, see Robert Middlekauff, *The Glorious Cause: The American Revolution, 1763–1789* (1982). As you would expect, there is a large body of literature on the failure of the Articles of Confederation and the debates over the Constitution. Among the best are Gordon S. Wood, *The Creation of the American Republic, 1776–1787* (1998) and Jack N. Rakove, *Original Meanings* (1997). Merrill Jensen's *The Articles of Confederation* (1959), though dated, is still a valuable resource. Michael Kazin's *The Populist Persuasion* (1995) examines the impact of the populist tradition on American politics.

3

January 24, 1848
Gold Rush

John Augustus Sutter spent much of his life traveling west in search of fortune. Born to Swiss parents in Baden, Germany, in 1803, he tried his hand in the dry goods business but failed. Heavily in debt and threatened with arrest, he decided to leave his wife and five children behind and remake himself in the United States. In May 1834, at the age of thirty-one, Sutter boarded a ship bound for New York. Over the next few months he slowly made his way to Missouri, reinventing himself along the way as a gentleman and former captain in the Swiss military. "He looked the part," one biographer wrote, "slim, handsome, dapper and military, sporting a pair of soldierly sideburns." A friend described him as "a man of medium or rather low stature, but with a marked military air." A thick mustache covered his lip. "His head was of a very singular formation, being flat and well shaped behind and rising high over the crown, with a lofty and expanded forehead."

After leaving the Missouri frontier, Sutter traveled extensively throughout the West and Pacific region. He spent time in Oregon before sailing to Hawaii. From there he backtracked, traveling to a

Russian colony in Alaska. Lured by the prospect of open land and mild climate, he finally settled in California on July 1, 1839. There he secured permission from the Mexican government to establish a fifty-thousand-acre settlement east of San Francisco that he called New Helvetia (New Switzerland). Sutter had finally achieved his piece of the American Dream—thousands of acres of land, thirteen thousand cattle, and a ten-acre orchard. He hired Native Americans to cultivate the land and work on his ranch. He built a large adobe fort with walls that were three feet thick and fifteen feet high and fortified by mounted cannons. Sutter's Fort, as it was widely known, stood on a slight rise at the junction of the American and Sacramento Rivers. It protected his supplies and provided living quarters for him and his workers. The site, which housed a bakery, carpenter's shop, gunsmith, and doctor's office, became a regular stopping place for Americans traveling to California.

According to John Bidwell, who worked at the fort, "Sutter was one of the most liberal and hospitable of men. Everybody was welcome." He was often generous to a fault, welcoming everyone who passed his way. "He employed men—not because he always needed and could profitably employ them, but because in the kindness of his heart it simply became a habit to employ everybody who wanted employment," Bidwell wrote.

James Marshall, a New Jersey native who traveled to California by wagon train in 1844, was one of the hundreds of men who found themselves at Sutter's Fort. Born in 1810 into a strict Methodist family, Marshall trained as a carpenter before family troubles and debts pushed him from his home to points farther west. After drifting through Ohio, Indiana, and Illinois, he settled in Missouri in 1837. Once in an area of the state called Platte County, Marshall farmed the marshy land near the Missouri

River. Ultimately, Marshall's health declined due to "fever and ague," an illness found predominantly in swampy areas in the United States and later more commonly identified as malaria. Hearing reports of a temperate climate in California, Marshall decided to travel west in the spring of 1844.

After a brief stop in Oregon, Marshall arrived at Sutter's Fort in July 1845. "He presented a strong and healthy appearance," a biographer wrote of Marshall's initial appearance at New Helvetia. "His well-proportioned body, a little above average height, was clad in buckskin, frontier style. His features were coarse but strong, indicating will power and courage. His blue eyes shone brightly." Sutter, then in need of skilled labor, hired Marshall as a carpenter for five dollars a day, to be paid in cattle, horses, and ammunition. Eventually, and with some additional assistance from Sutter, Marshall purchased his own land near the fort, where he used his payments of cattle to stock his own ranch. When the Mexican-American War broke out, Marshall sided with the Americans and served in John C. Frémont's California Battalion until March 1847. After Marshall returned to his land in northern California, he discovered that most of his cattle had disappeared or been stolen. Since the cattle were worth more than the land, Marshall was unable to continue his mortgage payments and, once again, returned to Sutter's Fort in search of work.

In early 1847, Sutter made plans to expand his New Helvetia empire. In May, Sutter directed Marshall to find a suitable site for a sawmill along the American River. Marshall found his spot forty-five miles up the south fork of the American River in a valley named Coloma in the foothills of the Sierra Nevada. Marshall's sawmill design required the digging of two long channels, a headrace and tailrace, to and from the river. Water would rush down the headrace toward the mill, where its current would turn the wheel of the mill before flowing out the tailrace and returning to the main body of the river.

Construction on the sawmill proceeded quickly, though heavy rains and flooding threatened to wash out the area. Each morning, Marshall walked the length of the tailrace, approximately two hundred yards long, and inspected it for any stones or gravel that had been washed away the night before. While inspecting the tailrace on the morning of January 24, 1848, Marshall noticed glittering yellow flakes in the riverbed. "My eye was caught by something shining in the bottom of the ditch," he reflected. "I reached my hand down and picked it up; it made my heart thump, for I was certain it was gold. The piece was about half the size and shape of a pea. Then I saw another. . . ." After a few days, Marshall decided it was time to share his discovery with Sutter, so he wrapped a few pieces of the precious metal in an old rag, stuck it in his pocket, and rode through a torrential downpour to New Helvetia.

Sutter was surprised to see Marshall, but he escorted him into his office. "Are we alone?" a fidgety and rain-soaked Marshall asked. "Yes," replied Sutter, who was growing increasingly concerned by his friend's erratic behavior. Marshall then demanded two bowls of water, a stick of redwood, twine, and sheets of copper. Reluctantly, Sutter gathered the requested materials. Marshall reached into his pocket and unfolded the rag, revealing his booty. "I believe this is gold," he said.

Sutter examined the metal closely while Marshall told him the story of how he discovered it. "Well, it looks like gold," Sutter said. "Let us test it." Deciding to apply his own test, Sutter went to his apothecary shop and brought back some nitric acid. If it was gold, the acid would have no impact. The metal passed that test.

Next came the weight test—gold is heavier than other metals. They placed silver Swiss coins on one side of the scale and the mystery metal on the other side, until they were perfectly balanced. Sutter then submerged the scales into the two bowls of water. The silver was clearly outweighed by the other metal. Finally, Sutter pulled a copy of the *Encyclopedia Americana* off the shelf and read the article about gold. "I declare this to be gold," he announced.

That night Sutter tossed and turned in bed as he considered the consequences of Marshall's discovery. He knew that some explorers had found modest traces of gold in California, but he also remembered the advice of a Swedish scientist who, after examining rumors of gold in California, warned: "Your best mine is the soil." If there were large deposits of gold, he reasoned, the Indians would have discovered them long ago. Sutter's most pressing concern was the impact that rumors of gold would have on his business. Gold could ruin his arrangement by luring away his workers and attracting strangers who would overrun his land. Sutter decided to pledge his employees to secrecy. "Of course I knew nothing of the extent of the discovery," he reflected, "but I was satisfied, whether it amounted to much or little, that it would greatly interfere with my plans."

There was another reason Sutter wanted to keep the gold a secret: he did not have title to the land where he was building the sawmill, which he believed belonged to the local Nisenan Indians. Without informing the tribe about the gold, he offered some shirts, hats, flour, and a few other items in return for a three-year lease of a dozen square miles. Next, he tried to get the government to recognize the lease. Since it was not yet accepted into the union as a state, California was ruled by a military governor.

The governor, however, said that it was impossible to figure out who actually owned the land. Until ownership could be confirmed—a process that could take years—he could not recognize any land titles.

Many people were initially skeptical of rumors that gold had been discovered. "People did not believe it," wrote a man named Findla. "They thought it was a hoax. They had found it in various places around San Francisco, notably on Pacific Street, specimens of different minerals, gold and silver among them, but in very small quantities, and so they were not inclined to believe in the discovery of gold at Sutter's Mill." "I have heard of it," wrote one San Franciscan. "A few fools have hurried to the place, but you may be sure there is nothing in it." In March 1848, the *Californian* buried the story at the bottom of page two. The rival *California Star* dismissed the stories about gold as "a sham" designed to "guzzle the gullible."

That changed on Friday, May 12, 1848, when Sam Brannan traveled to San Francisco carrying proof of the new discovery. Brannan had opened up a general store at Sutter's Fort around the same time that Marshall traveled upstream to begin construction of the sawmill. While Sutter may have wanted to keep the discovery of gold a secret, Brannan had a strong incentive to get as many people into the mountains as possible—gold or no gold. He was not interested in mining for gold; he planned to strike gold by selling equipment to eager miners. Brannan collected a sample of flakes and dust in a quinine bottle and left for San Francisco, where he gave the public irrefutable proof of the gold discovery, parading along Montgomery Street, waving his hat and carrying the bottle of gold flakes and dust, shouting "Gold! Gold! Gold from the American River!"

Brannan's theatrics turned San Francisco into a ghost town, as thousands flocked into the hills in search of gold. By July, four thousand people were out hunting gold—20 percent of the non–Native American population of California. Stores were emptied, ships were abandoned in port, and newspapers were shut down as three-quarters of the town's population fled. On May 29, the *Californian*, which had been the first newspaper to report rumors of a gold strike, shut down, because "the majority of our subscribers and many of our advertising patrons have closed their doors and places of business and left town." In Monterey, Walter Colton remarked on how gold fever swept his sleepy little town. "The blacksmith dropped his hammer, the carpenter his plane, the mason his trowel, the baker his loaf, the tapster his bottle. All were off to the mines, some on horses, some in carts, some went on crutches, and one went in a litter. The fever has reached every servant in Monterey; none are to be entrusted in their engagements beyond a week."

Among those who flocked to the gold were soldiers who abandoned their posts in pursuit of wealth. While stationed in towns like Monterey and San Francisco, they watched locals get rich while they earned six dollars a month on garrison duty. "The struggle between *right* and six dollars a month," said one soldier, "and *wrong* and seventy-five dollars a day is rather a severe one." The army in northern California lost 716 men out of a total of 1,290 in the first eighteen months of the gold rush. One soldier who gave in to the temptation wrote, "A frenzy seized my soul; piles of gold rose up before me at every step; thousands of slaves bowed to my beck and call; myriads of fair virgins contended for my love. In short I had a violent attack of gold fever."

For these early gold rushers, the pickings were often spectacular. California's gold was placer gold. Over the course of millions of years, geological forces had deposited placer gold in flakes and fragments among the many rivers and rocks in the region. Placer gold was often near the surface, at times freely exposed, and was easily dug up with only rudimentary tools such as a knife, spoon, pickax, or, if desperate, fingernails. Huge gold nuggets could even be found on the surface in some areas. Novice miners could learn to use pans to prospect in a very short period of time, and a more modest investment in a cradle or rocker could quickly improve their results. With only a small effort, individuals could count their gold tally in hundreds of dollars a day or week. At a time when most laborers earned a dollar for a day of work, prospectors were finding an ounce or two of gold every day and selling their finds for fifteen or sixteen dollars an ounce.

Word spread of men who dug gold with spoons, and each spoonful was worth $8 in gold. Another man who had a strip of land only four feet square got thirty pounds of gold in less than a month. Larger operations counted larger profits. During three months in the summer of 1848, a partnership of five miners collected $75,000 in gold. Another rancher, Pierson B. Reading, put his Native American laborers to work in the gold fields and collected $80,000 during the month of July.

Until the summer of 1849, Californians had the gold rush to themselves. Since there was not yet a transcontinental telegraph or railroad, it had been difficult to spread the news to the East Coast. Gradually, however, word spread and people flooded in from across America and, indeed, from around the world. In April 1848, Sam Brannan published two thousand copies of the *California Star*, promoting the riches of California, and had them shipped by pack mule to the Missouri frontier. In July, the military governor of California, Colonel Richard B. Mason, sent an official report to Washington, D.C., and gave numerous accounts of the wealth of the gold fields, which he estimated already held four thousand miners. Perhaps sensing the inevitable disbelief of faraway officials, Mason also sent along 230 ounces of Californian gold.

On December 5, 1848, President Polk delivered his final State of the Union message to Congress and confirmed the discovery of gold in California. "The accounts of the abundance of gold in that territory are of such an extraordinary character as would scarcely command belief were they not corroborated by the authentic reports of officers in the public service, who have visited the mineral district, and derived the facts which they detail from personal observation," he said. With that, Polk made the discovery official and the rush was on. "The El Dorado of the old Spaniards is discovered at last," declared the *New York Herald*. "We now have the highest official authority for believing in the discovery of vast gold mines in California, and that the discovery is the greatest and most startling, not to say miraculous, that the history of the last five centuries can produce." Just over two weeks later, London's *Times* reprinted Polk's message in full along with gold fever accounts taken from the *New York Herald* and *Washington Union*.

Stories of quick fortunes—most of them greatly exaggerated—inspired men to mortgage their homes, borrow from family members, and take out life insurance policies to finance or protect their investments in claims of mining land. Men quit their jobs, sold their businesses, and moved to California. They caught "gold fever," a term that seemed appropriate since many observers thought of it as a contagious disease. The Sioux holy man Black Elk called gold "the yellow metal that makes Wasichus [whites] crazy." The men—and they were mostly men—who traveled to California came to be known as forty-niners because of the year that the gold rush kicked into high gear. They often referred to themselves as Argonauts—the famed explorers of Greek mythology who sailed in search of the Golden Fleece. A popular miner's poem of the period read:

Like Argos of the ancient times,
I'll leave this modern Greece:
I'm bound to California mines
To find the golden fleece.
For who would work from morn to night,
And live on hog and corn:
When one can pick up there at sight
Enough to buy a farm.

The gold rush inspired perhaps the largest mass movement of people in world history. "Neither the Crusades nor Alexander's expedition to India (all things considered) can equal this emigration to California," wrote one forty-niner. In 1848, Henry Simpson outlined the best routes to California in his bestselling *The Emigrant's Guide to the Gold Mines*. He pointed out that Americans eager to journey to the gold fields could travel one of five overseas or overland routes. Overseas routes proved popular, especially for those who left from eastern ports, primarily because sea travel could occur during any season. These travelers had to choose between stopping in Panama or traveling around Cape Horn. The fourteen-thousand-mile-long Cape Horn route could take six to eight months, but it was a relatively simple and safe trip that American ships had been making for more than forty years. It had its share of hazards though, including rough seas, seasickness, and infested food. One passenger complained that "there were two bugs for every bean."

The trip through Panama included a three-to-four-day hike across the isthmus to the Pacific Ocean, where passengers would have to set sail again. These gold seekers paid as much as $450 for a ticket on a steamer from New York to Panama's Chagres River, where they were then forced to hike and canoe for three days to Panama City. There, if they were lucky, they boarded a steamship to San Francisco harbor. Assuming that there was a ship available for the trip from Panama City to California, the Panama route might take only six to eight weeks, but the traveler risked fever and illness when trekking through the jungle. In April 1849, the *New York Herald* reported that 14,191 people had taken the Cape Horn route during the preceding five months, compared to only 3,547 leaving for Panama.

As an alternative to sailing to California, overland travel offered its own perks and problems. Most were unprepared for the difficulties of the journey. Some used guidebooks like Lansford W. Hastings's *The Emigrants' Guide to Oregon and California,* which hopelessly underestimated the hardship of the journey and the amount of time it would take. Western terrain was nothing like that of the east. It was, noted a contemporary, a "land of extremes," containing the nation's "highest and lowest spots, its hottest and coldest, and its wettest and driest." Argonauts had to contend with either too much rain or too little. One traveler complained about sand fleas that "fill the atmosphere like dust," stinging "ears, nose, eyes and beard . . . face, neck, breasts . . . and wrists." Many travelers faced cholera outbreaks produced by the crowded and unsanitary conditions along the trails. As many as 1,500 travelers died from cholera along the Overland Trail in 1849. A Native American recalled a scene along the Platte River lined with "a solid mass of wagons" and "men digging graves on each side of the river; men dying in their wagons, hallooing and crying and cramping with the cholera, women screaming and hallooing and praying."

Some southern routes, such as the route that went through Texas, Santa Fe, and northern Mexico, could be traveled year-round. This route was longer for some and offered a potentially harsh trip through the desert, but at least ten thousand people made the journey in both 1849 and 1850. A more popular route was the Oregon-California Trail, which traveled west from the Missouri frontier. This trail had been well publicized since 1841, when large numbers of immigrants pursued land in the Pacific Northwest, but it offered a smaller time window of travel for the miners. In 1849 it took up to a hundred days to get from the Missouri frontier to California. On a good day, mule and oxen wagons would go twenty-five miles. If travelers left too early in the year, they risked high waters on the plains and a lack of prairie grass to feed their oxen. If travelers left too late, they risked arriving during California's rainy season in late September or, even worse, encountering the snow and harsh weather in the mountains. Despite these challenges, the Oregon-California Trail still proved the most popular overland route. Though difficult to estimate the exact number of travelers, figures suggest that more than thirty-two thousand traveled along the trail in 1849, more than forty-four thousand in 1850, and more than fifty thousand in 1851.

Americans were not the only ones immigrating to California. At first, word of the gold rush spread to Mexico and Hawaii, then toward South America before reaching the Far East and Europe. Sonora in northern Mexico, for instance, had one of the largest contingents of immigrants in 1848. Sonorans generally traveled in families and made mining into seasonal work, returning to Mexico in the fall. Within a year, there were more than six thousand Sonorans mining in the region. For Australians, California provided an additional port of trade along the Pacific rim. Once the first wave of Australian immigrants went home with their success stories in 1849, trade and immigration increased. In China, the Taiping Revolution in 1850 changed the agricultural landscape and freed an entire labor class. As a result, many young men left Asia for the gold fields, intending to work for a brief time before returning home with their wealth.

Europeans also flocked to California. Irish immigration to the United States, already at 100,000 a year in 1847, more than doubled to 220,000 by 1851. In France citizens organized *la sociétés*, or French versions of a joint-stock company, and by 1853 there were more than 28,000 Frenchmen in California.

The mining towns that sprang up almost overnight were raucous, violent, almost exclusively male places. Miners found their entertainment in the myriad taverns, gambling joints, and brothels that housed most of the few females in the vicinity. One prostitute in California boasted of making more than $50,000 in a year. A miner described a typical Sunday in the mining town of Coloma: "The principal street in Coloma was alive with crowds of moving men, passing and repassing, laughing, talking, and all appearing in the best of humor." They included blacks, Jamaicans, Hawaiians, Peruvians, Chileans, Mexicans, Frenchmen, Germans, Italians, Irishmen, Yankees, Chinese, and Native Americans. "It was," he concluded, "a scene that no other country could ever imitate. Antipodes of color, race, religion, language, government, condition, size, capability, strength and morals were there, within that small village in the mountains of California."

The gold rush helped colonize the country's open land, fulfilling the dreams of those who believed that America's manifest destiny was to create a nation that extended from coast to coast. In one of the most remarkable coincidences in American history, Marshall discovered his glittering rocks just nine days before the end of the Mexican-American War. Prior to the war, California was the northernmost territory of Mexico, then a fledgling country only a quarter-century removed from its own independence from Spain. On February 2, 1848, the two countries signed the Treaty of Guadalupe Hidalgo, which added a million square miles of territory to the United States—the rugged expanse that is now made up of the states of Texas, New Mexico, Arizona, Colorado, Nevada, and California. The United States paid Mexico $15 million in cash for the land. Massachusetts senator Daniel Webster excoriated President Polk for spending so much money to acquire the useless, arid land in the West. The discovery of gold, however, soon quieted Webster and other critics.

But California was not settled like other parts of the United States in a gradual, methodical movement of Anglo-Saxons; it was invaded by people from other parts of North America, Europe, Asia, and Latin America. In the words of one observer, "The world rushed in." In 1847, California was home to about 13,000 people, including 7,000 Californios—native-born Mexicans—and around 6,000 "foreigners," most of whom were Americans. At this time, many of these citizens lived in the coastal cities of California, such as Monterey, Los Angeles, Santa Barbara, San Diego, and Yerba Buena, a small port in northern California later renamed San Francisco. The discovery of gold attracted aspiring miners and adventurers from across the nation and from around the globe, creating, almost overnight, one of the most diverse and energetic cultures anywhere on the planet. By 1852, California's population had swelled to 260,000. By the time of the first federal census in 1860, it had grown to 308,000.

In only twenty-two years, the gold rush transformed San Francisco from a tiny port town into the tenth-largest city in the United States. One miner marveled that San Francisco "seemed to have accomplished in a day the growth of half a century." In January 1848, San Francisco had about eight hundred residents. Three years later it bragged a population of thirty thousand and claimed the title of the "great metropolis of the Pacific coast." It became a brawling city of tents and shacks occupied by derelicts, sailors, gamblers, and prostitutes. A survey of the area in 1853 revealed 537 liquor stores, 46 gambling houses, and 48 houses of prostitution. As the city lacked adequate sanitation, tuberculosis and dysentery were common, and the streets were often knee deep in mud and manure. "This is not a town, it is a quagmire," complained one Frenchman. Fires ripped though the city on a regular basis. In one year alone, the center of San Francisco burned down three times. With the influx of miner gold, it was rebuilt each time—finer, grander, larger.

San Francisco also became the most cosmopolitan city in America, with large numbers of French, Germans, Americans, Mexicans, and Chinese living, often uncomfortably, side by side. "It is a most wonderful town, sprung up, as it were, by magic," noted a new resident. "On every street we found halls, brilliantly lighted, where men of every description were gambling at monte, twenty-one, faro, roulette, and dice. Such piles of money I never saw before. . . . Every establishment is furnished with a bar at which liquors are sold at 25 cents a glass, and instrumental music is performed during the whole evening. I have seen men clinking their hands full of gold to the tune which was playing. As much as $160,000 has been ventured and lost on the turn of a single card." Charles Starkweather wrote to his family that "the whole world seems to flock here. The town is full of people, and full of goods, stowed anywhere, everywhere, on board vessels and piled in the streets. This is the dirtiest place in creation, so sandy and windy."

Although California attracted people from around the world and helped forge a new cosmopolitan culture, it also continued a familiar pattern of American racism and discrimination. The 1848 Treaty of Guadalupe Hidalgo had promised the Californios the "free enjoyment of their liberty and property." That promise was quickly broken. The Californios owned some of the largest and richest tracts of land in the state. At the time of the gold rush, two hundred Californio families owned almost fourteen million acres of prime real estate. The Anglos who moved to the mines treated local Californios with disdain, lumping them together with immigrants from Chile and Mexico and calling them "greasers." Many were forced out of the mines by threats of violence. Those who continued to work were required to pay a sixteen-dollar-a-month "foreign miners' tax"—even though they had lived in the region long before the Americans arrived. But banishment from the mines was only the beginning. As Anglos flooded into the area, they squatted on the land owned by Californios. The courts upheld the Californios' claims, but only after long and expensive litigation that forced many to sell the land to pay their legal bills. According to one account, a family that lost its land and saw three family members lynched "most justly complained of the bad faith of the adventurers and squatters and the treachery of American lawyers."

Chinese immigrants came to the United States in search of *Gam Saan*, "Gold Mountain." During the 1860s, two-thirds of the twenty-four thousand Chinese in America were working in the California gold mines. As their numbers increased, so too did native hostility. In 1852 the California legislature enacted another foreign miners' tax aimed specifically at the Chinese requiring any miner who did not want to become an American citizen to pay a monthly fee of three dollars. The Chinese were prevented from becoming citizens by a 1790 law that limited naturalized citizenship to "white" persons. By the time the law was voided in 1870, the state had collected five million dollars in taxes from the Chinese, a figure that represented nearly half of all state revenue. As the mines dried up, many of the Chinese laborers left the gold fields, worked on the railroads, or opened up stores in San Francisco's bustling Chinatown. Further pressure from California pushed Congress to pass the Chinese Exclusion Act in 1882, the first law ever to restrict immigration from a specific country. The act suspended all Chinese immigration for ten years. The Supreme Court upheld the constitutionality of the act, claiming that the Chinese were "impossible" to assimilate and that they "remained strangers in the land, residing apart by themselves, and adhering to the customs and usages of their own country." The Chinese, the court concluded, constituted "a menace to our civilization."

Foreigners often fell prey to the primitive system of justice that governed many mining towns. In Old Dry Diggings, often called "Hangtown," an impromptu jury of two hundred miners sentenced three foreigners to death for an alleged robbery and murder in another California town. None of the men spoke a word of English. The trial, judgment, and execution by hanging took less than thirty minutes.

In addition to drawing in immigrants from around the world, the gold rush led to the construction of a transcontinental railroad that would eventually knit the nation closer together at the same time that it would jump-start the industrial revolution. In 1862, four California businessmen—Collis Huntington, Mark Hopkins, Leland Stanford, and Charles Crocker—pressured Congress into passing the Pacific Railroad Act, which provided land grants for the construction of a transcontinental railroad. With the completion of the great iron highway, the still young state of California began to play an integral and an important role in a new continent-wide America and in a flourishing national economy. By 1890, railroads crisscrossed the nation, linking raw materials in the West to factories, markets, and consumers in the East. The nation was laced with thirty-five thousand miles of railroad in 1865; by 1900, two hundred thousand miles were in operation—more railroad mileage than in all of Europe. The surge in railroad construction also spurred the expansion of other industries, especially steel, stone, and lumber. In 1882, for example, the railroads purchased nearly 90 percent of all steel produced in the United States.

Marshall's discovery transformed the American Dream, replacing old Puritan notions with visions of instant wealth. The search for gold, with its unpredictable mix of risk and reward, was better suited to the emerging entrepreneurial culture than the older faith in thrift and sweat. The Puritan work ethic and the ideals of the Jeffersonian yeoman farmer, where success came in steady and modest doses, gave way to the expectations of quick riches, because the gold rush made immediate and vast wealth accessible and rewarded risk. In 1848, the minister E. L. Cleaveland delivered a sermon called "Hasting to Be Rich," in which he warned his flock of the spiritual dangers of seeking instant wealth. Solemnly, he quoted Proverbs 28:20: "He that maketh haste to be rich shall not be innocent." Similar sermons were given from pulpits across the country, invoking the Puritan work ethic and warning that being rich was not synonymous with being virtuous. Few followed the advice.

Failure was common, but the nature of California in 1850 softened the blow. More gold, after all, was just around the bend, down the river, or under another rock. "One man works hard all his life and ends up a pauper. Another man, no smarter, makes twenty million dollars. Luck has a hell of a lot to do with it."

The gold rush spawned new industries to provide services— food, clothing, hardware—to the thousands of miners who over-ran the region. What started out as small enterprises to aid the miners in some cases turned into major ventures that served the nation. For example, Levi Strauss invented the first blue jeans by stitching together cotton duck cloth originally meant for building tents. The rugged new material was ideal for the rough business of mining. In another example, an enterprising Hungarian immi-grant named Agoston Haraszthy planted dozens of varieties of grapes from Europe to start a wine business. He became the father of the California wine industry.

Not all the consequences of the gold rush have been beneficial to our country. Mining transformed the western environment. As miners moved from camp to camp, they left behind a blighted landscape—the hills stripped of trees, massive piles of gravel, and thousands of abandoned tents. The ground was littered with "empty bottles, oyster cans, sardine boxes, and brandied fruit jars." As the placers gave out, a great deal of gold remained, but it was locked in quartz or buried deep in the earth. Mining became an expensive business, far beyond the reach of independent prospec-tors. Tapping veins of gold or silver required huge mills to crush the ore and powerful machinery to move vast quantities of dirt and sand. Hydraulic mining depended on large-scale reservoirs and elaborate flumes delivering massive volumes of water at high pressure. The process washed mountains into streambeds, clog-ging rivers and killing fruit orchards. By the 1890s, the debris from mining had buried thirty-nine thousand acres of farmland.

At the same time, whole forests were destroyed to support the mines.

Gold seekers were lured with the promise of getting rich, but as hard-rock mining supplanted placer operations, more miners became laborers paid by the day or week to work in difficult and dangerous conditions underground. They suffered in underground temperatures that sometimes soared above 100 degrees. Poor ventilation often led to headaches and dizziness, while long-term exposure to quartz dust and lead produced fatal diseases of the lungs. Miners were in danger of misfired dynamite, cave-ins, and fires. For a time, so many accidents occurred that a worker died every week. In the late 1870s, accidents disabled one in thirty miners and killed one in eighty. As a whole, as many as 7,500 men died digging out silver and gold on the western mining frontier, and perhaps 20,000 more were maimed. Over time, the threatening working conditions in the mines produced angry, and frequently violent, confrontations between workers and mine owners.

Most important, the discovery of gold hastened America's drive toward civil war by forcing the federal government to confront once again the painful, and politically explosive, issue of slavery. The explosion in population in the West translated into demands for statehood. On June 3, 1849, California's military governor took the highly unusual step of issuing a Proclamation to the People of California. This proclamation called for an election of delegates to a constitutional convention and the eventual creation of either a territorial or state government. The forty-eight delegates who met in Monterey on September 1, 1849, represented the diversity of California in the years following the gold rush. Half of the delegates were younger than thirty-five. Seven delegates were native-born Californians (including one Native

American, Manuel Domínguez), six delegates were Europeans (including John Sutter), and thirty-five delegates were originally from the United States, though their time in California ranged from four months to twenty years. The delegates voted unanimously to prohibit slavery in the state. "Neither slavery, nor involuntary servitude, unless for the punishment of crimes," the group wrote into the California bill of rights, "shall ever be tolerated in this State." The new constitution also made a special effort to attract women to the state. In 1850, women made up less than 8 percent of California's population. The percentage was even lower in the gold fields. The new constitution guaranteed that all of the assets of the wife, whether acquired before or after her marriage, would remain her separate property.

Washington thought that it had developed a plan for dealing with the question of slavery that would delay the seemingly inevitable conflict for at least another generation. The Missouri Compromise of 1820 divided slavery along sectional lines by prohibiting the institution above the 36°30' latitude. With the gold rush and California's rush to statehood, the delicate sectional balance was upset. The South immediately laid claim to the new lands, most of which lay below the line established by the compromise. Georgia's Robert Toombs warned Congress "in the presence of the living God, that if by your legislation you seek to drive us from the territories of California and new Mexico . . . therby attempting to fix a national degradation upon half the states of this Confederacy, *I am for disunion.*" Northern abolitionists, however, were unwilling to cede the new territory. A Pennsylvania Democrat, David Wilmot, attached an amendment called the Wilmot Proviso to an 1846 appropriations bill declaring that no territory acquired from Mexico would be open to slavery.

Congress failed to pass the proviso, but it represented a symbolic watershed: it signaled that the question of slavery in the new territories would push the nation closer to civil war. The debate produced some of the finest speeches ever given in Congress, featuring the then aging triumvirate of Henry Clay, Daniel Webster, and John C. Calhoun. In January 1850, Clay, the architect of the 1820 compromise, presented his "comprehensive scheme" in a two-day address before the Senate. He received unexpected support from Webster, who shared his determination to save the union. Webster rose "to speak today not as a Massachusetts man, nor as a Northern man, but an American. . . . I speak today for the preservation of the Union."

The plan that Clay presented and Webster supported became known as the Compromise of 1850. According to the plan, California entered the Union as a free state and the slave trade was abolished in Washington, D.C., both of which were concessions to northern representatives. For the South, slavery in New Mexico and Utah would be determined by popular sovereignty, and the federal government would enact a Fugitive Slave Act that allowed slave owners the right to hunt down escaped slaves in the north. Popular sovereignty meant that citizens of the territory could determine if they wanted slavery or not, and this became the government's method for solving the issue in the West. "Faction, Disunion & the love of mischief are put under, at least, for the present, & I hope for a long time," Webster said of the compromise.

In reality, the compromise only temporarily derailed the march to civil war initiated by the end of the Mexican-American War and California's insistence on entering the Union as a free state. The battle over slavery in the new states fed fears on both sides: the South's of territorial and economic strangulation; the North's of the "slave power" conspiracy. But the Fugitive Slave Act was the

Achilles' heel of the compromise. Harriet Beecher Stowe's *Uncle Tom's Cabin*, which sold three hundred thousand copies in the first year after publication, brought home the evils of the new law. "His idea of a fugitive," she wrote of a typical northerner, "was only an idea of the letters that spell the word. . . . The magic of the real presence of distress,—the imploring human eye, the frail trembling hand, the despairing appeal of helpless agony,—these he had never tried. He had never thought that a fugitive might be a hapless mother, a defenseless child." The Supreme Court added to northern anger when it issued the infamous *Dred Scott* decision, which described blacks "as a subordinate and inferior class of beings, who . . . had no rights which the white man was bound to respect." Finally, the violence unleashed by forces on both sides over the admission of Kansas and Nebraska into the Union rendered moot the faith in popular sovereignty and made the war inevitable.

The spirit of the gold rush did not end with the Civil War. It extended well into the twentieth century. The audacious forty-niner spirit is reflected in modern-day high-tech Argonauts who mine the rich veins of science and technology. In the nineteenth century, California gave birth to a gold rush that added millions of dollars to the nation's wealth; in the twentieth century it was the birthplace of microchips and personal computers. It remains the most diverse state in the union, with a population that is 52 percent white, 30 percent Latino, 10 percent Asian/Pacific Islander, and 7 percent black—a clear legacy of the gold rush.

* * *

The gold rush added as much as $500 million to the nation's wealth. Unfortunately, neither James Marshall nor John Sutter benefited from their find. Squatters swarmed over Sutter's land, destroying crops and butchering his herds. "There is a saying that men will steal everything but a milestone and a millstone," Sutter later recalled; "they stole my millstones." By 1852, New Helvetia had been devastated and Sutter was bankrupt. He spent the rest of his life seeking compensation for his losses from the state and federal governments. As for Marshall, with everyone searching for gold, he could not find workers for his sawmill, which quickly failed, and he was unable to secure legal recognition of his claims in the gold fields. When Marshall died on August 10, 1885, he was living in a small cabin with a subsistence garden. The man who first discovered California's gold died with an estate valued at $549.70.

For Further Reading

H. W. Brands offers the most concise and lively discussion of the gold rush in his popular *The Age of Gold* (2002). Also valuable is J. S. Holliday, *Rush to Riches: Gold Fever and the Making of California* (1999); and Malcolm J. Rohrbough, *Days of Gold: The California Gold Rush and the American Nation* (1997). Kenneth N. Owens provides an international context for understanding the gold rush in *Riches for All: The California Gold Rush and the World* (2002).

For biographical information on the main players in the drama, see Richard Dillon, *Fool's Gold: The Decline and Fall of Captain John Sutter of California* (1967); Iris H. Engstrand, "John Sutter: A Biographical Examination," in *John Sutter and a Wider West*, edited by Kenneth N. Owens (1994); Theressa Gay, *James W. Marshall, the Discoverer of Californian Gold: A Biography* (1967); Will Bagley, ed., *Scoundrel's Tale: The Samuel Brannan Papers* (1999).

The best recent survey concerning the economic transformations occurring in the United States in the late nineteenth century is Walter Licht's *Industrializing America* (1995). A number of books address the importance of the railroad industry in shaping continued economic growth in the late nineteenth century. David Haward Bain offers the most comprehensive account in *Empire Express: Building the First Transcontinental Railroad* (1999).

4 September 17, 1862
Antietam

By the fall of 1862 it appeared that the South was on the verge of victory in the Civil War. "The winter of our discontent is turned to glorious summer," observed the *Richmond Examiner*. In the West, two southern armies under Generals Braxton Bragg and Edmund Kirby Smith swept through eastern Tennessee in August; by September, they were operating in Kentucky. But the more daring part of the Confederate offensive unfolded in the East. While General George B. McClellan's army was slowly being withdrawn from the Virginia peninsula, General Robert E. Lee turned quickly on the Union forces, led by General John Pope, that were stationed in Virginia to guard Washington. Concentrating his entire strength on Pope, Lee scored a brilliant victory in the Second Battle of Bull Run (August 29–30, 1862). "For the first time I believe it possible," wrote the *New York Tribune*, "that Washington may be taken." The southern offensive demoralized the North. The *New York Times* asked: "Of what use are all these terrible sacrifices? Shall we have nothing but defeat to show for all our valor?"

The South's bold strategy was in keeping with General Lee's approach to war. "His name might be 'Audacity,'" a southern officer said of his commander. "He will take more chances and take them quicker, than any other General in this country, North or South." A scion of the first families of Virginia and a 1829 graduate of West Point, Lee had distinguished himself during the Mexican-American War, leading U.S. commander General Winfield Scott to call him "the very best soldier that I ever saw in the field." In April 1861, Lincoln offered Lee command of the Union Army, forcing him to choose between the nation and his native state of Virginia, which had announced its secession from the Union. "I cannot raise my hand against my birthplace, my home, my children," he wrote. A few days later he resigned his commission in the army and accepted appointment as commander in chief of Virginia's military forces. Realizing that the North possessed greater resources and would win a war of attrition, Lee decided on a risky offensive strategy. He hoped that by winning a few decisive battles he could demoralize the North, embolden the peace forces, and pressure Lincoln to end the fighting.

In September 1862, with the enemy "weakened and demoralized," Lee led forty thousand soldiers across the Potomac into Maryland, stopping at the town of Frederick. "The present," he wrote to Confederate president Jefferson Davis, "seems to be the most propitious time since the commencement of the war for the Confederate Army to enter Maryland." Although officially a "border state," Maryland allowed slavery and had close southern ties. If he could convince residents to join the Confederacy, Lee could trap the Union capital of Washington, D.C., inside a Confederate state.

But it was a ragtag army that crossed the Potomac. According to one of Lee's officers, the soldiers had been "marching, fighting and starving" since June. The Confederates had little food and no supplies. Nearly a quarter of the men marched barefoot. In order to sustain the move north, Lee needed to capture the Union garrison at Harpers Ferry, which threatened his supply line. On September 9, Lee dictated Special Orders No. 191, dividing his army and sending "Stonewall" Jackson to secure Harpers Ferry while the remainder of his army marched toward Hagerstown, Maryland.

This bold and dangerous move left his army scattered and vulnerable to attack for the next five days. Lee had few worries that his Union counterpart, General McClellan, would take advantage of the opportunity. The Union general had recently returned to lead the Army of the Potomac after an embarrassing performance in the Seven Days campaign in June 1862, when Lee's forces had repelled his advances on the Confederate capital of Richmond, Virginia. "He is a very able general but a very cautious one," Lee told a fellow officer. A vain and powerful man of whom it was said that he could lift a 250-pound man over his head, McClellan, like Lee, was a hero of the Mexican-American War and the author of manuals on military tactics. "The true course in conducting military operations," McClellan declared, "is to make no movement until the preparations are complete." True to his philosophy, McClellan required a week to march his eighty-four-thousand-man army the fifty miles from Washington to Frederick.

In war, however, decisive battles are often determined as much by chance as by strategy. Lee had every reason to believe that the ponderous McClellan would be unable to take advantage of the opportunity. But on this occasion his Union counterpart would have the advantage. On Saturday, September 13, a soldier from the 27th Indiana, Corporal Barton W. Mitchell, decided to take a nap under the shade of a tree in a meadow east of Frederick,

Maryland. He saw a bulky envelope lying in the grass. When he picked it up he discovered three cigars wrapped in a piece of paper that read: "Headquarters, Army of Northern Virginia, Special Orders, No. 191." The paper contained Lee's orders announcing his audacious plan. A major on Lee's staff wrote: "The loss of this battle order constitutes one of the pivots on which turned the event of the war." Upon reading Lee's orders, an excited McClellan wired Lincoln: "I have the plans of the rebels, and will catch them in their own trap if my men are equal to the emergency. Will send you trophies."

Even though he soon discovered that his orders had fallen into enemy hands, Lee went ahead with the planned capture of Harpers Ferry. On September 15, Federal forces raised the white flag and 12,500 men surrendered. Thrilled by the victory, Lee decided to reunite his army and engage McClellan east of Sharpsburg, Maryland, near a little creek called Antietam. "We will make our stand on these hills," he said. The Confederates formed a line four miles long. There was one drawback: it forced them to fight with their backs against the Potomac, leaving only a shallow crossing as an escape route.

There was a great deal riding on this battle. The series of Confederate victories had pushed England and France toward recognizing the Confederacy. Lord Palmerston, the British prime minister, laid out the plan. "If the Federals sustain a great defeat," he said, "they may be at once ready for mediation, and the iron should be struck while it is hot. If, on the other hand, they should have the best of it, we may wait awhile and see what may follow." At the same time, morale in the North was low and Lincoln was facing increased pressure from peace forces in the upcoming elections. Lee's strategy was working. A government official wrote that the previous Fourth of July, 1862, had been "the gloomiest since the birth of this republic. Never was the country so low, and after such sacrifices of blood, of time, and of money."

By September 16, McClellan had amassed a force of nearly 75,000 men. Lee had half as many men, but McClellan assumed he had more—as many as 120,000. Although his army vastly outnumbered Lee's, the ever-cautious McClellan waited for reinforcements. The delay gave Lee the time he needed to build defenses and to welcome Stonewall Jackson's men back. Late in the afternoon, McClellan ordered Major General "Fighting Joe" Hooker to lead an assault on the Confederate left flank. Once they had Lee's forces occupied, McClellan planned to send Ambrose Burnside's IX Corps across Antietam Creek to attack on the right, cutting off Lee's route to the Potomac. He kept two divisions in reserve to take advantage of a Union breakthrough and to counter any Confederate offensive. The problem with the plan was that McClellan would never have more than half of his troops in combat at any time, essentially negating his superior numbers and firepower. The result was that Lee was able to shift his resources back and forth to the sector where they were needed most. After a brief skirmish, the two sides settled down for a restless night. "We are through for the night," Hooker said, "but tomorrow we fight the battle that will determine the fate of the Republic."

* * *

The roots of the Civil War could be traced back to 1607 when the first slaves arrived in Jamestown. By 1750 slavery had become standard practice in all the colonies. Slavery was the great contradiction at the heart of the new American republic. At the time that Thomas Jefferson penned the words "all men are created equal," he owned more than 220 slaves. The founders fought a revolution to preserve freedom, but they codified slavery in the Constitution, which included provisions that prevented Congress from ending slavery for at least twenty years and required free states to return fugitive slaves. Slavery was not an anomaly—it was the willful product of the democratic system, held in place by laws enacted by popularly elected officials. By 1830, most northern states had passed laws abolishing slavery, but south of the Mason-Dixon Line, the two million blacks living in slavery helped make cotton king. Slave owners invested more than $2 billion in their human property, making it the largest concentration of capital in the country.

The discovery of gold, and the westward expansion that it inspired, brought the long-simmering moral debate over slavery to a boil. When Lincoln won the election in November 1860, there were thirty-three states in the Union. By the time he took the oath of office in March 1861, only twenty-seven remained. Many secessionists, especially large slave owners, viewed Lincoln and the Republicans as revolutionaries determined to destroy the slaveholding system. Lincoln's election, declared a southern newspaper, "shows that the North [intends] to free the negroes and force amalgamation between them and the children of the poor men of the South." In fact, Lincoln's approach to the slavery issue was far from revolutionary, and he struggled to reassure the South that he wished only to prevent slavery's spread, not to abolish it. But even attempts to limit slavery's expansion frightened southern slaveholders, who believed that their peculiar institution needed to grow in order to survive. The Civil War would be fought over the fundamental question left unresolved following the American Revolution: Would the rights of freedom be extended to all Americans, or only a chosen few?

The Civil War began at 4:30 A.M. on April 12, 1861, when Confederate artillery opened fire on Fort Sumter. Each side believed that the war would be short and relatively bloodless. The Union defeat at the First Battle of Bull Run shattered that illusion, giving Americans their first taste of the carnage that lay ahead. Some 4,500 men were killed, wounded, or captured on both sides in this battle known as Bull Run to the North, which named battles after the land feature nearest to the fighting, and as Manassas to the South, which used the name of a nearby town.

The Civil War was more than a clash of armies; it was a battle between two societies. Each side went into the war with considerable advantages and liabilities. The North's chief assets were its enormous size and its thriving industrial economy. Nearly 21 million people lived in the North but only 9 million in the Confederacy, 3.5 million of whom were slaves. The North had more than twice as many miles of railroad track as the South. Most of the nation's heavy industry was concentrated in the North. In 1860, Union states produced 97 percent of the nation's firearms, 94 percent of its cloth, and 90 percent of its boots and shoes. One state, New York, produced four times as many manufactured goods as the entire South. The North in 1860 built fourteen out of every fifteen railroad locomotives manufactured in the United States.

The rebel states were not intimidated by the Union's advantages in human resources and industrial might. Confederate leaders had the psychological advantage, because their people were fighting to preserve their own territory. "Lincoln may bring his 75,000 troops against us," said vice president of the Confederacy, Alexander Stephens. "We fight for our homes, our fathers and mothers, our wives, brothers, sisters, sons and daughters!" For decades, southerners had dominated the nation's military academies and officers' corps, and Confederates could count on experienced military men defecting from the North to lead their army. Although the South had only 40 percent as many people as the North, the availability of slaves freed a much larger proportion of whites for military service.

With the obvious example of the American Revolution in mind, southerners believed that a determined nation could successfully win or maintain its independence against invaders with larger armies and more material resources. George W. Randolph, the Confederate secretary of war in the fall of 1861, confidently stated, "There is no instance in history of a people as numerous as we are inhabiting a country so extensive as ours being subjected if true to themselves." It was believed that, like George Washington's forces during the American Revolution, Southerners could lose most of the battles and still win the war, but only if they could convince their opponent that victory was too costly. Union armies had to penetrate deep into enemy territory, gain control of it, and eventually break the Confederate will to resist the reestablishment of federal power. This offensive strategy required larger numbers of troops than the defensive operation employed by the Confederacy.

Ironically, while drawing parallels between themselves and the American revolutionaries, the Confederates looked for support from an unlikely ally: Great Britain. The Confederacy hoped that Britain, which imported 80 percent of its cotton supply from the South in the 1850s, would rush to the South's defense once the flow of cotton was cut off by the combined effects of the Union blockade and a voluntary embargo in the South on cotton exports. The North, on the other hand, anticipated that a powerful antislavery sentiment in Britain and France would compel their leaders to oppose the slaveholding South.

Despite their differences, both sides called upon a common history and a shared language to justify the war. People living in both the North and South believed they were the true heirs of the American Revolution. The Confederates used the language of individual freedom and liberty to justify their support of slavery and explain their secession. Initially, Lincoln used similar language to explain his hostility toward slavery and his desire to preserve the Union. The contradiction between liberty and slavery built into the foundation of the republic had torn an irreparable breach in the American experiment.

Most young men who marched off to battle in early 1861 held a romanticized image of war and glory. The average age of a soldier in either army was twenty-five. Law set the minimum age for enlistment at eighteen, but recruiters frequently ignored it. As many as eight hundred thousand underage soldiers signed up to fight. Charles E. King, believed to be the youngest soldier in the war, was twelve when he enlisted in the Pennsylvania Volunteers. He was barely a teenager when he died at Antietam. In the initial enthusiasm for war, whole towns rushed to sign up. The Tenth Michigan Volunteers was filled entirely by Flint men; their commander was the mayor.

Religious faith also inspired soldiers in both armies, shaping their understanding of the conflict and the need to fight and, perhaps, die for their cause. Union and Confederate soldiers often prayed to the same God, read from the same Bible, and were equally convinced that God was on their side. "I believe our cause to be the cause of liberty and light," observed a Unionist, "the cause of God, and holy and justifiable in His sight." On the other end of the battlefield, a Confederate declared, "Our cause is Just and God is Just and we shall finally be successful whether I live to see the time or not."

The early battles of the war dashed any hope of quick victory for either side. The North scored some victories in the West and gained the upper hand on the sea, but the Army of the Potomac was bogged down in the East, where Confederate forces scored a series of victories in defense of their capital at Richmond. By the time the two armies gathered on opposite sides of Antietam Creek in September 1862, the harsh reality of war and death had shattered the illusion of a quick and painless victory.

* * *

The battle commenced on the morning of September 17 with Hooker's three divisions attacking at dawn, charging into a thirty-acre cornfield. "It was never my fortune to witness a more bloody, dismal battlefield," said Hooker. Three divisions on either side waged the battle. "Men were knocked out of the ranks by the dozens," recalled Major Rufus Dawes. "But we jumped over the fence, and pushed on, loading, firing, and shooting as we advanced. There was, on the part of the men, great hysterical excitement, eagerness to go forward, and a reckless disregard of life, of every-thing but victory." A chorus of cannon fire on both sides created what one Confederate called "artillery hell." The cornfield became the scene of bloody combat, with both sides surging back and forth through the shattered stalks. "In the time I am writing," Hooker reported, "every stalk of corn in the northern and greater part of the field was cut as closely as could have been done with a knife, and the slain lay in rows precisely as they had stood in their ranks a few moments before."

While Hooker's division fought without backup, Lee managed to throw three additional divisions into the battle. "Never have I seen men fall as fast and thick," observed a soldier from South Carolina. The 6th Wisconsin managed to fight their way past the cornfield and push the Confederates back, "loading and firing with demoniacal fury." The Confederate line was dangerously thin and near collapse when the 2,300-man division of Brigadier General John Bell Hood stormed out of the woods and pushed the Federals back into the cornfield. Hood's offensive, which he described as "the most terrific clash of arms, by far, that has occurred during the war," prevented an early Union victory. Both sides suffered heavy losses in the battle. In less than twenty minutes, 186 of the 226 men in the 1st Texas regiment were killed or wounded. By 9 A.M. more than 8,000 Americans had been killed or injured— and the fighting had only just begun.

New military technology had recently made the battlefield a much more dangerous place. The most important single innovation was a new bullet. For centuries infantry had been equipped with smoothbore muskets that required a solider to ram a bullet down the barrel after each firing. In the 1850s, an American adoption of a French invention produced the "minie ball," a bullet sufficiently smaller than the rifle barrel to permit relatively rapid loading and reloading. The new bullet expanded into a gun barrel's rifled grooves and spun at great speed from the muzzle. The minie ball from a rifled barrel could kill at half a mile and was accurate at four hundred yards—five times as far as any earlier one-man weapon. Despite the new lethal bullets, the traditional infantry charge remained a standard tactic. The result was often mass slaughter. Frontal assaults in compact formations were suicidal in the face of accurate, long-distance rifle fire. It was not uncommon for regiments to experience battlefield casualties in excess of 50 percent in a single engagement. Faced with the high probability of death, many soldiers wrote out their own "identification tags" before going into battle, pinning scraps of paper to their uniforms with their names, next of kin, and civilian addresses.

While the battle in the cornfield remained stalemated, the Union was making progress a couple hundred yards to the west. Major General Edwin Sumner, at sixty-five the oldest general in the northern army, sent a division across the cornfield and into the West Woods. The rebels fell back, allowing Sumner's men to penetrate the woods unopposed. But in reality, Sumner had walked into an ambush. Confederates popped up from behind trees, bushes, and fencelines, raining bullets on the confused Union troops. "All hands ran for dear life," wrote a Union soldier. "Where the line stood the ground was covered in blue," wrote a Georgian. The Union division began to collapse. Rookie regiments in the rear brigades began firing frantically into the backs of their own troops. Among the men wounded was Captain Oliver Wendell Holmes Jr., who survived a bullet through the neck at Antietam and eventually became an associate justice of the U.S. Supreme Court. By the time Sumner managed to get all of his men out of the West Woods he had lost nearly half his division—2,255 men dead, wounded, or missing.

The fiercest battles that day took place on Bloody Lane, a sunken farm road at the center of Lee's forces. The trench provided the Confederates with an exceptionally strong defensive position. They waited patiently for the Union soldiers to come within firing range. Colonel John B. Gordon of the 6th Alabama recalled what happened next. "With all my lung power I shouted, 'Fire!' My rifles flamed and roared in the Federals' faces like a blinding blaze of lightning accompanied by the quick and deadly thunderbolt. The effect was appalling. The entire front line, with few exceptions, went down in the consuming blast." Wave after wave of Union soldiers was beaten back. Among those participating in the assault was the colorful Irish Brigade, which advanced up the slope under their emerald flags, their Catholic chaplain shouting the words of absolution for those about to die.

Not until noon, after two hours of fighting, did the Confederate line break, and not before leaving behind a ghastly scene. "In the road the dead covered the ground. It seemed, as I rode along, that it was the Valley of Death," recalled a soldier. "I think that in the space of less than ten acres, lay the bodies of a thousand dead men and as many more wounded." It was not just men who suffered. A Union lieutenant described "hundreds of horses too, all mangled and putrefying, scattered everywhere." The Confederates were in full retreat. "Lee's army was ruined," observed a Confederate, "and the end of the Confederacy was in sight." McClellan, ever fearful that Lee had perhaps an entire division in reserve, feared exposing himself by sending in his reserves.

In the afternoon the fighting shifted to Lee's right, where Ambrose Burnside's men forced their way across a heavily guarded bridge, rolling back the Confederates after more fierce fighting and large casualties. One of Burnside's regiments, the 23rd Ohio, included two future presidents of the United States: Lieutenant-Colonel Rutherford B. Hayes and Sergeant William McKinley. By 3 P.M. Burnside had eight thousand Union troops advancing on a front three-quarters of a mile wide across the hills and fields of Sharpsburg. They outnumbered the Confederates by more than four to one. One of Lee's officers watching the Union Army advance from a hill near town wrote that "the earth seemed to tremble beneath their tread." The battle, and the war itself, hung in the balance. At just the moment when Burnside appeared on the verge of capturing Harpers Road and cutting off Lee's escape,

Major General A. P. Hill, and his division of three thousand seasoned men, came riding to the rescue. Lee's light division had ridden seventeen miles in eight hours to arrive just in time to save their general and crush the exhausted Union troops. Routed, Burnside pulled his troops back to the west bank of the Antietam.

By nightfall, 2,108 Union solders lay dead along with between 1,546 and 2,700 Confederates. Between 17,301 and 18,573 men were wounded or injured. "No tongue can tell, no mind can conceive, no pen portray the horrible sights I witnessed," a Union soldier reflected. By comparison, more men lost their lives at Antietam than in all the wars the nation fought in the nineteenth century. Four times as many men died on the battlefield near Sharpsburg than were killed in the D-day invasion of Normandy in World War II. The next day another eyewitness noted, "The most appalling sights upon the battlefield . . . the ground strewn with the bodies of the dead and the dying . . . the cries and groans of the wounded . . . the piles of dead men, in attitudes which show the writhing agony in which they died—faces distorted . . . begrimed and covered with clotted blood, arms and legs torn from the body or the body itself torn asunder."

Despite the carnage, the Union commander could finally claim a victory. He had blunted the Confederate offensive and Lee was forced to retreat. "God bless you and all with you," Lincoln wired his commander. "Destroy the rebel army if possible." With thirty thousand fresh troops in reserve, McClellan could have crushed Lee's battered army. But he was, as historian Stephen W. Sears wrote, "so fearful of losing that he would not risk winning." The Confederate Army slipped back south across the Potomac, defeated but intact, capable of fighting for another horrific two and a half years. Lincoln told his Cabinet that "the action of the army against the rebels has not been quite what I should have best liked," and soon afterward he fired McClellan. Lee's retreat, however, turned a tactical stalemate into a strategic victory for the Union.

* * *

The Civil War would continue, but the nature of the war changed on that day. Before Antietam, Lincoln's objective was solely to preserve the Union. "If I could save the Union without freeing any slave, I would do it," he said, "and if I could save it by freeing all the slaves, I would do it, and if I could save it by freeing some and leaving others alone, I would also do that." On September 22, 1862, just five days after the battle, however, Lincoln issued his preliminary Emancipation Proclamation. He had wanted to do so earlier but had accepted the counsel of Secretary of State William Seward to delay "until you can give it to the country supported by military success." He told his Cabinet that he had made a promise "to myself, and to my Maker" to issue the proclamation if Lee was forced to retreat from Maryland. "I think the time has come now," he said. The proclamation warned Confederate states that unless they returned to the Union by January 1, 1863, their slaves "shall be then, thenceforward, and forever free." "Perhaps no consequence of Antietam was more momentous than this one," observed the historian James McPherson.

On the promised date of January 1, 1863, Lincoln issued the official Emancipation Proclamation. The historian Brooks Simpson called it "a revolutionary document cloaked in conservative terms." As of that day, the document declared, the three million slaves in the rebellious states "shall be then, henceforth forever free." As critics were quick to point out, the proclamation did not set free a single slave on the day it was issued. Believing that he derived the power to declare emancipation from his war powers,

Lincoln was careful to limit the immediate impact of the proclamation to those slaves living in the rebellious states, or in parts not
under Union control. Excluded from the provisions were slaves
living in the border states that remained in the Union—Delaware,
Kentucky, Maryland, and Missouri—as well as those living in
Union-controlled areas of Tennessee, Louisiana, and Virginia.
"The Government liberates the enemy's slaves as it would the
enemy's cattle," blustered the *London Spectator*, "simply to weaken
them in the coming conflict. . . . The principle asserted is not that
a human being cannot justly own another, but that he cannot own
him unless he is loyal to the United States."

Despite its limitations, the proclamation set off wild rejoicing
among white and black abolitionists. For the first time, the government had committed itself to freeing slaves. "We shout for joy,"
wrote Frederick Douglass, "that we live to record this righteous
decree." In Washington, D.C., a crowd of blacks gathered in front
of the White House to cheer the president, who appeared at the
window. To Charlotte Forten, a young black woman living in
South Carolina, "it all seemed . . . like a brilliant dream." There
was even jubilation among the slaves in loyal border states who
were exempted from the proclamation's provisions.

The Emancipation Proclamation transformed the war to preserve the Union into a struggle over the meaning of freedom. "We
all declare for liberty," Abraham Lincoln declared, "but in using
the same word we do not all mean the same thing." Jefferson
Davis enunciated the Confederacy's views of freedom when he
declared that the South was "forced to take up arms to vindicate
the political rights, the freedom, equality, and State sovereignty
which were the heritage purchased by the blood of our revolutionary sires." Lincoln initially equated freedom with the preservation of the Union, but after Antietam freedom came to mean

the abolition of slavery. Antietam, he said, was God's sign that "he had decided this question in favor of the slaves." In his message to Congress on December 1, 1862, Lincoln said: "Without slavery the rebellion could never have existed, without slavery it could not continue."

The evolving war goals soon changed the military strategy on the ground. "This government cannot much longer play a game in which it stakes all, and its enemies stake nothing," Lincoln observed. The president turned to General Ulysses S. Grant to execute the new strategy of "total war" that would eventually defeat and devastate the South. "There is now no possible hope of reconciliation," General Henry Halleck wrote Grant. "We must conquer the rebels or be conquered by them." By fighting a coordinated war on all fronts, Grant hoped to exploit the North's advantage in numbers and resources. He recognized that victory would result not from winning individual battles but from destroying the resources and morale of the Confederacy. Ultimately, the capacity of Confederate armies to wage war depended on the economic and psychological support they received from the civilian population. To win this war of conquest, Grant led the Union to target civilians as well as Confederate armies. Grant did not intentionally harm innocent civilians, but he directed his soldiers "to consume everything that could be used to support or supply armies." "Whatever happens," Grant assured Lincoln, "we will not retreat."

News of the Antietam loss doused southern hopes for European intervention. Antietam was, in the words of a rebel representative in London, "a bitter draught and a stunning blow" to the Confederacy. British newspapers viewed the battle as a major military victory for the North. "These battles in Maryland have rather set the North up again," British prime minister Lord Palmerston reasoned. "The whole matter is full of difficulty, and can only be cleared up by some more decided events between the contending armies." Not only were the Europeans unwilling to be on the losing side of another war on the North American continent, but Lincoln's Emancipation Proclamation made it difficult for them to justify supporting the South. As one American diplomat wrote, "Everyone can understand the significance of a war where emancipation is written on one banner and slavery on the other."

Antietam, on the other hand, boosted northern morale. "We have whipped and dispirited them terribly," exclaimed a Union soldier. The *New York Times* used bold headlines to announce the "Great Victory" at Antietam. Before the battle, antiwar Democrats, tapping in to public frustration with the war effort and anger at Lincoln's use of executive powers to wage it, planned to gain control of Congress. Although Democrats picked up seats, winning the governorship of New York and New Jersey and a net gain of thirty-four seats in the House, they failed to significantly alter the political balance of power in the North. The party of Lincoln maintained a majority of twenty-five in the House, actually gained five seats in the Senate, and retained the governorships of sixteen of the eighteen northern states.

In 1863, a number of decisive moves on the battlefield broke the military stalemate. Union victories at Gettysburg, Vicksburg, and Chattanooga opened the way to subduing the South. In September 1864 Sherman captured Atlanta, setting the stage for the final Union victory. The war ended when Lee and Grant met in a Virginia farmhouse at Appomattox Court House on April 9, 1865.

The Civil War was America's defining moment. Since the days of Daniel Shays, Americans had worried whether the republic was strong enough to hold together. The Union victory in the Civil War ended any doubts. Even the language used to describe the United States changed. Before the Civil War, most people referred to the United States as a union, federation, or a confederation. The phrase "the United States are" was common. In his first address to Congress as president, Lincoln used the word *union* twenty times. Not once did he refer to a nation. By the end of the Civil War, Lincoln spoke of a nation, rarely of a union. After 1865, the new usage "the United States is" symbolized a fundamental shift in how Americans saw themselves. The Civil War, Woodrow Wilson said in his 1915 Memorial Day address, "created in this country what had never existed before—a national consciousness."

The legacy of the battle at Antietam would shape the nation for decades to come. The war devastated southern society. The countryside, said one observer, "looked for many miles like a broad black streak of ruin and desolation." Most major southern cities were gutted by fire. A northern visitor called Charleston a place of "vacant houses, of widowed women, of rotting wharves, of deserted warehouses, of weed-wild gardens, of miles of grass-grown streets, of acres of pitiful and voiceless barrenness." Beyond the razing of cities, the Civil War shattered an entire generation of young men in the South. In Alabama, 29 percent of the 122,000 men who bore arms died. One-third of Florida's 15,000 soldiers failed to return. An estimated 23 percent of South Carolina's white male population of arms-bearing age were killed or wounded. Many of those who survived were maimed in battle. In 1866 the state of Mississippi spent a fifth of its revenues on artificial arms and legs for Confederate veterans.

The war also ruined the South's economic health. The region's best agricultural lands lay barren. It would take more than a decade for the staples of the southern economy—cotton, tobacco, and sugar—to recover from the wartime devastation. Union forces had destroyed or dismantled most factories and torn up long stretches of railroad. According to some estimates, the South's per capita wealth in 1865 was only about half what it had been in 1860. All Confederate money became worthless. But the most unsettling of all the changes to the southern economy resulted from the end of slavery. Slave property, which was estimated at over $2 billion in 1860, completely disappeared.

In contrast, the North emerged from the Civil War with new prosperity and power. The Republicans who had dominated the wartime Congress enacted a uniform system of banking and a transcontinental railroad. They also fueled the North's economy through generous appropriations for internal improvements. Railroads thrived by carrying troops and supplies; the meatpacking and textile industries soared in response to demands from troops for food and uniforms. The per capita wealth of the North doubled between 1860 and 1870. The number of manufacturers increased by 80 percent, and property values increased from $10 billion to more than $25 billion. In 1870 the per capita wealth of New York State was more than twice that of all eleven ex-Confederate states combined.

On the political landscape, war-born hostility shaped the competition between the two parties long after the war had ended. Republicans depended on hatred of southern rebels to cement their biracial coalition. "The Democratic party," proclaimed Indiana governor Oliver P. Morton, "may be described as a common sewer and loathsome receptacle, into which is emptied every element of treason, North and South." Democrats appealed to their natural constituency of former slave owners by charging that Republicans were the defenders of economic privilege and political centralization, and a threat to individual liberty. Stressing the potent message of white supremacy, southern Democrats also drove an ideological wedge between freed slaves and poor whites.

The balance of power in the nation was fundamentally altered as a result of the war. Before 1861, the slave states had achieved an extraordinary degree of power in the national government. In 1861 the United States had lived under the Constitution for seventy-two years. During forty-nine of those years, the country's president had been a southerner—and a slaveholder. After the Civil War, a century passed before another resident of the Deep South was elected president.

The war gave birth to the modern American state, dominated by a national government far more powerful than anything the nation had known previously. The federal budget for 1865 exceeded $1 billion (twenty times the budget for 1860), and with its new army of clerks, tax collectors, and other officials, the federal government became the nation's largest employer.

The Civil War era witnessed the passage of three constitutional amendments that would redefine the meaning of American citizenship. The Thirteenth Amendment, passed in December 1865, abolished slavery. The Fourteenth Amendment to the Constitution, passed in June 1866, represented the first national effort to define American citizenship. It declared that "all persons born or naturalized in the United States" were "citizens of the United States and of the State wherein they reside" and were guaranteed "equal protection" and "due process" under the law. By asserting that the national government played a role in guaranteeing individual rights, this amendment established an important foundation for future challenges to the states' rights doctrine. The Fifteenth Amendment, passed in March 1870, forbade states to deny their citizens the right to vote on the grounds of "race, color, or previous condition of servitude." Abolitionists like Frederick Douglass announced that blacks now would "breathe a new atmosphere, have a new earth beneath, and a new sky above." It would take another century, however, for the nation to fulfill the ideals of freedom won on the bloody battlefields of the Civil War.

"In a war with several crucial turning points, the battle of Antietam was the pivotal moment for the most crucial of them all," wrote the historian James McPherson. Yet the outcome of the battle was far from certain. If it had not been for the discovery of Lee's orders, it is unlikely that the perpetually ponderous McClellan would have mounted the attack that he did. And what if the battle had gone the other way? In all likelihood, a successful foray north by Lee would have been perceived as a major embarrassment for the Union. England and possibly France would have intervened on the side of the Confederacy, and Lincoln would have been forced to sue for peace—just as Lee had planned. There would have been no Emancipation Proclamation, slavery would have continued in the South, and the fragile American republic would very likely have been torn apart.

For Further Reading

The starting point for understanding Antietam are two books by James McPherson. *Crossroads of Freedom: Antietam: The Battle That Changed the Course of the Civil War* (2002) is the best brief volume on the battle and its consequences. *Battle Cry of Freedom: The Civil War Era* (1988) puts Antietam, and the Civil War itself, into the larger context of nineteenth-century America. Also valuable is Stephen W. Sears, *Landscape Turned Red: The Battle of Antietam* (1983).

The literature on the Civil War is enormous. The best brief treatments can be found in Brooks Simpson, *America's Civil War* (1996); William L. Barney, *Battleground for the Union: The Era of Civil War and Reconstruction, 1848–1877* (1990); and Allen C. Guelzo, *The Crisis of the American Republic: A History of the Civil*

War and Reconstruction Era (1995). Geoffrey C. Ward's *The Civil War: An Illustrated History* provides a lucid and colorful account of the war. *In the Presence of Mine Enemies: The Civil War in the Heart of America, 1859–1863* (2003), Edward Ayers shows the impact of national events on two counties on opposite sides of the Mason-Dixon Line.

The most thorough military history from the Confederate viewpoint is Shelby Foote's three-volume work *The Civil War: A Narrative* (1958–1974). For a northern perspective, *How the North Won: A Military History of the Civil War* (1983) by Herman Hattaway and Archer Jones treats all aspects of the northern war effort. The experience of the common soldier is explored in Gerald Linderman's *Embattled Courage: The Experience of Combat in the American Civil War* (1988). The politics of the Emancipation Proclamation are addressed in two studies, LaWanda Cox's *Lincoln and Black Freedom: A Study in Presidential Leadership* (1981) and Robert Durden's *The Gray and the Black: The Confederate Debate on Emancipation* (1972).

5 July 6, 1892
The Homestead Strike

E arly on the morning of July 6, 1892, two covered barges, the *Iron Mountain* and the *Monongahela,* floated down the Monongahela River toward Andrew Carnegie's Homestead steel plant. Located about six miles upriver from Pittsburgh, Homestead was the crown jewel in Andrew Carnegie's vast steel manufacturing empire. The customized barges contained enough food to last several weeks, as well as 300 pistols and 250 rifles. The boats also carried some 300 Pinkerton "detectives." With their symbol of an open eye, and their slogan "We Never Sleep," the Pinkertons gave birth to the term "private eye." In reality, they were a well-armed mercenary army of private police officials used to crush labor strikes. On this day they had come to bust the union of steel workers. *Harper's Weekly* noted that the agency "hired themselves out, and fought more or less bravely on whatever side of a contest they found the best pay and the most tempting booty, without taking the slightest interest in the merits or demerits of the cause they fought for or against."

The industrial revolution produced wrenching changes for American workers who felt trapped in a new industrial order that had turned them into cogs in a wheel. "They no longer carried the keys of the workshop, for workshops, tools and keys belonged not to them, but to their master," observed union leader Terence Powderly. The friction reached a boiling point in the 1870s and 1880s when workers organized an unprecedented number of protests and strikes. In 1877 railway workers organized the first national strike in American history to protest salary cuts. Nine years later unions battled with McCormick Reaper Works, a confrontation that culminated with a deadly bomb exploding in Chicago's Haymarket Square, killing seven policemen and injuring sixty bystanders. For these deaths, eight anarchists were put on trial and seven were convicted of conspiracy to commit murder. The Haymarket riot, which produced a national backlash against labor radicalism and strengthened the hand of business, cast a dark shadow over labor-management relations for the rest of the century.

The confrontation at Homestead pitted against each other two of the most powerful players in the new industrial order. If any union could resist the growing corporate tide it was the Amalgamated Association of Iron, Steel, and Tin Workers, the most powerful craft union in the country at the end of the nineteenth century. Earlier in 1892 the *Pittsburgh Post* called the union "the most powerful independent labor organization in the world." Formed in 1876 by the merger of three groups, the iron and steel union boasted of having nearly twenty-four thousand members, nearly a quarter of the eligible workers in the industry. The membership was made up largely of skilled workers of northern European descent—Irish, English, Scottish, and Welsh—who felt little kinship with less skilled laborers, blacks, or recent immigrants from southern and Eastern European countries. The union leadership tried winning the confidence of business leaders by presenting themselves as moderate and mainstream, and were always careful to distinguish themselves from more radical organizations. They often cooperated with management and opposed strikes "for frivolous purposes."

Despite their conservative approach, business leaders feared the growing power of this union and felt the time had come to force a confrontation that would diminish the union and establish once and for all the power of corporate management to control the workplace. The confrontation "was not so much a question of disagreement as to wages, but a design upon labor organization," opined the *Homestead Local News*.

No one epitomized the concentration of corporate wealth and power better than Andrew Carnegie. Born in Scotland, Carnegie immigrated to the United States with his impoverished parents in 1848. He gradually climbed the American industrial pyramid, starting out as a messenger boy in a Pittsburgh telegraph office. In 1873, at the age of thirty-eight, he used money earned from investments to build the giant J. Edgar Thomson Steel Works in Pittsburgh. Mingling the Puritan doctrine of stewardship with ruthless business practices, Carnegie managed to keep his prices low and drive competitors out of business. To guarantee adequate supplies, Carnegie acquired sources of iron ore for pig iron to produce his steel and of coke and coal to fire the furnaces, and he developed a fleet of steamships and a railroad for transporting the raw materials directly to his mills. "From the moment these crude stuffs were dug out of the earth until they flowed in a stream of liquid steel in the ladles," noted a Carnegie contemporary, "there was never a price, profit, or royalty paid to an outsider."

As tensions between labor and capital escalated during the 1880s, Carnegie billed himself as the friend of labor. He expressed his sympathy toward labor, emphasized peaceful cooperation, and denounced the use of strikebreakers. "There is an unwritten law among the best workmen," Carnegie penned. "Thou shalt not take thy neighbor's job." In public he considered worker organization a "sacred right," said industry should "meet the men more than half way," and preached the wonders of arbitration. In practice, however, Carnegie was often a ruthless businessman who celebrated the benefits of better goods and lower prices that resulted from competition, although he also insisted that the rich were obligated to spend some of their wealth to benefit their "poorer brethren."

Carnegie's tough-minded business practices were on open display at Homestead. In June 1892, Henry Clay Frick announced that the company would no longer recognize the union and would sign individual contracts with workers. Frick, who made a fortune in the coke industry before managing Carnegie's plant, had a well-earned reputation as a fierce opponent of organized labor. Although he stood only five feet three inches, Frick was an intense and intimidating figure. "You see that his head is there, placed on that body, for his triumph and your defeat," noted a contemporary. Realizing that the union would never accept this demand, Frick prepared for the inevitable battle, surrounding the mill with a three-mile-long, twelve-foot-high fence topped with barbed wire. Workers, knowing the company planned to use the fence to protect strikebreakers, named Homestead Works "Fort Frick." On June 29, Frick closed down the mill, locking out 3,800 workers. The two sides braced themselves for a bloody confrontation. "It is evident there is no bluffing at Homestead," observed the *New York Times*. "The fight there is to be to the death."

The mill workers suspected that management might employ Pinkertons and try to bring in nonunion workers. The Homestead workers set up a wide reconnaissance network, watching every approach to town, twenty-four hours a day. They created a workers' advisory committee consisting of forty members who organized the mill on "a truly military basis." They divided the four thousand workers and townspeople into three divisions that watched the town in rotating eight-hour shifts. There was no trouble getting volunteers. Nearly every adult citizen clamored to participate. They were fighting to protect their jobs. If the Pinkertons gained control of the mill, management would then import nonunion workers, whom union members dismissed as "scabs," to perform their jobs. "To be confronted with a gang of loafers and cutthroats from all over the country, coming there, as they thought, to take their jobs, why, they naturally wanted to go down and defend their homes and their property and their lives, with force, if necessary," recalled one worker.

In the early morning hours of July 6, a watchman posted on a bridge in Pittsburgh spotted the Pinkertons. Within minutes operatives sent telegrams warning the people of Homestead of the impending invasion. To alert the town, union men sounded a powerful steam whistle and set off fireworks. Riders sped through the mill town waking up the residents. A journalist observed that at 3 A.M. a "horseman riding at breakneck speed dashed into the streets of Homestead giving the alarm as he sped along." Within minutes, thousands of Homestead plant workers rushed toward the riverbank, tearing down sections of the wooden fence surrounding the mill. "There was no method, no leadership apparent. . . . It was an uprising of a population," wrote a reporter for the *Chicago Tribune*. Looking out over the riverbank, one detective saw "what appeared to be a lot of young men and boys on the bank, swearing and cursing and having large sticks."

The workers needed to keep the Pinkertons from establishing

a beachhead. As long as they could keep the attackers bottled up on the barges, they could win. The Pinkertons, who carried not sticks but the latest Winchester rifles, had the advantage in firepower, but the workers had superior numbers. Workers scoured the town for weapons, gathering together an assortment of old rifles and small arms. No one knows who fired the first shot, but once the firing started, it continued for hours. One observer estimated more than one thousand shots were fired in the first ten minutes.

Homestead workers even discovered a twenty-pound cannon—an old piece of Civil War weaponry that had just been a part of the Fourth of July celebrations in the town—and put it to work. Just before 8 A.M. on July 6, as the Pinkertons tried to land, workers blasted the cannon at the barges. They missed their target, so they sent a railroad car loaded with burning barrels of oil at the barges. It stopped short. Next, the workers pumped oil onto the surface of the river and attempted to light the slick to encircle the barges. It was only lubricant oil and would not light. Finally, the union members tossed dynamite onto the barge roofs and bombarded the barges with Roman candles left over from the July Fourth celebrations.

As the sun rose over the town the heat in the barges became almost unbearable. The terrified Pinkertons cowered belowdecks, hungry, thirsty, tired, and scared. "The noise that they made on shore was awful, and it made us shake in our boots," one Pinkerton said. "We were penned in like rats and we went at the fighting like desperate wild men. . . . All of our men were under the beds and bunks, crying and trembling."

"It was a place of torment," said another. "Men were lying around wounded and bleeding and piteously begging for someone to give them a drink of water, but no one dared to get a drop, although water was all around us. . . . It is a wonder we did not all go crazy or commit suicide."

After an intense battle lasting twelve hours, the Pinkertons raised a bullet-ridden white flag of surrender. At 4 P.M. the workers finally accepted the Pinkertons' surrender. "Victory! We have them now," shouted a union leader. "They surrender." The workers guaranteed the detectives would not be harmed. By this time, however, thousands of townspeople had turned out to witness the victory. Wives and children, workers, toughs, and even an occasional anarchist were milling around the dock. According to one account, the joyous crowd formed itself "into two lines, 600 yards long, between which the men from the barges had to pass." The crowd assaulted the detectives as they walked the gauntlet. A woman used her umbrella to punch out the eye of one man. "The men screamed for mercy," wrote the *New York World*. "We were clubbed at every step," one Pinkerton recalled. "Sticks, stones, and dirt were thrown at us. The women pulled us down, spat in our faces, kicked us, and tore our clothing off while the crowd jeered and cheered." Held in the local jail for their safety the rest of the afternoon, the Pinkertons rode the night train out of town.

At the end of that hot July day, three Pinkertons and seven mill workers lay dead; dozens more were injured. The next day, the workers and the entire community mourned their dead and looked for meaning in what had happened. The Reverend J. J. Mc-Ilyar, spiritual leader of the Methodist Episcopal Church, blamed the company for failing to recognize the legitimate needs of the town's workers. "The mill men were organized in an association that enabled them to obtain just and adequate remuneration for their services," he told mourners. "The existence of this union of men was threatened by a body of Pinkertons, employed by somebody for that purpose. This is what has put this blessed man in his coffin today: a perfect citizen; an intelligent man; a good husband who was never lacking in his duty; a brother who was devoted and loyal and who will surely find his reward."

Many who attended the service and listened to Reverend McIlyar believed that the union men had not only repelled the Pinkertons, but seized the mill, gaining control over the town and saving their jobs. Now if they could keep the state from using the militia to break the strike, the workers believed they could reverse the growing power of big business, force Carnegie to compromise, and reinvigorate the flagging labor movement. Homestead workers had articulated an alternative vision of democracy. "The employees," noted the Homestead Advisory Committee, "have built there a town with its homes, its schools and its churches; have for many years been faithful co-workers with the company in the business of the mill; have invested thousands of dollars of their savings in said mill in the expectation of spending their lives in Homestead." Therefore, they argued, the strikers "have equitable rights and interests" in the mill, declaring that "it is against public policy and subversive of the fundamental principles of American liberty" that workers be denied the right to employment and full participation in the affairs of the mill.

Sometimes it takes decades to discern the significance of a historical event. That was not the case at Homestead. Everyone—strikers, management, reporters, people on the street—realized that the outcome would profoundly impact the American way of life. As one contemporary put it, "The shots fired that July morning at the Pinkerton barges, like the shots fired at Lexington, were 'heard around the world.'" The future of workplace democracy in America hung in the balance. On one side of the divide were the workers who believed in community control of the factory and the surrounding town. They envisioned a system where union members would participate as equals in making all major decisions at work and in the community. The union expected to be on equal footing with its employers, becoming "owners" of the factory where they toiled twelve hours a day, six or seven days a week. On the other side were the new corporate managers who, in an effort to promote efficiency and increase profits, created clear divisions between management and labor, relegating workers to second-class citizenship in the factory.

The workers had won the day, but their victory would be short-lived. Homestead management remained strong in its determination to break the union. On July 7, Carnegie cabled Frick from Scotland: "All anxiety gone since you stand firm. Never employ one of these rioters. Let grass grow over works. Must not fail now. You will win easily next trial." The workers may have scored a victory in the "Battle for Homestead," but the war for workplace democracy was just beginning.

*　*　*

In 1889 economist David A. Wells announced, "An almost total revolution has taken place, and is yet in progress, in every branch and in every relation of the world's industrial and commercial system." Wells was observing the second industrial revolution. Unlike the first industrial revolution, which started in Britain in the late eighteenth century, the second emerged in Germany and the United States during the 1870s. Whether in Berlin or Pittsburgh, the economic transformation shared common features: a growing population, the development of new inventions, the expansion of the railroads, and the emergence of a national marketplace that kindled consumer demand. This favorable environment invited entrepreneurs and government to launch ambitious experiments in harnessing the nation's industrial potential.

The second industrial revolution also produced wrenching changes for American workers. "There is no permanent class of hired laborers among us," Abraham Lincoln said in the 1850s. Twenty years later Lincoln's statement seemed antiquated. Before the Civil War the United States was an overwhelmingly agricultural nation. About 60 percent of all workers toiled on a farm; only 30 percent were involved in nonagricultural pursuits. By the end of the century, those numbers had reversed. The nation's growing urban areas of the Northeast and Midwest saw their manufacturing workforce quadruple, from 1.5 million workers in 1860 to nearly 6 million in 1900.

Labor not only moved from agriculture to manufacturing, it transitioned from small shops to large factories. "Of the nearly three millions of people employed in the mechanical industries of this country, at least four-fifths are working under the factory system," a statistician estimated in 1880. In the South, where cotton mills and tobacco factories were the largest industrial employers, the average factory work force doubled between 1870 and 1900. The Cambria Iron Works in Johnstown, Pennsylvania, employed a thousand workers in 1860; by the end of the century, that number had swelled to nearly ten thousand. In many cities, huge factories employing thousands of workers became commonplace. By 1910, General Electric employed fifteen thousand workers at its plant in Schenectady, New York, as did the Pullman Palace Car Company and International Harvester in Chicago. The transformation from small shop production to factory wage earner robbed many workers of their sense of independence. Workers who had been self-employed now depended on large companies to pay their wages. In 1860 as many people were self-employed as earned wages. By 1900, two of every three Americans relied on wages.

Also during this time, corporate managers were experimenting with new ways to organize and control the workplace that inevitably limited worker freedom. Many turned to the new ideas of "scientific management." Pioneered by an engineer named Frederick W. Taylor, scientific management imposed a new level of regimentation on factory life by promising to allow companies to lower costs and increase profits by subdividing manufacturing into small tasks. Taylor used a stopwatch to dissect the "millions of different operations" that factory workers performed. With these time-motion studies, he was able to determine the simplest, and cheapest, way of performing each job. Taylor's system resulted in the standardization of work procedures that made many factory tasks painfully monotonous. "The different branches of the trade are divided and subdivided so that one man may make just a particular part of a machine and may not know anything whatever about another part of the same machine," machinist John Morrison told a Senate committee in 1883.

The new emphasis on organization also burdened workers with a tighter system of discipline. Employers often forbade singing, drinking, joking, smoking, or conversation on the job. Foremen imposed fines for even minor infractions. Many companies denied immigrant workers time to celebrate their holidays and holy days. Companies enamored of the rigors of scientific management abolished older work patterns, which included periods of heavy work followed by leisurely breaks, and institutionalized a continual pace of work synchronized with machines. "In the factory there is no chance to read," complained one man, "and the noise and hum of machinery prevent general conversation, even when the rules and discipline do not positively forbid it."

Not surprisingly, contemporary accounts of worker attitudes are filled with expressions of resentment toward the new industrial system. Workers resisted many of the new restrictions by forming cooperative alliances and organizing wildcat strikes, but most felt helpless against the onslaught of industrialization. "That a deep-rooted feeling of discontent pervades the masses, none can deny," Terence Powderly wrote in 1885. Two years later, after surveying working-class opinion in his state, a government official in Connecticut commented on "the feeling of bitterness which so frequently manifests itself in their utterances," their "distrust of employers," and their palpable "discontent and unrest."

The confrontation at Homestead resulted from Carnegie's ongoing efforts to streamline his process and cut labor costs. By the late 1880s, Homestead employed roughly three thousand people, produced tons of steel daily, and generated millions of dollars for Carnegie and his company. In the previous decades, technology had dramatically changed the way steel was produced, and Carnegie wanted to reorganize the labor force to reflect these new realities. In 1855, a British inventor, Henry Bessemer, developed a new method for mass producing high-grade steel. The process involved using blasts of air to remove particles of carbon from iron. The invention led to a tenfold increase in steel production between 1877 and 1892, but it also represented a serious threat to the powerful steel workers' union, since it required fewer laborers and eliminated the need for skilled workers. Thus, the technology allowed Carnegie to reduce costs by reducing his dependence on skilled labor. As one commentator put it: "Whatever can be done by machinery, let machinery do, for it at least is insensible to Fourth of July, Washington's birthday, political meetings, pay-days and whisky."

Because of preexisting contracts, skilled workers benefited from the new technology since they were paid by the ton. As production soared, their pay increased even as their skills became obsolete. By the late 1880s, Carnegie focused on countering this trend by replacing the existing salary structure with a "sliding scale" based on the market cost of steel. Labor vigorously opposed the plan, realizing that it could dramatically cut wages and provide Carnegie with an excuse to hire fewer skilled workers. Confrontation seemed inevitable. The first clash took place at the J. Edgar Thomson Steel Works. In 1888, after a series of work stoppages had forced him to accept the union's demand for an eight-hour day, Carnegie closed the plant, fired all union workers, and reopened it with nonunion labor protected by Pinkerton guards. Anyone wishing to work at Thomson was required to sign the Carnegie "ironclad" contract renouncing union membership. The plant then returned to two twelve-hour shifts. Pay was based on the sliding scale controlled by the fluctuating price of steel. The result was longer hours at lower pay.

In 1889, Carnegie turned his attention to Homestead, where he presented workers with the same terms as those at Thomson Works—no union members, a twelve-hour day, and a pay scale that amounted to a 20 to 25 percent cut. The Amalgamated Association at Homestead went on strike in an attempt to get more favorable wages under the sliding scale, to force the company to recognize their union, and to assert their right to advise the company on hiring, firing, and adding new technology. When William Abbott, the manager of Homestead, attempted to bring in nonunion labor, the workers rounded them up and ran them off the property. Eventually, Abbott gave in to union demands. The union agreed to sign a three-year contract that accepted a sliding scale of wages, but set a minimum price of $25 per ton. Most observers considered the settlement a major victory for the workers.

Carnegie, however, was furious with the arrangement, and resolved to produce a different result when the union contract expired in three years. "The great objection to the compromise is of course that it was made under intimidation—our men in other works now know that we will 'confer' with law breakers," Carnegie wrote Abbott. For the new negotiations, Carnegie replaced Abbott with Henry Clay Frick, who was notorious for resorting to violence to break strikes at his coal and coke companies prior to coming to Homestead.

In January 1892, Frick asked the union to submit its proposals for a new contract. The union asked only for a renewal of the previous contract. While the two sides engaged in "negotiations," the fact was that Frick had no intention of compromising, or offering any deal acceptable to the union. While labor argued that they had certain rights because they invested their lives and labor into the company, Frick firmly believed that the company's titled ownership was the only justification needed for hiring whomever at whatever wage the company wanted. Frick believed that labor had no right to force the company into negotiating with an independent organization—a union—over wages, and wanted laborers to work for the mill as individuals only. The unions, Frick had decided, no longer had a place at Homestead.

Not surprisingly, the unions rejected Frick's initial offer, which slashed wages across the board but had its greatest impact on skilled craftsmen. They felt justified in their rejection; after all, they were not asking for more money, just a reaffirmation of the status quo. Not only that, the union leaders now felt confident that a strike might be effective because the company had just received a lucrative contract from the U.S. Navy to provide armor plate for the USS *Monterey* and USS *New York*. Union leaders reasoned that Frick would not want to jeopardize a highly profitable relationship with the government.

Frick gave the union a June 24 deadline to accept his offer. If they refused, he would import nonunion workers. Carnegie, vacationing in the Scottish Highlands, sent Frick a note encouraging a hard line. "We all approve of anything you do, not stopping short of approval of a contest. We are with you to the end." On June 28, he sent another cable to Frick. "Cables do not seem favorable to a settlement at Homestead. If those be correct, this is your chance to reorganize the whole affair." The union understood clearly that Frick was trying to force a confrontation. It called his proposal "a proposition by the firm that they knew we would not accept." It said, however, that it was willing to accept wage cuts if management could show cuts were necessary. "We want to settle it without trouble," they declared. Although the union assured Frick they "don't want a strike," they set up a special strike committee and prepared to stand firm.

Now Frick was making plans for a lockout. He pushed workers throughout May and June to generate a stockpile of steel goods in case the mill had to quit operations. Then, in a move that affirmed the worst fears of the Amalgamated Association, Frick commissioned the erection of a twelve-foot-high wooden fence. A rhyme that began to circulate around Homestead in June of 1892 captured the situation:

> *There stands today with great pretense*
> *Enclosed within a whitewashed fence*
> *A wondrous change of great import,*
> *The mills transformed into a fort.*

The June deadline of the twenty-fourth came and went, and talks broke down completely. True to his word, Frick shut down the armor plate mill on June 29—eight hundred workers were sent home; the lockout had begun. That night Frick was burned in effigy all over Homestead. The next day, a mass meeting of roughly three thousand workers convened at the town meeting hall and defiantly resolved to stand firm. On July 2 notices were posted around Homestead stating that the company's current contract with the workers would no longer be honored; anyone who wanted to return to work had to do so as nonunion labor. The mood was somber at the July 4 celebrations in the town when "Honest John" McLuckie, burgess of the town and a mill worker, addressed the crowds: "We can't celebrate the Fourth until we know whether or not the Declaration of Independence is still in force in this country." Both sides were locked in an ideological struggle to assert what each considered their rights as American workers and entrepreneurs.

On July 5, Frick sent Allegheny County sheriff William McCleary to take possession of the mill. McCleary arrived in Homestead on July 5, followed by a force of deputies and rumors of the approaching Pinkertons. The union and town were galvanized. Led by Hugh O'Donnell and John McLuckie, the union convinced the sheriff that the law was not needed and proceeded to escort his force out of town. A few hours later, early on July 6, scouts spotted the Pinkertons approaching the town.

* * *

Events at Homestead enraged organized labor all across the United States. In a show of solidarity for their brethren, three other Carnegie mills in Pennsylvania went on strike. The solidarity lifted spirits, but the workers at Homestead knew that while they could defeat Carnegie's private army, they were no match for the state's well-trained militia. On July 8, a union delegation met with the state's governor, Robert E. Pattison, to convince him that the workers were protecting the mills and that the state should not intervene in a private labor dispute. Their appeals fell on deaf ears. Two days later, the governor ordered the state militia to Homestead. On Monday, July 11, a train carrying eight thousand soldiers arrived in ninety-five cars, pitching their white tents on the side of a hill overlooking the town, strategically positioning their cannons facing the mills. "It means just this," said one worker, "that the entire National Guard of the State of Pennsylvania has been called out to enable the Carnegie company to employ scab labor."

The workers held fast; they believed they had done nothing wrong and hoped to convince the militia to protect them against another Pinkerton attack. The union sent a welcoming committee to greet the troops with four brass bands. Their efforts failed to engender goodwill. "I don't want any brass-band business while I'm here," said the commanding officer. "I want you to distinctly understand that I am master of this situation." He announced that Homestead was now under martial law. The militia's purpose was to break the strike and to protect the property rights of the Carnegie corporation.

Within three days, the Homestead mills were back in operation, protected by soldiers wielding rifles with fixed bayonets. The company had accepted applications from old workers who had not participated in violence. Many refused to submit applications, but there were plenty of other potential laborers eager for jobs. "There is always an army of unemployed in the United States, and upon these as well as underpaid workers in various lines—clerks, struggling young professional men and others—who were tempted by the high wages said to be paid at Homestead the firm could and did draw freely," observed a local journalist. By mid-August the mill was back in full swing, employing 1,700 replacement workers.

Public sympathy for the union eroded further on July 23 when Russian anarchist Alexander Berkman, after posing as an agent for nonunion laborers, burst into Frick's office and shot him twice. "Murder!" Frick cried. "Help!" A wrestling match ensued. Berkman then pulled a knife, stabbing Frick three times in the hip and left leg. Although seriously wounded, Frick continued the fight until aides rushed in and subdued his attacker. Doctors worried whether Frick would live, but he refused to leave his office, forcing them to probe his neck and back for bullets without the aid of anesthesia. After the bullets were removed and the wounds stitched, Frick finished his paperwork. "This incident will not change the attitude of the Carnegie Steel Company toward the Amalgamated Association," he told the press. "I do not think I shall die, but whether I do or not, the Company will pursue the same policy and it will win." Frick recovered and became even more determined to win: "I will fight this thing to the bitter end. I will never recognize the Union, never, never!"

In August, Berkman was convicted of attempted murder and sentenced to twenty-one years in prison. When the press reported the story it had two devastating effects on the workers of Homestead: it raised the specter of radicalism penetrating Pennsylvania's steel mills and it elicited public sympathy for Frick. "It would seem that the bullet from Berkman's pistol, failing in its foul intent, went straight through the heart of the Homestead strike," noted a union leader.

In an unprecedented move, Chief Justice Edward Paxson of the Pennsylvania Supreme Court indicted labor organizers on charges of treason in October. The union's main leaders, including McLuckie, were barred from the steel industry, and their fate mirrored the path industrial unions would take in and around Pittsburgh for the next forty years. After the summer of 1892,

McLuckie fled the state, charged with murder and treason stemming from the violence of July 6. He last visited Homestead in 1894. Apparently unable to find work, he disappeared and was last seen working as a miner in Mexico.

The now strong alliance between big business and state power doomed any hope of victory for the workers. The *Homestead Local News* reported on October 15 that more than two thousand men were working in the mill, including one hundred former employees. Based on this report, the paper reached two conclusions: "First, the Carnegie Company is gradually succeeding. Second, the great Homestead strike is gradually dying out." In mid-November, the union conceded. Three hundred locked-out men applied for work and were rehired. Many more were blacklisted. Those returning were emasculated, forced to sign a pledge of loyalty and a statement declaring that the applicant had not been on company grounds, had not participated in the rioting, and did not know anyone who had. With the union crushed, Carnegie slashed wages, imposed twelve-hour workdays, ceased extra pay for working on the Sabbath, and eliminated five hundred jobs. "Our victory is now complete and most gratifying," Frick wrote in a congratulatory note to Carnegie, who crowed from Italy, "Life worth living again—Cables received—first happy morning since July."

The battle at Homestead broke the spirit of the town. Visiting Homestead the year after the strike, author Hamlin Garland painted a bleak picture in *McClure's Magazine*. "The town was as squalid and unlovely as could well be imagined, and the people were mainly of the discouraged and sullen type to be found everywhere where labor passes into the brutalizing stage of severity," he wrote. "Such towns are sown thickly over the hill-lands of Pennsylvania. . . . They are American only in the sense in which they represent the American idea of business." He was surprised to find that few of the workers expressed support for either the strike or the strikers. "We can't hurt Carnegie by six months' starving. It's *our* ribs that'll show through our shirts. A man working for fourteen cents an hour hasn't got any surplus for a strike."

The tough response from big business and the state government to the Homestead strike also helped to revitalize the steel industry and laid the foundation for America's industrial supremacy in the twentieth century. In 1896 the company produced more than 25 percent of all steel produced in the United States, making it the largest steel manufacturing facility in the world. By 1910, the United States was making more than 28 million tons and was by far the number-one producer of steel in the world. During peacetime, that steel forged the infrastructure of economic progress, creating bridges and tunnels, cars and locomotives, skyscrapers and factories. During wartime, it transformed the nation into the "arsenal of democracy," producing the tanks, bombs, and guns that would overwhelm its enemies.

America's industrial supremacy came at a great cost, however. The Homestead strike delivered a crippling blow to organized labor and its vision of a working-class democracy in America. Carnegie used his success at Homestead to lead a union-busting campaign across the nation. His competitors followed his example. In less than twelve months the iron and steel union lost nearly ten thousand members. Breaking the union allowed Carnegie to replace skilled workers with nonskilled labor. By 1907, almost two-thirds of the Carnegie employees in Allegheny County, Pennsylvania, were foreign born—mostly Eastern Europeans. The increased diversity produced intense ethnic and racial tension, weakening organized labor by making it more difficult to build a sense of class solidarity among workers who shared little else in common. "Oh that Homestead blunder," Carnegie wrote a friend. "But it's fading as all events do & we are at work selling steel one pound for a half penny."

The strike made clear that in labor disputes government would intervene decisively on the side of capital. For most of the nineteenth century the federal government had remained small and ineffectual, delegating most domestic responsibilities to the states. Homestead removed any doubt that government would now side with business in its confrontations with labor.

Just two years after Homestead the nation was gripped by a crippling depression. With wages slashed and factories closing, many workers went on strike. During the first year of the depression, 1,400 strikes sent more than half a million workers from their jobs. In 1894, Jacob Coxey, accompanied by his wife and infant son, Legal Tender Coxey, led five hundred unemployed men, women, and children from Ohio to Washington. Coxey and his followers planned to present government leaders with "a petition with boots on," in support of a public works program of road building. Having learned the lessons of Homestead, President Cleveland had a hundred mounted policemen greet Coxey as he entered the capitol grounds.

While Coxey's army was calling for government aid to the unemployed, workers at the Pullman Palace Car Company went on strike when the company refused their requests for higher wages. Under the dynamic leadership of Eugene Debs, the union forged a powerful alliance of all railroad workers and organized a boycott of the railroad. Under pressure from the business community, Cleveland decided to put an end to the boycott and promptly dispatched two thousand troops to Chicago to "restore law and order." Many people criticized Cleveland for his tactics, but not future president Theodore Roosevelt, who was then serving as a civil service commissioner. He advised his fellow citizens that such radical sentiment could be suppressed only "by taking ten or a dozen of their leaders out, standing them against a wall and shooting them dead."

In the 1830s, Alexis de Tocqueville observed that the unbridled pursuit of self-interest presented a grave threat to the proper functioning of a democracy. He warned the "friends of democracy" to "keep their eyes anxiously fixed" on the growing power of the "manufacturing aristocracy." The Homestead battle resolved, at least in the workplace setting, the tension in American democracy between individual rights and public good. Workers believed that it was the responsibility of the government to protect community standards and quality of life. Management believed that government should enforce the property rights of business leaders like Andrew Carnegie. The state's response to Homestead clearly established that Carnegie's rights outweighed the general rights of any residents of Homestead. Any hope of creating a working-class democracy in America died on that bloody July day in Pennsylvania.

For Further Reading

For anyone interested in reading more about the Homestead conflict of 1892, Arthur Burgoyne's 1893 monograph *The Homestead Strike of 1892* is the place to start. Another useful primary source is David P. Demarest Jr.'s *"The River Ran Red": Homestead, 1892* (1992). Joseph Frazier Wall has published the "definitive" biography of Andrew Carnegie (*Andrew Carnegie* [1989]). Anyone interested in Henry Clay Frick should read Samuel A. Schreiner Jr.'s *Henry Clay Frick: The Gospel of Greed* and Kenneth Warren's *Triumphant Capitalism: Henry Clay Frick and the Industrial Transformation of America*. Also valuable is Martha Frick Symington's

Henry Clay Frick: An Intimate Portrait (1998). On the complicated relationship between Carnegie and Frick see Les Standiford, *Meet You in Hell* (2005). The best modern historical treatment of the Homestead conflict is Paul Krause's *The Battle for Homestead: 1880–1892* (1992). William Serrin's *Homestead: The Glory and Tragedy of an American Steel Town,* takes the story of Homestead into the late twentieth century—when the Homestead mill was finally closed.

For good overviews of the period see H. W. Brands's *The Reckless Decade: America in the 1890s* and David Montgomery's *The Fall of the House of Labor.* Perhaps the most insightful and thought-provoking work on this period is an article by Herbert G. Gutman titled "Work, Culture, and Society in Industrializing America, 1815–1919," published in *The American Historical Review* in 1973.

6 September 6, 1901

Murder at the Fair: The Assassination of President McKinley

I t was appropriate that President William McKinley, the most popular president since Abraham Lincoln, appear at the Pan-American Exposition in Buffalo. The Exposition celebrated America's technological prowess and paid tribute to its emergence as an industrial and world power. The Exposition also signaled the dawn of the American century. It was an America in transition from a rural, agricultural past to an urban, industrial future. In 1901, eight thousand automobiles shared the streets of American cities with 18 million horses. Of the 76 million residents, nearly nine of ten were of European origin; eight of ten professed some form of Protestantism; and 63 percent lived in places of fewer than four thousand people. The nation was still relatively homogeneous.

But that was changing. Between 1860 and 1900, almost 14 million immigrants came to the United States and another 14.5 million would join them over the next two decades. In 1860, Pittsburgh had a population of 67,000; by 1900 it had 450,000. The nation's urban population increased from 14 million to 42 million between

1880 and 1910. Jacob Riis estimated in 1890 that 330,000 people lived in one square mile of the Lower East Side of New York. Expanding cities and a swelling population of new immigrants speaking different languages and worshipping different gods produced a host of troubling new problems—crime, congestion, cultural conflict, and a growing gap between the rich and poor.

The federal government lacked the power and expertise to tackle many of these problems. The executive staff of the White House numbered ten people, of whom four were bookkeepers and messengers. The secretary of agriculture complained in 1900 that more men worked for George Vanderbilt on his North Carolina estate than worked for the entire Department of Agriculture. Tocqueville had noted that democracy succeeded in America because most people were able to balance competitive individualism with their concern for their local community. By the first decade of the twentieth century, however, the forces of urbanization and industrialization threatened that balance. Whether or not they favored the changes taking place around them, most Americans would have agreed with Harvard historian Henry Adams: "My country in 1900," he wrote, "is something totally different from my own country in 1860. I am wholly a stranger in it. Neither I, nor anyone else, understands it."

William McKinley embodied the contradictions of the nation moving forward while still clinging to its past. McKinley was working as a teacher in Poland, Ohio, when the Civil War broke out in 1861. He was the first volunteer from his hometown, serving in the Poland Company E of the 23rd Regiment of Ohio volunteers. As a commissary sergeant, he served under another future president, Major Rutherford B. Hayes, at the battle at Antietam. After the war he worked as a lawyer before winning a seat in

Congress in 1876. After losing his seat in a close election in 1890, he won election as governor, and in 1896, won the Republican nomination for president.

While his political career was remarkably successful, McKinley's private life was full of pain and loss. In 1871, he married Ida Saxton, an attractive and fashionable woman from a prominent local family. In 1867, she was working as a cashier at a bank in Canton, Ohio, when she caught the eye of Major McKinley, who had just opened a new law practice. The couple's two daughters died in childhood. Many observers felt that these premature deaths devastated the already fragile Mrs. McKinley, who sank into a deep depression. She would remain in poor health, suffering from a host of illnesses, including epilepsy, an incurable and untreatable disease at the time. She spent most of her days sitting in an old Victorian rocking chair crocheting bedroom slippers for family and friends.

McKinley remained deeply devoted to his troubled wife. When elected governor, he purchased a house directly across the street from his office so he would never be far away. At three o'clock every day, no matter what he was doing, he would walk to the window and wave to her. When he ran for president in 1896, he refused to leave her side. Instead, his campaign manager, Mark Hanna, arranged to have voters come to him, hence the famous "front porch campaign." Once in the White House, McKinley insisted that his wife accompany him to important state functions despite her frequent seizures. Contrary to protocol, he always had her sit next to him so he could intervene in the event of a seizure. When one occurred, he would casually cover her face with a white lace handkerchief, pretending that nothing had happened.

In style and substance McKinley was a product of America's

rural, small-town past who embodied the social and political conservatism of the Republican Party in the late nineteenth century. While many members of his own party were clamoring to use federal power to address the new problems produced by the nation's burgeoning cities—poverty, sanitation, crime, education—McKinley remained focused on the two big issues left over from the political battles of the previous century. He vigorously defended using high tariffs to protect American industry and resisted efforts of farmers to abandon the gold standard in favor of a looser, more inflationary money policy. In 1900, after defeating William Jennings Bryan for a second time, he announced that his administration was "standing firm against demands that it become an engine for social betterment." He presented himself as "the embodiment of conservatism."

McKinley's trip to the Buffalo exposition on September 4, 1901, got off to a rocky start. Arriving on a special presidential train, he and his wife were greeted with full military honors, including an artillery salute. Unfortunately, an inexperienced officer placed the cannons too close to the train tracks. The explosions blew out the windows and knocked people to the floor.

The next morning, on September 5, McKinley entered the fairgrounds in a horse-drawn carriage followed by an elaborate procession of troops, military bands, and a mounted honor guard. Later that day, McKinley gave what was to be the last speech of his presidency. Noting that "expositions are the time keepers of progress," he laid out a future vision for the United States that included constructing a great fleet of ships for commerce and empire, building a canal allowing for easier transport between the Atlantic and Pacific Oceans, and the laying of a transpacific undersea cable. "Isolation is no longer possible or desirable," he said.

"The period of exclusiveness is past." The *New York Times,* remarking on the president's rejection of isolationism, wrote, "Unquestionably the President has learned much in the last few years." But while McKinley showed a capacity for rethinking America's role in the world, he promised no changes to America itself, pledging continued fealty to the protective tariff and rejecting calls for a federal income tax.

McKinley did not know that among those in the crowd that day was Leon Czolgosz, a twenty-eight-year-old self-avowed anarchist. One of eight children born to Polish-German immigrants in Michigan, Leon lived much of his early childhood in crushing poverty. With no formal education, he started working at the age of ten. Two years later, after his mother died, the family moved to Cleveland. Leon and two of his brothers worked at the American Steel and Wire Company until management fired all workers in a labor dispute. The experience radicalized Leon, making him increasingly angry about the inordinate power of business and embittered by the government's reluctance to aid working people. He declared himself an anarchist and began reading socialist newspapers and radical magazines.

In 1898, Czolgosz suffered an emotional breakdown. He returned to his father's house, becoming increasingly reclusive. When an Italian-American immigrant named Gaetano Bresci assassinated King Humbert I of Italy in July 1901, Czolgosz hailed him as a hero and a role model. On August 31, Czolgosz traveled to Buffalo, where he rented a cramped room for $2 a week. "I had made up my mind that I would have to do something heroic for the cause I loved," he said later. "I thought of shooting the President but had not yet formed a plan."

McKinley spent an enjoyable day on September 6, 1901, taking a morning trip to Niagara Falls and viewing the river's massive hydroelectric project. He did not visit the Canadian side, however, since custom then dictated that a sitting president not leave U.S. soil while in office. Late in the afternoon, McKinley attended a reception at the ornate redbrick Temple of Music. His security force, worried they could not properly protect the president in such a large crowd, requested that he cancel this appearance. McKinley, in a decision that would change the course of American history, decided to ignore the concerns. "Why should I?" he asked. "Who would want to hurt me?"

Once inside the temple, McKinley greeted throngs of citizens. Many of the men wore stiff collars and bowler hats; the women wore fancy bonnets. Since it was a hot, humid day, some held handkerchiefs to dab the sweat from their foreheads. Even the president was carrying extra handkerchiefs that day. As citizens filed past him in an orderly line, the president shook hands and kissed babies. In the background, an organist played Bach's Sonata in F. Czolgosz stood patiently in line, inching ever closer to the president. In his right hand he grasped a .32-caliber Iver Johnson revolver concealed beneath a bandage. He briefly caught the eye of McKinley guard George Foster, who was scanning the crowd for possible threats. Foster later recalled that he briefly looked at one man with a "pale complexion" who looked like "a mechanic out for the day to the exposition." His right hand was wrapped in what appeared to be a bandage or handkerchief, not at all unusual for the crowd that day.

By 4:07 P.M., Czolgosz was standing directly in front of the president. As McKinley extended his hand, Czolgosz pushed it aside and thrust the revolver toward the president's torso. Holding the weapon just inches from the president, he fired two shots into McKinley's stomach. "The noise was like that made by firecrackers, which have been softened by dampness," explained a security guard. Soldiers rushed in and started beating Czolgosz while others grabbed the gun from his hand. "I would have shot more but I was stunned by a blow in the face, a frightful blow that knocked me down and then everybody jumped on me!" Czolgosz later said.

All eyes turned to McKinley. "The president did not fall," a reporter observed. "He raised his right hand and felt his breast, and seemed to be maintaining his upright position only by a wonderful effort." The president was helped to a chair while a handful of men stood around him fanning him with their hats. McKinley's first words were of concern for his wife: "I trust Mrs. McKinley will not be informed of this; at least I hope it will not be exaggerated." A local official went to the home where the McKinleys were staying and disconnected the telephones. Mrs. McKinley was taking an afternoon nap. The police blocked all traffic near the house so as not to wake her up.

While calls went out to the most qualified doctors and surgeons, the president was tended to by Dr. Edgar Wallace Lee, who had been visiting the Buffalo Bill Cody exhibit at the Exposition. He was soon joined by Dr. Peter W. Van Peyma, a Buffalo obstetrician. "As soon as I saw the President I was struck with his condition," said Dr. Lee. "There was a pallor in his face, and upon examination it was found his pulse was abnormally high. There was every indication that he was dangerously wounded and that an immediate operation was necessary." Later another physician, Dr. Herman Mynter, examined the wounds and determined that the president needed immediate surgery. They located a leading surgeon who specialized in gynecology, Matthew D. Mann, who was getting a haircut in a nearby barbershop. Although he had never dealt with gunshot wounds, Mann was the best qualified to operate on the president.

McKinley was taken by electric ambulance to the expo's emergency hospital. At 5:20 P.M., one hour and thirteen minutes after the shooting, McKinley was administered ether as he recited the Lord's Prayer. Mann, assisted by two surgeons, began the emergency operation by cutting open the president's stomach. Ironically, despite the presence of tens of thousands of electrical fixtures at the expo, the doctors relied on the sun for light. Mann also searched in vain for the bullet in McKinley's abdomen, relying on his own hands and eyes rather than having the X-ray machine, on display at the expo, help locate the slug. These were hardly the best conditions: a gynecologist operating on the president in a makeshift hospital with limited facilities. Mann repaired what damage he could find, and then cleaned and stitched up the president's wounds. The doctors seemed confident that they had done all they could and reported to the press that they had "entire confidence" in McKinley's recovery. After his surgery, McKinley was transported to the home of John G. Milburn, the Exposition president.

Mrs. McKinley, now aware of her husband's injury, slept in a separate bedroom. More than 250 journalists assembled in Buffalo—at that time the largest collection of newspeople ever assembled for a major event. The shooting of the president by a self-avowed anarchist sent shock waves through a nation already on edge after a decade of violent unrest. McKinley was the third American president killed in thirty-six years. Assassins' bullets had already struck down Abraham Lincoln in 1865 and James Garfield in 1881. Many Americans now believed that McKinley's shooting was part of a larger international conspiracy carried out by a small group of radicals determined to destroy the institutions of modern civilization. Over the previous two decades, anarchists were responsible for assassinating Czar Alexander II of Russia, French president Marie-François-Sadi Carnot, and Humbert I, the king of Italy. Now the American president had fallen victim.

The Cabinet, along with Vice President Theodore Roosevelt, rushed to Buffalo to be near the president. The White House turned the second floor of Milburn's house into a hospital ward and transformed the horse stables into a communications center. That evening, McKinley's physicians issued the following bulletin: "The President was shot about 4 o'clock. One bullet struck him on the upper portion of the breast bone, glancing and not penetrating; the second bullet penetrated the abdomen five inches below the left nipple, and one and a half inches to the left of the median line." The second bullet, which was still inside the president, posed a grave threat. While the doctors had sewn up the damage from the impact, there was always risk of an infection.

Over the next few days all the reports suggested that McKinley was improving and would make a full recovery. "I feel certain President McKinley will get well," said the renowned Dr. Roswell Park on Sunday, September 8. "This is not 1881, but 1901, and great strides have been made in surgery in the past twenty years." By Monday, the president was asking for food and wanted to read the daily newspapers. "I'm feeling much better," he told his doctors. By Tuesday many members of the president's Cabinet felt comfortable enough to leave and return to their daily schedules. "You may say that I am absolutely sure that the President will recover," Roosevelt told reporters. "So sure, in fact, that I leave here tonight." There was reason for optimism: McKinley's pulse was strong, his temperature was down, and he was getting progressively stronger. "The crisis has passed," said the *New York Times* on

September 10. "President McKinley will fully and speedily recover from the wounds inflicted upon him by the Anarchist Czolgosz."

In reality, a lethal infection was spreading through the president's bloodstream. By noon on Thursday, McKinley's pulse weakened. He slipped into shock. His heart began to fail. Those close to the president went to his room to say their good-byes. A Secret Service agent cabled his office in Washington: "All hope seems to be gone." By Friday evening McKinley was slipping in and out of consciousness. He asked to see his wife for the last time. "The easy chair was drawn close to the bedside, and she was seated there," recalled a nurse. "She took his hand, the hand which in one short week had become emaciated and thin, and held it." She kissed him and stayed close so she could hear his voice, now only a whisper. "I want to go too," she said to him. "We are all going, we are all going," he responded. He began to whisper the words of his favorite hymn, "Nearer, My God, to Thee." Weeping uncontrollably, she hugged him the last time before being escorted out of the room. The president's oxygen tube was then removed. William McKinley, the twenty-fifth president of the United States, died quietly at 2:15 A.M. on September 14, 1901.

The nation honored the slain president with five days of mourning. A special train carried McKinley's body from Buffalo to Washington for services in the nation's capital. He then returned home to his final resting place in Canton, Ohio. Silent crowds lined the train route; bells tolled as the flag-draped coffin passed. Occasionally, the muffled sounds of the president's favorite hymn, "Nearer, My God, to Thee," filled the air. At exactly 2:30 P.M. on September 17, in big cities and small towns, Americans stopped what they were doing and offered five minutes of silence. In normally bustling downtown Chicago, trains stopped and cable cars came to a halt. Men and women flooded into the streets, bowing their heads in silent prayers. "Never in history had the Union of the States been joined in such universal sorrow," noted an observer.

The president's death crushed his already fragile wife. After attending the funeral and burial ceremonies, she remained in Canton, where she spent most of her time knitting and taking care of a younger sister. She visited her husband's grave nearly every day until her own death six years later, in May 1907.

Justice was swift for McKinley's assassin. Czolgosz went on trial just nine days after the assassination. The trial lasted two days before the jury, after deliberating for thirty-four minutes, declared him guilty of first-degree murder. Early on the morning of October 29, less than two months after he pulled the trigger, Leon Czolgosz was strapped into an electric chair in Auburn Prison in upstate New York. A sponge soaked with water was tucked below his knees. As he was strapped into the chair he said his final words: "I shot the President because I thought it would help the working people and for the sake of the common people. I am not sorry for my crime. That is all I have to say." The same electrical system that powered the expo provided the current that electrocuted McKinley's assassin. "The rush of the immense current threw the body so hard against the straps that they creaked perceptively," reported the *New York Times*. "The hands clinched suddenly, and the whole attitude was one of extreme tension. For forty-five seconds the full current was kept on, and then slowly, the electrician threw the switch back, reducing the current volt by volt until it was cut off." The assassin died at 7:12 A.M. He was buried in a black-stained pine coffin in the prison cemetery. His clothing was burned and sulfuric acid was poured over his body before it was lowered into the ground.

* * *

Sorrow at McKinley's death was matched by fear about the future. Panic swept Wall Street. "A cold wind of change seemed to blow with McKinley's passing," noted the historian Margaret Leech. "Americans anxiously queried whether plenty and prosperity were destined to endure, while they waited for some word from the new President, the unknown quantity, the X in the equation of the American future."

The "X" in the equation of America's future was none other than Theodore Roosevelt. It would be his destiny to usher in the twentieth century with his own swaggering style of bravado and a towering ego that, in a very real sense, was a reflection of the new America itself. Teddy Roosevelt's accidental presidency, made possible by an assassin's bullet, profoundly changed the course of the century. The conservative barons of Republican politics understood the threat posed by Roosevelt. Power broker Mark Hanna muttered that McKinley's assassination had put "that damned cowboy in the White House." "In a sense," wrote the historian Eric Rauchway, "William McKinley had two killers: the man who shot and destroyed his body, and the man who succeeded him and erased his legacy." Roosevelt assured worried Republicans that he would continue McKinley's conservative policies. "In this hour of deep and terrible national bereavement I wish to state that it shall be my aim—to continue absolutely unbroken the policy of President McKinley for the peace, the prosperity, and the honor of our beloved country," he said in the hours following the president's death. It was just a matter of time, however, before Roosevelt made his mark on the office and helped change the course of American history.

At forty-two, TR was the youngest man ever to serve as president, and he was the fifth to take the oath because of the death of a sitting president. As a child, Roosevelt watched the funeral procession of Abraham Lincoln as it passed beneath his New York City home. Born into a distinguished New York family, Roosevelt had plunged into state politics in 1880, winning election as a Republican state assemblyman after his graduation from Harvard. However, a profound personal tragedy struck on February 13, 1884, when his wife and mother died on the same day. "The light has gone out of my life," he wrote in his diary. Roosevelt then sought refuge in the Dakota Badlands, where he worked as a rancher before returning to New York to resume his climb up the political ladder. In 1889 he became a member of the state Civil Service Commission, and in 1895 he became president of the New York City Police Board. In 1897 President McKinley appointed him assistant secretary of the Navy. He resigned this office to fight in the Spanish-American War. As commander of a volunteer regiment known as the Rough Riders, the young officer led a heroic charge that helped secure strategic San Juan Hill. "The only trouble" with the conflict, he said later, "was that there was not enough war to go around." In 1898 he returned from that war a hero and was elected governor of New York. In his spare time, Roosevelt managed to read voraciously and to write ten books, including five works of history.

During his two years as governor, Roosevelt angered party bosses with his public criticism of powerful trusts and his strong support of land conservation. Republican leaders nominated the upstart to be McKinley's running mate in 1900, hoping to remove Roosevelt from the limelight. It was a risky strategy, as Mark Hanna understood when he wrote McKinley that "your duty to the Country is to live for four years from next March." Roosevelt complained that he would "a great deal rather be anything, say professor of history, than Vice-President." But he realized that accepting the offer and serving four years as vice president would improve his chances of winning the party's nomination in 1904. Reluctantly, he accepted the offer.

Overnight, McKinley's death transformed the nation by elevating Roosevelt to the presidency. America was at a critical time in its history. Roosevelt conceived of the president as "a steward of the people" and argued that he had the right to use any power not specifically forbidden by law or the Constitution. "There adheres in the Presidency more power than any other office in any great republic or constitutional monarchy of modern times," he wrote, and, in truth, he became the dominant political figure of his time. Most presidents had outlined their goals in speeches and messages to Congress. Roosevelt sent drafts of legislation to Congress and actively lobbied on behalf of that legislation. He fed the public's interest in the presidency, encouraged the public to expect the president to speak out about important issues, and used the office as a "bully pulpit" to cultivate public opinion.

Understanding the value of his personality to attract media attention, Roosevelt maintained public interest by feeding reporters a steady diet of colorful antics. A man of boundless energy—"a steam engine in trousers," a contemporary called him—he packed two hundred pounds of muscle on his five-foot-eight-inch frame. He loved to exercise, read, write, and talk. Secretary of State John Hay once calculated that in a two-hour dinner at the White House, Roosevelt's guests were responsible for only four and a half minutes of conversation. He became the first president to ride in an automobile, fly in an airplane, and be submerged in a submarine. On one occasion he went swimming naked in the Potomac River. The public responded to Roosevelt's exuberance. He came to be known affectionately as "Teddy." His cultural influence was so great that when a toy manufacturer heard a story of the president's protecting a bear cub, he introduced the "Teddy bear" to his line of stuffed animals. "You must always remember," said a close friend, "the president is about six." Secretary of War Elihu Root told the president on his forty-sixth birthday in 1904, "You have made a very good start in life, and your friends have great hopes for you when you grow up."

By focusing attention on himself, Roosevelt helped elevate the Progressive movement from the state to the national level. Both politically and culturally, McKinley had shared little in common with Progressive reformers who were working to tame the consequences of industrialism and urbanization. Although their goals were different, sometimes even contradictory, Progressives shared a moralistic view of the world, which saw political issues as a clash between right and wrong, and an agenda for using government to rein in the trusts and empower the people. Roosevelt shared the Progressive temperament, bringing with him a sense of style and a well-developed political philosophy appropriate for the new urban and industrial age.

Like most Progressives, Roosevelt believed in the environmental roots of human behavior. Poverty, hopelessness, and lack of opportunity served as breeding grounds for crime and radicalism. He was determined to use the power of the presidency to ameliorate the social conditions that produced men like Leon Czolgosz, who was a product of America's failure to respond to the challenges of industrialism. Fearing both the excessive power of corporate wealth and the dangers of working-class radicalism, Roosevelt planned to mediate disputes and uphold the public interest. "The unscrupulous rich man who seeks to exploit and oppress those who are less well off is in spirit not opposed to, but identical with, the unscrupulous poor man who desires to plunder and oppress those who are better off," he said.

This approach revealed itself when Roosevelt dealt with one of the central questions of the time: how should government deal with the trusts? The process of corporate consolidation, which began in the late nineteenth century, picked up steam in the early twentieth century. By 1904, 1 percent of American companies produced 38 percent of all manufactured goods. A few corporate giants dominated the industrial landscape. J. P. Morgan's U.S. Steel controlled 80 percent of the market, while his International Harvester Company monopolized 85 percent of the farm-equipment business.

Roosevelt regarded centralization as a fact of modern economic life. "This is an age of combination," he said in 1905. However, he made the distinction between "good" trusts—those that did not abuse their power and contributed to economic growth—and "bad" trusts—those few companies that used their market leverage to raise prices and exploit consumers. He earned a reputation as a "trustbuster" largely because of his prosecution of J. P. Morgan's Northern Securities Company, which controlled nearly all the long-distance railroads west of Chicago, eliminated competition, and created the threat of higher rates. Morgan tried to bargain, telling the president to "send your man to my man and they can fix it up." Roosevelt resisted, and in 1904 the Supreme Court, siding with the president, ordered the combination dissolved. During his administration, the president employed the Sherman Antitrust Act twenty-five times, prosecuting some of the country's largest corporations, including Standard Oil of New Jersey and the American Tobacco Company.

A similar faith in the regulatory power of the federal government shaped Roosevelt's approach to labor. In 1902 the president intervened with much fanfare to support Pennsylvania coal miners who went on strike to demand a 20 percent wage increase, an eight-hour day, and recognition of their union. Roosevelt spoke out publicly in support of the miners and summoned both sides to the White House, where he asked them to accept impartial federal arbitration. When the mine owners refused to compromise, Roosevelt lashed out at their "arrogant stupidity" and threatened to send in ten thousand federal troops to seize the mines and resume coal production. The operators finally relented. Arbitrators awarded the strikers a 10 percent wage increase and reduced the workday to nine hours, but they refused to grant recognition to the union. Afterward, Roosevelt boasted that he had offered both sides a "square deal." The phrase stuck and became a familiar label for his policies as president.

Roosevelt's colorful style and Progressive policies earned him the enmity of Republican power brokers but the affection of the American public. He easily won his party's nomination in 1904 and crushed a lackluster Democratic opponent. His 336 electoral votes were the most ever won by a candidate to date. The breadth of TR's victory stunned even his supporters. "What are we going to do with our victory?" asked a Republican senator.

Roosevelt had no doubts about the significance of the election. "Tomorrow," he cried the day before his inauguration, "I shall come into my office in my own right. Then watch out for me." With public desire for bolder federal action increasing, Roosevelt announced his support for an ambitious social agenda including regulation of the railroads, increased federal power to regulate commerce, and passage of a range of legislation to improve working conditions. In 1906 he pushed through Congress the Hepburn Act, which authorized the Interstate Commerce Commission to establish shipping rates. With Roosevelt's support, Congress passed the Pure Food and Drug Act of 1906. The legislation made it a crime to sell adulterated foods or medicines and provided for correct and complete labeling of ingredients. Capitalizing on the publication of Upton Sinclair's powerful novel *The Jungle* (1906), Roosevelt won passage of the Meat Inspection Act, which led to more effective supervision of meat processing.

As president, Roosevelt was also committed to using his office to bolster the American conservation movement. While western business interests advocated unrestrained exploitation of the nation's natural resources, the growth of congested cities and the closing of the frontier raised public concern about the environment. In his first message to Congress on December 3, 1901, Roosevelt argued that national forests should be enlarged and "set apart forever, for the use and benefit of our people as a whole and not sacrificed to the shortsighted greed of a few." He promoted a three-part program that involved the reclamation of arid lands via irrigation—claiming that "the western half of the United States would sustain a population greater than our whole country today if the waters that now run to waste were saved and used for irrigation"—the setting aside of timber to create forest reserves, and the creation of wildlife refuges. Roosevelt used his executive authority to add 150 million acres of virgin forest lands in the western United States to the national forests, an area that exceeded the total acreage of France, Belgium, and the Netherlands.

No one was more eager to assume the responsibilities of world power than Theodore Roosevelt, and his presidency laid the foundation for America's emergence as a world power in the new century. A student of the writings of naval strategist Captain Alfred Thayer Mahan, Roosevelt was committed to establishing American control in the Western Hemisphere and opening new trade routes to Asia. To this end, he oversaw the building of the Panama

Canal and established the Roosevelt Corollary to the Monroe Doctrine, which stated that the United States would intervene to guarantee that nations in the Western Hemisphere did not invite "foreign aggression to the detriment of the entire body of American nations." McKinley had been a reluctant imperialist, forced into war against Spain. Roosevelt was unapologetic about his imperial ambitions. "There is a homely adage that runs 'Speak softly and carry a big stick; you will go far,' " he noted in 1901. Roosevelt told a foreign diplomat that the United States was "becoming, owing to our strength and geographical situation, more and more the balance of power of the whole globe."

In addition to his expansion of presidential power, and his push to make the United States a major world power, Roosevelt oversaw the first total renovation of the White House since its initial construction. By 1901, the building was sorely in need of renovation and was approaching the status of national disgrace. The pipes were still made of wood, the heating system was bad, the wiring was sub-par, the elevator was faulty, and servants lived in substandard attic rooms. Guests at state dinners and other functions had to put their coats and wraps on the floor because the building lacked even a basic cloak or dressing room. First Lady Edith Roosevelt, among her many complaints, stated that living in the White House was "like living over the store." In fact, the "White House" was not even officially called the White House prior to Roosevelt; it was known as the "executive mansion." He banned the term *executive mansion* and officially began using the term *White House,* thus making official the more common term utilized by the people and the press of the era.

By expanding the power of the presidency and the national government, Roosevelt foreshadowed both the New Deal and the Great Society, making clear that the era of big government had begun. He adopted the ideas of *New Republic* founder Herbert Croly, who warned Progressives to abandon their older Jeffersonian notions of small government, recognize the inevitability of economic concentration, and provide government with broad powers to regulate business. In Roosevelt's hands, Croly's ideas would become the philosophical springboard for a new democratic nationalism that would be the dominant spirit of the twentieth century. Roosevelt claimed to be "a Jeffersonian in my genuine faith in democracy and popular government," but "a Hamiltonian in my governmental views, especially with reference to the need of the exercise of broad powers by the National Government." He urged Progressives to recognize that only a strong federal government could protect the public's interest. Democracy was not incompatible with increased government; indeed, only government could guarantee true freedom and democracy.

In 1908, Roosevelt decided not to seek another term, entrusting the office to his hand-picked successor, William Howard Taft, before leaving for safari in Africa. Within a few years, however, Roosevelt was convinced that Taft had betrayed his Progressive principles and decided to again seek his old office, running against Taft in the Republican primaries. "My hat is in the ring!" he declared with typical exuberance. "The fight is on and I am stripped to the buff!" As a sitting president, Taft controlled the party convention, which denied Roosevelt the nomination. Never one to walk away from a fight, Roosevelt formed the Progressive Party and ran as a third-party candidate in the 1912 election. In his acceptance speech for the nomination delivered before thousands of frenzied supporters, Roosevelt pronounced himself "as strong as a bull moose" and delivered a spirited "Confession of Faith" in which he criticized Democrats and Republicans for protecting "the interests of the rich few." In keeping with the New Nationalism philosophy, the Progressive Party platform, called a "Covenant with the People," advocated a bold list of new reforms, including strict regulation of corporations, a national presidential primary, the elimination of child labor, a minimum wage, and universal women's suffrage.

With the Republicans divided, the Democrats nominated New Jersey governor Woodrow Wilson to lead the party. The 1912 campaign developed into a two-way contest between the moralizing Wilson and the crusading Roosevelt. With the Republicans divided between Taft and Roosevelt, Wilson held a slim lead as the campaign entered its final months. Roosevelt, who loved the thrill of battle, continued his crusade. Nothing, not even a would-be assassin's bullet, could stop him from campaigning. On October 14, as he entered an automobile in Milwaukee, a lone attacker fired a single bullet into Roosevelt's chest. It fractured a rib and lodged below his right lung. Roosevelt first ordered the crowd not to harm his assailant, then insisted on attending a previously scheduled rally, where he spoke to a stunned crowd for more than an hour. "It takes more than that to kill a Bull Moose," he told them.

The Republican split allowed Wilson to win the election. In many ways, however, Roosevelt won the debate. His spirit shaped American society and politics for the rest of the century. He helped the nation make the transition from a rural republic to a world power, and for that reason his face is carved in stone on the side of Mount Rushmore along with George Washington, Thomas Jefferson, and Abraham Lincoln. He served as a role model for his fifth cousin, Franklin D. Roosevelt, who told friends that "Uncle Ted" was the greatest man he had ever known. Franklin not only drew inspiration from his cousin's example, he adopted many of his ideas about enlarged federal power to launch his New Deal reform program. At the same time, TR's muscular internationalism and his visions of America as a world power inspired FDR's response to the threat from Nazi Germany.

Nearly a century after his death, Theodore Roosevelt remains one of the most popular and influential American presidents. A Republican, he has now risen above partisanship to be embraced by the leaders of both parties. Republicans invoke his assertive internationalism; Democrats cite his willingness to use federal power to promote the public good. Three modern presidents— George H. W. Bush, Bill Clinton, and George W. Bush—have each invoked Roosevelt's name and legacy to support their agendas. Clinton, a Democrat, hung Roosevelt's portrait by the entrance of his private study and posthumously awarded Theodore Roosevelt the Congressional Medal of Honor in 2001—exactly one hundred years after an assassin's bullet had elevated him to the presidency.

For Further Reading

Eric Rauchway's *Murdering McKinley: The Making of Theodore Roosevelt's America* (2003) deals directly with the impact of the assassination. On the assassination itself see Sarah Vowell, *Assassination Vacation* (2005). Lewis Gould challenges the conventional wisdom about McKinley in *The Presidency of William McKinley* (1981) and *The Modern American Presidency* (2003).

There is a large body of literature on TR and his impact on American politics. Edmund Morris's two volumes—*The Rise of Theodore Roosevelt* (1979) and *Theodore Rex* (2002)—remain the best and most readable. John Morton Blum offers a brief but insightful portrait in *The Republican Roosevelt* (1954). Lewis Gould's

The Presidency of Theodore Roosevelt (1991) is the best one-volume treatment of TR's presidency. John Milton Cooper Jr.'s *The Warrior and the Priest* (1983) is an excellent comparative biography of Wilson and Roosevelt.

The Progressive Era has one of the most robust bodies of literature of any period in American history. Richard Hofstadter's *The Age of Reform* (1955) remains one of the classic surveys of the Progressive movement. For a look at reform on the state level, see David Thelen's *The New Citizenship* (1972) and Carl Burgchardt's *Robert M. La Follette, Sr.: The Voice of Conscience* (1992). Robert Wiebe provided the seminal study of the new, professional middle class and its response to industrialization and urbanization in *The Search for Order, 1877–1920* (1967). *A Very Different Age* (1998) by Steven J. Diner is a recent synthesis that includes social and political topics.

7

July 21, 1925

Scopes: The Battle Over America's Soul

On January 10, 1955, hundreds of people crammed into a packed Broadway theater to see the opening of the new play *Inherit the Wind*. Set in a time "not long ago," it was based loosely on the Scopes trial three decades earlier, but many of the play's themes were as relevant to the witch-hunting fifties as they were to the "roaring" twenties. The drama opened with a courageous high school teacher, Bertram Cates, being imprisoned in the small town of Hillsboro for teaching evolution to his students. A three-time Democratic presidential candidate, the pompous and dogmatic Matthew Harrison Brady, arrives in town to prosecute the case to chants of "Give me that old-time religion." A famous defense attorney, the enlightened and humane Henry Drummond, endures the hostility of the local residents to defend both Cates and the principle of free speech. "You murder a wife, it isn't nearly as bad as murdering an old wives' tale," he tells the jury. The play ends with a dramatic courtroom scene in which Drummond calls Brady to the stand, humiliates him by exposing the dangers of his rigid and literal interpretation of the Bible, and

149

closes with a dramatic appeal for open minds and free speech. Although the jury delivers the inevitable guilty verdict, and the judge levies a token $100 fine, Drummond wins the day: freedom of thought has triumphed over religious dogma.

A hit at the box office, the play inspired a highly acclaimed 1960 movie starring Spencer Tracy, as well as numerous adaptations for stage and screen. *Inherit the Wind,* in all its various incarnations, reinforced the traditional view of the Scopes trial as a triumph of enlightened science over Christian fundamentalism, and reason over faith. In 1926, the year after the trial, the *Christian Century* observed: "Looking at it as an event now passed, anybody should be able to see that the whole fundamentalist movement was hollow and artificial," predicting that it would be "a disappearing quantity in American life."

The reality of the trial and its legacy are, however, more complex. This infamous "monkey trial" represents a turning point in American history not for what it resolved, but for what it revealed: a deep cultural fault line in society between doubter and devout, between elite opinion and common belief, and between city and country. Instead of being the decisive victory depicted in *Inherit the Wind,* the Scopes trial represented only the first skirmish in an ongoing culture war that would shape American politics and culture for the rest of the century and beyond.

* * *

The Scopes trial was a product of the conflicting cultural crosscurrent of the era. At the time, dazzling technological changes were transforming the way Americans lived and worked, forcing a confrontation between old values and new realities. Americans were bombarded with new appliances that changed the daily habits of millions: refrigerators, radios, washing machines, automatic ovens, vacuum cleaners, electric toasters. The number of telephones doubled to more than 20 million between 1915 and 1929. But the most significant innovation was the automobile. By the end of the 1920s more than half of all American families owned a car. New York City alone had more cars than the entire continent of Europe. The car gave Americans new mobility, and highway development opened up new areas for settlement and business. Paved roads helped establish a wider sense of community, connecting small towns with larger cities, and bringing people who had lived in geographic isolation in touch with a larger universe.

The 1920s also witnessed the birth of a national culture as millions of Americans for the first time shared identical experiences: they watched the same newsreels and films, listened to the same radio broadcasts, and read similar style newspapers. By 1925, there were twenty thousand theaters dotting the nation. For fifty cents people could watch a silent movie along with a live stage show. In 1929, Chicago theaters had enough seats for half the city's population to attend a movie every day. Moviegoers in small towns and big cities flocked to see stars such as Douglas Fairbanks, Charlie Chaplin, Clara Bow, and Joan Crawford. At the same time, Pittsburgh-based radio station KDKA provided the nation's first public radio broadcast when it reported the presidential election of 1920. Millions of Americans listened to radio programs such as *The Maxwell House Hour* and *The General Motors Family*.

The 1920 census revealed another milestone: for the first time in the history of the United States, a majority of Americans (51.4 percent) lived in cities. Not only were cities transforming the geographic landscape, they were producing a new cosmopolitan culture that threatened the moral verities of America's rural past. Mass communication forced a confrontation between these two competing cultures. In *A Preface to Morals* (1929), the journalist

Walter Lippmann referred to the "acids of modernity" to describe the forces that were corroding the stability and certainty of American life. Among the most corrosive acids was a new morality that was eating away at Victorian notions of womanhood. In many cities, teenage girls adopted the "flapper" image: they wore cosmetics, cut their hair short, hemmed their skirts above the knee, drank openly, and even played golf. The virtual legalization of birth control information and devices in many states permitted a substantial number of Americans to put into practice the radical idea that sex could be a source of pleasure detached from procreation. Birth control, wrote Lippmann, "is the most revolutionary practice in the history of sexual morals." A survey in 1925 showed that 60 percent of women used contraceptives; for middle-class women, the figures were even higher. Popular culture began to reinforce the emphasis on sex. People turned on the radio to hear songs with titles like "Hot Lips," "I Need Lovin'," and "Burning Kisses." Popular movies of the time included *Sinners in Silk, Women Who Give,* and *Rouged Lips.*

The mass media brought the values of this rising urban culture into previously isolated rural towns and villages, producing a potent backlash in the process. Prohibition, which became law with passage of the Eighteenth Amendment to the Constitution banning the sale of alcohol, became a rallying cry for those Americans who were fearful of the changes transforming the nation and hopeful of returning to a simpler past. Despite evidence that Prohibition was a failure, many provincial, largely rural, Protestant Americans continued to defend it. In their minds, Prohibition had always been about more than alcohol. It represented an effort to defend traditional American values against the growing influence of an urban, cosmopolitan culture. Throughout the decade, "wets" and "drys" battled to define America.

As a further result of the cultural conflict, the early 1920s saw millions of Americans joining the "new" Ku Klux Klan. The Klan of the 1920s, although strong in the South, was stronger still in Indiana, Illinois, and Ohio. The Invisible Empire gained legitimacy by fashioning itself as a middle-class Protestant populist movement crusading for social purity and against vice, crime, and deteriorating morality. On August 8, 1925, more than fifty thousand Klan members marched down Pennsylvania Avenue in Washington, D.C., in a brazen demonstration of strength.

Scientific thought that challenged older religious notions about the origins of man added to the anxiety that traditional values were under assault. In 1859, Charles Darwin posited in his famous *Origin of Species* that man evolved over a period of several million years. He followed with a second book, *The Descent of Man,* which argued that "man is descended from a hairy, tailed quadruped, probably arboreal in its habits, and an inhabitant of the Old World." His theory of evolution was at odds with God's seven-day creation of the world described in the Bible's book of Genesis. Initially, many Christians reconciled themselves to Darwin's theory, accepting the Bible as divinely inspired but not literally true. By the 1920s, however, fundamentalists, who believed in the infallibility of the Bible, had gained broad appeal. Fundamentalists were so numerous during the 1920s, especially in the rural South, that celebrated journalist H. L. Mencken noted that you could "heave an egg out of a Pullman and you will hit a Fundamentalist almost everywhere in the United States."

During the Progressive period, as states passed mandatory attendance laws, schools became the new battleground between science and religion. In 1890, two hundred thousand students were enrolled in public high school; by 1920, that number had swelled to 2 million. Tennessee, the location of the Scopes trial, had only ten thousand high school students in 1910, but it had fifty thousand in 1925. In the early 1920s, fundamentalists crusaded for laws that would prohibit the teaching of Darwinism in public schools. By 1923, six southern and border states had considered enacting anti-evolution laws, but only two minor measures were passed—Oklahoma banned the purchase of texts that taught evolution and Florida had a nonbinding resolution that said that "it is improper and subversive to the best interest of the people" for schools "to teach as true Darwinism or any other hypothesis that links man in blood relationship to any form of lower life."

On January 21, 1925, Tennessee state representative John Washington Butler, a first-term legislator and Baptist lay leader, introduced a bill banning the teaching of evolution in the public schools. His bill barred the teaching of "any theory that denies the Story of the Divine Creation of Man as taught in the Bible, and [holds] instead that man has descended from a lower order of animals." It provided that the teachers who violated the law be fined between $100 and $500. The bill left many questions unanswered: What did it mean to "teach" evolution? Did a teacher have to specifically mention evolution, or teach evolution as the only "truth"? Most members of the legislature would have preferred to avoid voting on the controversial and poorly drafted bill, but they feared a public backlash if they went on the record opposing legislation that in theory supported biblical teaching. In the end, the legislature passed the bill without debate. The governor had little enthusiasm for the legislation, but feared a veto would jeopardize passage of a broad education reform package designed to centralize the state's school system. In March, he signed it into law, predicting that "the law will never be applied."

His prediction may have been realized had it not been for an aggressive new organization, the American Civil Liberties Union

(ACLU). Founded in 1920, the ACLU grew out of the efforts of groups fighting to protect the right of pacifists from serving in World War I, but later expanded its agenda to address the broad concerns of preserving minority rights from majority power. Hoping to stem a tide of anti-evolution state laws, the ACLU planned to challenge Tennessee, claiming it represented a violation of free speech and academic freedom. The organization sent out a press release, carried in local papers, asking for a teacher to volunteer to violate the law. The ACLU agreed to cover all the costs associated with the challenge.

In Dayton, thirty-one-year-old George Rappleyea, a transplanted New Yorker who opposed the Butler Act, saw the ad in the local paper. He believed that a legal test case might force the courts to strike the law, but, more important, it would bring national attention, tourists, and even jobs to Dayton. It would, he said famously, "put Dayton on the map." The city needed all the help it could get. Sitting midway between Chattanooga and Knoxville in the foothills of Tennessee, Dayton had once been a booming coal and railroad town. At the turn of the century, its population was 3,000. Soon afterward, however, the coal company closed its doors, and while farmers still produced healthy fruit and strawberry crops, the population had dwindled to around 1,800 by 1925.

Eager to share his plan, Rappleyea went to Robinson's drugstore, which served as a social center in Prohibition-era Dayton. The store's owner, Fred E. Robinson, just happened to be the head of the town's school board, as well as its major textbook supplier. "You are always looking for something that will get Dayton a little publicity, I wonder if you have seen the morning paper," Rappleyea said, pointing to the ACLU ad. Robinson liked the idea, as did the local school superintendent, Walter White. They had different views on evolution and on the merits of the Butler

Act, but they shared dreams of large crowds, throngs of reporters, and ballooning retail sales in their town. Now all they needed was a teacher who would be willing to violate the law.

The plotters decided to summon John Scopes, a sandy-haired, twenty-four-year-old math and science teacher and part-time football coach. They explained that by teaching evolution he had been in violation of the new law. "John, would you be willing to stand for a test case?" they asked. After some persuasion, Scopes agreed. Although he taught general science, Scopes had once substituted for the regular biology teacher. He could not recall mentioning evolution in the classroom, but the textbook he used, Hunter's *Civic Biology*, which had been adopted by the state and sold at the local drugstore, included a discussion of Darwin's theory. Unaware that he had just agreed to be the defendant in what would eventually become known as "the world's greatest court trial," Scopes left the drugstore to play a game of tennis. Rappleyea then wired the ACLU, telling them that Dayton had a test case. Another of the conspirators told the local *Chattanooga News* about the case, proudly proclaiming, "Something has happened that's going to put Dayton on the map!"

Initially, both the prosecution and the defense planned their legal strategies for winning the battle in the courtroom, not in the media. The prosecution, headed by the present and former attorneys general for eastern Tennessee, A. T. Stewart and Ben B. McKenzie, hoped to focus on one simple question: Did Scopes violate the Butler Act? They did not want to address the constitutionality of the act or engage in a debate over the relative merits of Darwin versus the Bible. For them, the case was not about religion but about enforcing the law. The ACLU assembled its own talented legal team, including Dudley F. Malone, who had once served as assistant secretary of state; John Neal, an eccentric law school dean from Knoxville; and ACLU general counsel Arthur Garfield Hays. They too hoped to avoid getting pulled into a heated public exchange about the role of religion in public education. Instead, they wanted to convince either the jury in Dayton, or the Tennessee Supreme Court on appeal, that religious belief and evolution were not incompatible, and efforts to limit discussion infringed on free speech and academic freedom. Both sides hoped to wage the courtroom battle squarely in the responsible legal center, avoiding a highly charged, polemical debate that would alienate moderate opinion. After all, both sides were fighting to sway a jury of local residents who were by most accounts noncommittal on the subject.

That legal strategy became moot when William Jennings Bryan volunteered his services for the prosecution. Subtlety was never his strong suit. Bryan had burst on the national political scene in 1896 when he delivered his famous "Cross of Gold" speech at the Democratic National Convention, perhaps the finest convention speech ever given. Despite waging an energetic campaign on a populist platform by calling for regulation of the railroads and loosening of the money supply, Bryan lost the election to William McKinley. He won the Democratic nomination two more times— in 1900 and 1904—but lost both times in the general election. In 1913, he accepted Woodrow Wilson's offer to serve as secretary of state, but resigned in protest of Wilson's growing involvement in World War I. After the war, Bryan used his oratorical skills and boundless energy as a leading evangelical Christian and anti-evolution advocate. The *Chicago Tribune* complained that Bryan had "half the country debating whether the universe was created in six days."

What united Bryan's progressive politics and his religious conservatism was an underlying faith in democracy. "The essence of democracy is found in the right of the people to have what they want," he wrote. "There is more virtue in the people themselves than can be found anywhere else." For Bryan, the central issue in the Scopes trial was the right of taxpaying parents to decide what their students will learn in the classroom. "If it is contended that an instructor has a right to teach anything he likes, I reply that the parents who pay the salary have a right to decide what shall be taught," he declared. Like many religious opponents of Darwinism, Bryan claimed that evolution was "the greatest menace to civilization as well as to religion," because "belief in God is the fundamental fact in society; upon it rest all the controlling influences of American life. Anything that weakens man's faith in God imperils the future of the race." A champion of the "common man," Bryan saw Darwin's concept of "survival of the fittest" as justification for the rich to oppress the poor and the strong to dominate the weak. For him, Darwinian theory represented "man as reaching his present perfection by the operation of the law of hate—the merciless law by which the strong crowd out and kill off the weak."

Famed defense attorney Clarence Darrow claimed that the minute he heard that Bryan had joined the prosecution team, "at once I wanted to go." So irresistible was the chance to battle "the idol of all Morondom," that Darrow agreed "for the first, the last, the only time in my life" to volunteer his services. At sixty-eight, Darrow was at the height of his powers. He had earned his reputation by defending unpopular political radicals and wealthy criminals, including two wealthy Chicago teenagers, Nathan Leopold and Richard Loeb, who were accused of kidnapping and killing an unpopular classmate just to see if they could get away with it. The sensational trial ended with Darrow's delivering a spellbinding two-day plea for the jury to give his clients life in prison rather than the death penalty.

Darrow personified the skeptical modernist who relied on science and reason, not religion and superstition. For him the trial provided an opportunity to ridicule Christianity before a national audience. Like many other intellectuals, he was suspicious of democracy, preferring rule of the elite—of people like him. He did support Bryan's Progressive politics and voted for him in his campaign for president, but Darrow did not share Bryan's faith in small-town democracy. Darrow viewed fundamentalists as representative of the dark populist mentality of small-town America—what H. L. Mencken called the "vulgar democracy" of America. In his mind, science and skepticism were both antithetical to religion and faith and essential to social progress. "The modern world is the child of doubt and inquiry," he concluded. Religious "fanaticism," he warned, threatened public education and the spirit of scientific inquiry necessary for civilization to sustain itself.

Many members of both the prosecution and the defense teams protested the celebrity additions, but local lawyers welcomed them. What better way to get attention for Dayton than by showcasing two of the most famous men of the era in a clash over the origins of life? Neither Bryan nor Darrow were interested in the specific legal issues and instead saw the case as an opportunity to promote their own strongly held beliefs. Their presence transformed a serious trial about weighty legal issues into a media circus. ACLU president Roger Baldwin realized that once Darrow came on board "it was immediately apparent what kind of trial it would be: the good book against Darwin, bigotry against science, or, as popularly put, God against monkeys."

As Baldwin suspected, Dayton had become the new battleground in America's first culture war. The nation had been divided over issues in the past. There were still people alive in 1925 with personal memories of the Civil War. That struggle had been between North and South. The new fault line in the twentieth century was between the values of an older rural past and that of a rising urban culture—a battle that would be fought in the full glare of a national media that often exaggerated differences and highlighted conflict. The trial, observed Arthur Garfield Hays, "was a battle between two types of mind—the rigid, orthodox, accepting, unyielding, narrow, conventional mind, and the broad, liberal, critical, cynical, skeptical, and tolerant mind."

The entire town mobilized to promote the upcoming event. The Progressive Dayton club spent $5,000 promoting local business development during the trial. They also issued a commemorative coin depicting a monkey wearing a straw hat. Dayton's shop owners hung signs with monkeys and apes in their windows. The town's constable put a sign that said MONKEYVILLE POLICE on his bike, and a local delivery van had MONKEYVILLE EXPRESS emblazoned on it. Fred Robinson began offering "simian sodas" at his drugstore, stocked up on fundamentalist books, and hung a large sign on his storefront that said WHERE IT STARTED. The Aqua, the finest hotel in town, put cots in its halls for the expected overflow crowds, and the Ladies' Aid Society offered dollar meals at a downtown church.

John T. Raulston, the media-friendly judge in the case, made special allowances for the reporters and the crowds, ordering the courthouse painted, adding five hundred seats, constructing a platform for movie cameras, and installing new toilets. Town officials roped off six blocks of downtown as a pedestrian mall, the space quickly filling with hucksters and proselytizers. One man offered tourists the opportunity to have their pictures taken with his pet chimpanzee. Another claimed to have a piece of "the missing link." Viewing the spectacle in Dayton, a *New York Times* reporter noted that "whatever the deep significance of the trial, if it has any, there is no doubt that it has attracted some of the world's champion freaks."

Just as the city boosters had hoped, reporters poured into Dayton as the trial approached, coming from as far away as Hong Kong. Collectively they penned more than two million words during the trial. News organizations utilized the latest in modern technology to cover events in Dayton, stringing thousands of miles of telegraph wires, filming events for newsreels, and pioneering live radio broadcasts. They sent twenty-two key operators to relay telegraph signals. For the first time, radio carried live and continuous coverage of a courtroom trial. Many of the reporters brought to Dayton their own biases about small-town life. Many unfairly painted the town as a fundamentalist stronghold, reinforcing the view that the trial represented a clash between religious dogma and free speech.

No one did more to convey this notion than H. L. Mencken, the iconoclastic editor of *American Mercury* and a columnist for the *Baltimore Sun*. Mencken, who once described himself as "absolutely devoid of what is called religious feeling," was a caricature of the skeptical eastern elitist who mocked the rural ways of people in Dayton. "Civilized life," he charged, was not "possible under a democracy" because it placed government in the hands of common people. His venomous daily reports, which he wrote while sipping Prohibition-banned scotch, dismissed Dayton residents as "the local primates" and referred to the trial as "a religious orgy." He saved his most vicious attacks for Bryan. "It is tragedy indeed, to begin life as a hero and to end it as a buffoon," he wrote.

Bryan set the stage when he arrived in Dayton a few days before the trial. Speaking to the Dayton Progressive club, he foreshadowed the arguments he planned to use in the courtroom. "Who made the courts? The people who made the Constitution!

The people. The people can change the Constitution and if necessary they can change the decisions of the court." Darrow arrived on the last train the night before the trial and was was promptly embraced by Scopes. The scene, caught on film, played in newsreels all over the country. "Scopes is not on trial, civilization is on trial," Darrow told reporters. "Nothing will satisfy us but broad victory, a knockout which will have an everlasting precedent to prove that America is founded on liberty and not on narrow, mean, intolerable, and brainless prejudice of soulless religio-maniacs."

The trial opened on July 10, 1925—the twenty-ninth anniversary of Bryan's "Cross of Gold" speech—with hundreds of people flooding into the Rhea County courthouse during one of the hottest summers on record. By 8:45 A.M. all the seats were occupied and the crowd overflowed into the hallways. The judge could barely squeeze down the aisle when he arrived at 9 A.M. These were not, however, the rich tourists the town boosters had hoped to attract to the trial. According to the *New York Times,* they were "farmers in overalls from the hillside farms, silent, gaunt men."

Inside the sweltering courtroom, Judge Raulston allowed the attorneys to remove their coats and ties. He refused to allow smoking, however, so spittoons were placed around the courtroom for the many people who chose to chew tobacco instead. The trial opened with a long prayer by a fundamentalist minister who took the opportunity to attack the defense team. The prosecutors respectfully bowed their heads; Darrow stared out the window. Most of the first day was devoted to jury selection. The entire jury pool consisted of about a hundred white males—a fact that was remarked upon by the African American press but little mentioned in the white media. Following jury selection, the court adjourned for the weekend.

When court resumed on Monday, the judge swore in the jury and then promptly excused them so he could consider a defense motion to dismiss the case on constitutional grounds, claiming the Tennessee law was too vague and violated both separation of church and state and free-speech provisions of the state constitution. With the jury absent, prosecutor Stewart countered the defense motion, arguing that the democratically elected legislature had the right to regulate public schools and exclude what it regarded as "dangerous beliefs." There was no freedom of speech violation, he claimed. "Mr. Scopes might have taken his stand on the street corners and expounded until he became hoarse, but he cannot go into the public schools . . . and teach his theory." Legislators "who are responsible to the constituents, to the citizens of Tennessee" should control public education, he charged.

The day ended with Darrow giving a long, eloquent, prepared speech that mesmerized those in the courtroom. An observer described Darrow as he slowly rose from his chair, his "huge head, leathery lined face, square jaw, his twisted mouth of the skeptic, softened by the quizzical twinkle of his deep-set eyes." Pacing the courtroom, tugging on his lavender suspenders, Darrow, unable to hide his contempt for religion, called the law "foolish, mischievous, and wicked." It represented "as brazen and as bold an attempt to destroy learning as was ever made in the Middle Ages." Darrow said that the Tennessee anti-evolution law made the Bible "the yardstick to measure every man's intellect, to measure every man's intelligence, to measure every man's learning."

On Wednesday morning the judge read his carefully argued response to the defense motion. Asserting that the Butler Act did not violate either the Tennessee or the United States Constitution, he ordered the case to proceed. Judge Raulston stated that the law "gives no preference to any particular religion or mode of worship." After lunch, the real trial commenced before the seldom-seen jury. The prosecution questioned the superintendent of schools and two of Scopes's students, who confirmed that Scopes had used Hunter's *Civic Biology* textbook in his class. They also testified that Scopes taught that man had evolved from one-celled organisms. Drugstore owner Fred Robinson then took the stand to confirm that Scopes had said that "any teacher in the state who was teaching Hunter's *Biology* was violating the law." It was a simple case: Scopes had violated the law. The prosecution rested its case.

Then the defense opened its case by calling one of its many experts, Dr. Maynard Metcalf, a zoologist from Johns Hopkins University. The testimony of prominent scientists was central to Darrow's strategy of using the trial to showcase the latest scientific reasoning on evolution and embarrass the creationists. The prosecution objected, arguing that testimony about evolution was not relevant to the issue of whether Scopes violated the law. Uncertain how to proceed, Judge Raulston initially allowed Metcalf to testify. On Thursday morning, however, as Metcalf prepared to take the stand again, the prosecution insisted that Raulston rule on the issue of admissibility. He agreed to hear arguments on both sides. Bryan, in his first speech in the courtroom, was supposed to make the case for denying experts. Instead, he delivered a rambling diatribe that included his familiar attacks on scientific experts and praise for the wisdom of common people.

Bryan's sermon prompted what many courtroom observers believed was the most eloquent and passionate speech of the entire trial. But it came from Dudley Malone, not Clarence Darrow. Malone had once worked for Bryan in the State Department and still referred to him as "chief," but he was troubled by his former boss's claim that the Bible and evolution were incompatible. Genesis and evolution were not in conflict, he argued, and it was important that the defense be able to present expert witnesses, many of them good Christians, who could make that point. Besides, he thundered, simple fairness required that Scopes be able to present evidence that could maintain his innocence. He closed with a moving tribute to the power of truth:

> The truth always wins and we are not afraid of it. The truth is no coward. The truth does not need the law. The truth does not need the forces of government. The truth does not need Mr. Bryan. The truth is imperishable, eternal, and immortal and needs no human agency to support it. We are ready to tell the truth as we understand it and we do not fear all the truth that they can present as facts. We are ready. We are ready. We feel we stand with progress. We feel that we stand with science. We feel that we stand with intelligence. We feel that we stand with fundamental freedom in America. We are not afraid. Where is the fear? We meet it. Where is the fear? We defy it. . . .

The courtroom erupted in applause, and Bryan later said it was the best speech he had ever heard. But it failed to convince Judge Raulston, who once again sided with the prosecution. He maintained that the experts' opinions on evolutionary theory would "shed no light" on the issue at hand in the trial—whether Scopes violated the state's anti-evolution laws. The trial was not about the scientific merits of evolution, he declared. In a small concession to the defense, he allowed the expert witnesses to compile their testimony in written affidavits that could be entered into the court record. The jury never heard the expert witnesses, but the press provided extensive coverage of their statements, providing Darrow with a partial victory in his efforts to turn the trial into a national seminar on evolutionary theory.

At this point, the prosecution essentially assumed they had won the case. Many journalists packed their bags and left town. On Sunday, the *Nashville Banner* noted that "it does not seem possible that anything can transpire to make the trial of John T. Scopes interesting again." Even H. L. Mencken did not wait around for the verdict. "All that remains of the great cause of the State of Tennessee against the infidel Scopes is the final business of bumping off the defendant," he wrote in his last report.

It was so hot and crowded in the courtroom in Dayton on Monday, July 20, that Judge Raulston decided to move the trial outside under the trees. "The floor may give way," he said. "The plaster is cracking downstairs. This floor was never intended to hold so many people." Frustrated by the judge's rulings that prevented him from placing the law itself on trial, and unable to call expert witnesses on evolution, Darrow made a bold move: he would call an expert on the Bible instead. He summoned William Jennings Bryan to the stand. The prosecution team erupted, pleading with Bryan not to take the stand. This move was unheard-of grandstanding, but Bryan, taking the stand, set the stage for one of the great courtroom confrontations, and helped define a national debate for all time. The *New York Times* called the Darrow-Bryan contest "the most amazing courtroom scene in Anglo-American history."

On Monday morning, the crowd swelled to nearly three thousand when it learned that Bryan was about to testify and defend religion. The two combatants took their places on the crude wooden platform as children hawked refreshments to the crowd. Darrow, jacketless and wearing his trademark purple suspenders, began his interrogation of Bryan with a quiet question: "You have given considerable study to the Bible, haven't you, Mr. Bryan?" Bryan replied, "Yes, I have. I have studied the Bible for about fifty years." Thus began a series of questions designed to undermine a literalist interpretation of the Bible. The crowd clearly favored Bryan, cheering wildly whenever he spoke or answered a question.

BRYAN: I believe everything in the Bible should be accepted as it is given there; some of the Bible is given illusively.

DARROW: . . . But when you read that . . . the whale swallowed Jonah . . . How do you literally interpret that?

BRYAN: . . . I believe in a God who can make a whale and can make a man and make both of them do what he pleases. . . .

DARROW: . . . but do you believe he made them . . . that he made such a fish and it was big enough to swallow Jonah?

BRYAN: Yes sir, let me add, one miracle is just as easy to believe as another.

Darrow then moved on to the Great Flood, which the Bible says took place in 4004 B.C. How, he asked, could such a calculation be made? By this point, the crowd was beginning to laugh at Bryan's defensive answers. Darrow was methodically accomplishing his mission. He continued on the question of how time was measured in the Bible. If the sun was not made until the fourth day, how did they measure the length of a day for the first three days of creation?

Eventually, Bryan admitted that the biblical account of creation could have involved "millions of years," since there was no way of knowing how long the first three "days" lasted. "I do not think they were twenty-four-hour days," he said. Bryan did not realize that this answer totally undermined his literal interpretation of the Bible. Although he had successfully humiliated Bryan on the stand, Darrow grew more aggressive and belligerent as Bryan became more rattled and defensive. At one point the exasperated Bryan said, "I do not think about things I don't think about." Darrow asked, "Do you think about the things you do think about?" Bryan responded, to the derisive laughter of spectators, "Well, sometimes." Darrow said that the Scopes trial was about "preventing bigots and ignoramuses from controlling the education of the United States and you know it, and that is all."

Realizing that Darrow was winning the exchange, the prosecution tried throwing in the towel, but Bryan refused to stand down. "I am simply trying to protect the word of God against the greatest atheist or agnostic in the United States," he shouted, pounding his fist in rage. "I want the papers to know I am not afraid to get on the stand in front of him and let him do his worst." Eventually, both men were standing, shaking fists at each other, until the judge finally intervened.

On Tuesday, court resumed while a light rain fell outside, so the judge moved the proceedings back inside. Given the devolution of the trial into a shouting match between Bryan and Darrow the prior day, Raulston ordered that Bryan give no further testimony and ordered that the trial record be expunged of all mention of the exchange. Because they wanted a guilty verdict so they could pursue the case on appeal, the defense refused to make a closing statement, essentially telling the jury that it should return a guilty verdict. The move frustrated Bryan, who had spent days preparing his own dramatic closing speech for the jury (and the assembled reporters). Now there would be no closing arguments.

The jurors left the courtroom to deliberate. They did not even bother sitting down. After huddling together in the hallway for nine minutes they returned to the courtroom to deliver their verdict. Before they did, Bryan turned to Malone and said, "I am not a gambling man, but if I was I would bet that the verdict is guilty." He was right. The jury found Scopes guilty. The judge set the fine at $100.

As the historian Lawrence Levine has noted, if Bryan felt humiliated by the trial, "he did a masterly job of concealing it during the five days of life remaining to him." With characteristic enthusiasm he embarked on an ambitious speaking campaign around the state of Tennessee. He rewrote his never-delivered closing argument into a fiery stump speech. After Sunday services at the Methodist church, where he gave morning prayers, and eating a heavy meal, Bryan lay down for a nap. He never woke up. His funeral became a national event and thousands lined the funeral train's route. He was buried in Arlington National Cemetery with the words "He Kept the Faith" inscribed on his tombstone. Darrow was vacationing in the Smoky Mountains when he learned the news of Bryan's death. He showed no sympathy for his former antagonist. Bryan had not died from a bad heart, he said, but from "a busted belly." Wasn't it ironic, he said, that "a man who for years had fought excessive drinking lay dead from indigestion by overeating."

The Scopes case quickly dropped from public view. The Tennessee Supreme Court threw out the appeal on a technicality. Eager to put an end to the controversy, it instructed the Tennessee attorney general not to retry Scopes because there was "nothing to be gained by prolonging the life of this bizarre case." The hopes of local city boosters to transform Dayton into a bustling new city went unrealized. They did, however, build a new college—Bryan

College, named after William Jennings Bryan. Local officials offered John Scopes his old teaching job, but he realized that living
in Dayton would never be the same. Scopes went on to graduate
school at the University of Chicago, where he studied geology. He
received many lucrative movie offers, but he disliked the celebrity
culture and consciously avoided the spotlight in favor of "peace
and emotional stability." Afterward, he accepted a job with Gulf
Oil and spent the rest of his career working in the oil and gas
industry.

*　*　*

Despite the short-term humiliation that Bryan endured on the
witness stand, the real losers were the secularists who believed
they had won the final battle over fundamentalism. While Darrow
succeeded in making Bryan look foolish on the witness stand, he
also alienated many liberal Christians with his sneering contempt
for religion. Writing in the *New York World,* Walter Lippmann
noted that "in his anxiety to humiliate and ridicule Mr. Bryan,"
Darrow "convinced millions" of open-minded Christians "that
Bryan is right in his assertion that the contest at Dayton was for
and against the Christian religion." The ACLU, which had fash-
ioned a legal strategy designed to highlight the compatibility of
religion and science, now found itself labeled antireligious.

Within a few years, religious conservatives pushed anti-
evolution bills through the legislatures of North Carolina, Washington, Minnesota, Missouri, Kansas, Florida, North Dakota, and
Virginia. By 1930, 70 percent of high schools in the United States
omitted any reference to evolution. In 1955, when *Inherit the Wind*
premiered on Broadway, the Butler Act was still on the books. The
state repealed the law in 1967.

Despite their legislative success, fundamentalists found themselves on the defensive in the decades following the Scopes trial. The stock market crash and the Great Depression that followed pushed the social issues that had dominated the 1920s off the public agenda. At the same time, most fundamentalists were embarrassed by the Scopes episode and chose to withdraw from the mainstream. Instead of trying to change public institutions, they decided to build their own schools, churches, and community centers. Viewing the world as corrupt, they adopted a "separatist" approach, believing they should be "in the world but not of the world."

In retrospect, however, Scopes forged a temporary break, not a full-scale retreat, in the fundamentalist assault on modernist thought. After the trial, H. L. Mencken observed that conservative Christianity was a "fire still burning on a far-flung hill, and it may begin to roar again at any moment."

That fire roared to life in the 1970s. That decade witnessed a dramatic increase in the number of self-identified evangelical Christians who had experienced a "born again" conversion, believed in a literal interpretation of the Bible, and accepted Jesus Christ as their personal savior. The number of Americans who identified themselves as "born again" increased from 24 percent in 1963 to nearly 40 percent in 1978. More than 45 million—one of every five Americans—considered themselves fundamentalists by the end of the decade. Many fundamentalists were converted by television preachers who used mass media to preach a return to traditional values. The three most successful televangelists—Jerry Falwell, Pat Robertson, and Jim Bakker—reached an estimated 100 million Americans each week with fire-and-brimstone sermons about the evils of contemporary life. America, they preached, confronted a crisis of the spirit, brought on by the pervasive influence of "secular humanism," which stressed material well-being and personal gratification over religious conviction and devotion to traditional Christian values.

The opening salvo in the new culture war had been fired in 1962 when the Supreme Court outlawed prayer in the schools, and it continued with decisions legalizing contraception and abortion. Paul Weyrich, a conservative political strategist, described the battle between the Christian fundamentalists and secular liberals, in language reminiscent of Bryan, as "the most significant battle of the age-old conflict between good and evil, between the forces of God and the forces against God, that we have seen in our country." Fundamentalists blamed themselves for the problems, claiming their withdrawal from public life created a moral vacuum, which the liberals filled. "The withdrawal for too many years by too many evangelicals from society and political engagement has led to many of our nation's problems," said Richard Land of the Southern Baptist Convention. "I believe that if there was more hell preached in the pulpits, there would be less hell in our schools, and less hell in the streets and less hell in the homes."

During the 1980s and 1990s, with a rejuvenated fundamentalist movement reengaged in the public debate, the nation found itself once again deeply divided between reason and religion, individual expression and moral righteousness. Some of the unresolved issues from the 1920s remained—immigration restriction and the role of religion in public schools—but the nation now had to contend with a host of new, morally complicated issues, such as abortion and gay rights.

On evolution, science has won most of the court battles, but it has made little progress in changing broader cultural attitudes. In 1968, the year after Tennessee repealed its anti-evolution statute, the Supreme Court ruled in *Epperson v. Arkansas* that bans on teaching evolution violated the Establishment Clause of the United States Constitution. In two decisions in the 1980s, the court expanded its original ruling, holding that "creation science" was not really science but religion in disguise, and striking down a law requiring biology teachers to discuss "creation science" along with evolution. In 2005, the justices declared that placing stickers on biology textbooks stating "Evolution is a theory, not a fact," violated the First Amendment.

These rulings did not quiet the fundamentalists, however. Instead of marking the triumph of secular thought over religious dogma, the Scopes trial revealed the enduring power of religious faith in America. Polls show Americans to be among the most religious people on earth. According to some polls, as many as 85 percent of Americans call themselves Christian. By comparison, Israel is 77 percent Jewish. The social divisions exposed during the trial have changed little in the intervening decades. In 1983 Stephen Jay Gould wrote that "sadly, any hope that the issues of the Scopes trial had been banished to the realm of nostalgic Americana have been swept aside by our current creationist resurgence." A 2005 Pew Forum Survey found that 78 percent of Americans believe that God created life on earth. A plurality—48 percent— say that humans evolved over time. Almost as many—42 percent—believe that God created humans in the present form. In 2006, just as in 1925, people with high education, liberals, and those who seldom attend church are more likely to support evolution. Conservatives, those with little education, and those who attend church regularly are most likely to oppose evolution. This ongoing debate over evolution versus creationism is a uniquely American problem. Polls show that more than 75 percent of Danish and French citizens and more than 60 percent of adults in

Germany, Austria, Britain, Spain, Italy, and the Netherlands have said they believe evolution is "definitely" or "probably" true.

The latest incarnation of the battle between science and religion is over "intelligent design," which, ironically, is strikingly similar to the position Darrow argued in the Scopes trial. It maintains that science and religion are not incompatible. Since Darwin's theory of natural selection cannot explain the complexity of nature, an "intelligent designer" must be involved in creation. The most recent version of Scopes played out in 2005, in Dover, Pennsylvania, where eleven parents sued the local school board after it voted that intelligent design be presented in biology classes as an alternative to evolution. The parents, represented by the ACLU, charged that intelligent design promoted religion and therefore violated constitutional freedom-of-religion protections. The school board, defended by the Thomas More Law Center, a Christian legal center, countered that intelligent design did not promote religion but simply presented an alternative to Darwin. In December 2005, a federal judge ruled against using intelligent design as an alternative to evolution. "The overwhelming evidence is that intelligent design is a religious view, a mere relabeling of creationism and not a scientific theory," the judge wrote in a scathing 139-page decision. "It is an extension of the fundamentalists' view that one must either accept the literal interpretation of Genesis or else believe in the godless system of evolution."

It seems unlikely that this case will resolve the questions raised in the "trial of the century." Unlike most turning points in history, the Scopes trial is important for the questions it raised, not for the answers it provided. It exposed the ongoing fault line in American democracy between majority rule and minority rights, at the same time that it opened a new cultural chasm between rural piety and urban cynicism. Americans are still struggling with the legacy of

Scopes, trying to reconcile their traditional values with the realities of social change. Events over the next few decades, including a startling and deadly new scientific discovery, would only complicate that process.

For Further Reading

For a superb survey of American life and thought in the period see Robert and Helen Lynd's *Middletown* (1929). Frederick Lewis Allen's *Only Yesterday* (1931) appraised the Roaring Twenties from the depths of the Great Depression. For the intellectual development of fundamentalism, see George Marsden's *Fundamentalism and American Culture* (1980).

The best single volume on the Scopes trial and its legacy is Edward Larson, *Summer for the Gods: The Scopes Trial and America's Continuing Debate over Science and Religion* (1997). Other useful historical accounts include: Paul K. Conklin's *When All the Gods Trembled: Darwinism, Scopes, and American Intellectuals* (1998) and Kary Doyle Smout's *The Creation/Evolution Controversy: A Battle for Cultural Power* (1998). For an excellent collection of essays, see Jerry R. Tompkins, *D-Days at Dayton: Reflections on the Scopes Trial* (1965). More recent views can be found in David C. Lindberg and Ronald L. Numbers, *When Science and Christianity Meet* (2003). Ray Ginger, *Six Days or Forever?: Tennessee v. John Thomas Scopes* (1958) remains the most readable popular account of the trial. It is instructive to read contemporary accounts of the trial and its immediate aftermath. H. L. Mencken summarized his views in *Treatise on the Gods* (1930). Walter Lippmann penned two books that dealt with the trial: *American Inquisitors: A Commentary on Dayton and Chicago* (1928) and the influential *A Preface to Morals* (1930).

There is an extensive body of literature by and about the main protagonists. S. T. Joshi has assembled Clarence Darrow's writings on religion and science in *Closing Arguments: Clarence Darrow on Religion, Law, and Society* (2005). Robert W. Cherny provides insight into the mind of Bryan in *A Righteous Cause: The Life of William Jennings Bryan* (1995). John Scopes produced a memoir about the case in *The World's Most Famous Court Trial: Tennessee Evolution Case* (2000). The Pew Foundation has placed online survey data on recent American attitudes toward science and religion. See http://pewforum.org/surveys/origins/#3.

8 July 16, 1939
Einstein's Letter

O n August 6, 1945, a B-29 named the *Enola Gay* opened
its bomb-bay doors and released a nine-thousand-pound
cigar-shaped bomb dubbed "Little Boy" on Hiroshima, Japan. At
8:15 A.M. it detonated 1,850 feet above the city. The sky exploded.
Survivors called it "Pika-don," meaning "flash of light, tremen-
dous sound." The world's first atomic bomb struck with the force
of twelve thousand tons of TNT, flattening forty-seven square
miles. Reaching temperatures of 100 million degrees at ground
zero, the explosion pulverized buildings and turned people into
ash. It killed about a hundred thousand people instantly, and
thousands more died later of burns, shock, and radiation poison-
ing. "What you remember most are the screams for water," recalled a survivor of the bomb. On August 8, Russian army units
invaded Manchuria and Korea. The day after Russia entered the
war, the United States dropped a second atomic bomb, called "Fat
Man," on Nagasaki, incinerating forty thousand people and oblit-
erating much of the city. The world had entered the nuclear age.

President Truman's decision to drop the atomic bomb literally shook the world. While historians debate the necessity of using the bomb, especially on a civilian population, few doubt that the United States would have developed the weapon before the end of the war if it had not been for the persistence of an eccentric Hungarian-born physicist named Leo Szilard and his more famous colleague, Albert Einstein. Sometimes something as simple as a letter can change the course of history.

Born in 1898, Szilard served briefly in World War I before moving to Berlin at the end of the war to study physics. At the beginning of the century, Germany was the Mecca of great scientists, especially physicists. Before 1933, it had won ninety-nine Nobel Prizes for science, compared to eighteen for England and only six for the United States. By the 1920s, however, the Nazis' rise to power carried with it a rising tide of anti-Semitism. Nazi students tried intimidating the faculty. A group called the Working Party of German Scientists for the Preservation of Pure Scholarship dismissed many of the new theories being developed as "Jewish physics." The Nazi secret police published a weekly newsletter attacking prominent Jewish scientists.

Szilard saw the writing on the wall and fled to Vienna and, later, to London, where he headed up an effort to bring refugee scientists to British universities. When he was not trying to find homes for other scientists fleeing Germany, he was thinking about theoretical physics. In 1933, the same year that Hitler came to power, Szilard had a revelation while sitting at a traffic light in London: perhaps it was possible to split a nucleus with a neutron and create a chain reaction of energy known as nuclear fission. Over the next few years he tried various experiments to achieve this result, but they all failed, largely because he was trying to split the wrong atoms. But theoretically he knew it was possible; he just had to find a way to prove it.

In 1939, German physicists Otto Hahn and Fritz Strassmann bombarded the nucleus of a single uranium atom with a neutron beam, splitting the atom in half and creating an intense burst of energy. The experiment demonstrated the viability of nuclear fission, perhaps the most significant scientific discovery of the twentieth century. The news both elated and scared Szilard. On January 25, 1939, he wrote a fellow scientist that the latest scientific breakthrough could lead to discoveries that "might make it possible to produce power by means of nuclear energy [that might also] lead to a large-scale production of energy and radioactive elements, unfortunately also perhaps to atomic bombs."

Szilard tried duplicating the fission experiments by bombarding uranium with neutrons in his lab at Columbia University. In theory, if the conditions were right, the scientists would see a series of fast flashes on an oscilloscope. These flashes would represent the presence of fast neutrons, essential for a quick chain reaction and necessary for a working atomic bomb. Later, Szilard would note that "we saw the flashes. We watched them for a little while and then we switched everything off and went home. That night there was very little doubt in my mind that the world was headed for grief."

For Szilard it was already clear that another world war was coming. Hitler, repudiating the Versailles Treaty, withdrew from the League of Nations in 1933 and unilaterally announced that Germany would rearm. On March 7, 1936, Hitler ordered German troops into the Rhineland, the strategic buffer that lay between France and Germany. Two years later, he pressed Europe to the brink of war, proclaiming the German nation's right to *lebensraum*, or living space. "Germany's problems could be solved only by means of force," he told his aides. In March he forced Austria into *Anschluss* (union) with Germany. In the fall Hitler threatened to invade Czechoslovakia when it refused to give him its Sudeten-land, a mountainous region bordering Germany and inhabited mostly by ethnic Germans. British prime minister Neville Chamberlain and French premier Edouard Daladier hastily scheduled meetings with Hitler in Munich on September 29–30, 1938. Hitler reassured the Western leaders by promising, "This is the last territorial claim I have to make in Europe." Hoping to avoid confrontation, the West sacrificed the Sudetenland on the altar of appeasement, agreeing to a gradual transfer to German control.

Szilard was by now consumed by the fear that Hitler could get his hands on a new weapon of terrifying destructive potential. The scientific genie was out of the bottle. Over the past few years scientists working in independent labs around the world had published their breakthroughs. German scientists had access to all this information. Szilard, who never owned a home and lived most of his life out of a suitcase, staying at hotels and the homes of friends, became obsessed with preventing Hitler from getting the bomb. He urged scientists outside Germany to withhold publication of their fission-related research.

When he learned that Germany blocked exports of uranium ore from occupied Czechoslovakia, Szilard was convinced that Hitler's scientists were busy at work turning the most important scientific discovery of the century into a weapon of mass destruction. How else to explain Hitler's reckless behavior? How else could Hitler believe that he could defeat the combined armies of the West? Since Belgium possessed the only other stockpiles of uranium, he needed to warn that government not to export uranium to Germany. But Szilard was relatively unknown and it was unlikely the Belgium government would listen to his appeal. He needed to find someone who could serve as a messenger—someone with such a stellar reputation that his warning would have to be taken seriously.

He turned to a former teacher, Albert Einstein. Szilard had worked with Einstein in the 1920s in Berlin, where they patented a refrigerator pump with no moving parts that would later be used in nuclear reactors. Oddly enough, Szilard contacted the most brilliant scientist of his age not for his intellect but for his political connections. Szilard recalled that Einstein was close friends with the queen of Belgium. They often played music together—she played piano; he the violin. It was not typical for physicists to socialize with European royalty, but Albert Einstein was not a typical physicist. He was the "Pope of Physics" and a celebrated international celebrity. With his rumpled clothes and unruly hair, he became a caricature of the modern scientist. He was quoted in newspapers, appeared in film newsreels, and was more popular than many Hollywood stars. When asked to name the most popular figure in the world, New York University's graduating class of 1930 ranked Einstein second behind Charles Lindbergh.

Born in the small German city of Ulm on March 14, 1879, Albert revealed few signs of his later brilliance as a child. He did not start speaking until the age of two and he was only an average student in school. The authoritarian German school system, which stressed rote memorization, bored him. Since he showed no interest in sports, many of his classmates called him *Biedermeier,* or "nerd." When his father asked the school headmaster what profession young Albert should choose, he responded, "It doesn't matter; he'll never make a success of anything." He attended the Federal Polytechnic Institute in Switzerland, one of the top science universities in the world, but was unable to get a teaching job when he finished.

In 1905, while working as a patent clerk, Einstein published three theories that would change the world of science, making it the single most significant year in science since 1666 when Isaac Newton discovered the laws of gravity. He revealed his revolutionary equation ($E = mc^2$) showing that mass and energy were interchangeable, which meant that a small amount of matter could be converted into huge amounts of energy. This insight would provide the theoretical underpinnings for the atom bomb. That same year he proposed his theory of relativity, which showed that space and time could be altered. He expanded on his ideas a few years later in his general theory of relativity, which showed that gravity and acceleration were related. When, on November 6, 1919, the Royal Society and the Royal Astronomical Society in London verified Einstein's new theory of gravity, he was transformed into a world figure. The head of the academy called Einstein's discovery "one of the greatest achievements in the history of human thought." His insight changed the Newtonian world of science and created a new understanding of time and space. The theory of relativity earned Einstein a Nobel Prize for Physics in 1921 and worldwide renown.

In December 1932, just a few weeks before Hitler came to power, Einstein left Germany for the United States. An outspoken pacifist, and a Jew, who opposed German rearmament at the end of World War I, Einstein had become an obvious target of the growing Nazi movement. As early as 1922 his name had appeared on a "Nazi hit list" for promoting ideas that challenged the notion of Aryan supremacy. In 1931, Nazi sympathizers published a pamphlet called *One Hundred Authorities Against Einstein*, which was filled with anti-Semitic slander. Einstein quipped that it would not take a hundred authorities to prove relativity wrong. One simple fact would do the trick. As they left their country home in Caputh, Germany, he said to his wife, "Turn around, you will never see it again." As expected, the Nazis seized his property, burned his books in public, and put a price of $50,000 on his head. When asked about the price on his life, Einstein said, "I didn't know I was worth so much."

Although he had offers from leading universities around the world, Einstein accepted a position at Princeton University, which he described as "a quaint ceremonious village of puny demigods on stilts." Many of his colleagues warned him against living permanently in the United States, which lagged far behind Western Europe in science. Einstein, however, announced that he would stay in the United States because "as long as I have any choice in the matter, I shall live only in a country where civil liberty, tolerance, and equality of all citizens before the law prevail."

Hitler's rise to power had forced Einstein to reconsider his pacifist beliefs. With the German army poised to overrun Europe, Einstein said that Belgium and France had no choice but to rebuild militaries. Many involved in the pacifist movement criticized him for his change in position, but he felt he had no choice. "With the rise of fascism, I recognized that one could not maintain such a [pacifist] point of view except at the risk of allowing the whole world to fall into the hands of the most terrible enemies of mankind," he said. "Organized power can be opposed only by organized power. Much as I regret this, there is no other way."

In July 1939 Szilard and a colleague, Princeton physicist Eugene Wigner, learned that Einstein was staying at a cottage owned by a Dr. Moore in Great Peconic Bay on the eastern shore of New York's Long Island. On Sunday morning, July 16, 1939, Wigner picked up Szilard—who never learned to drive—at the King's Crown Hotel in a 1936 Dodge coupe. The two scientists drove out of Manhattan over the Triborough Bridge. Ironically, as the pair left the city, they drove by the grounds of the recent world's fair, which featured a "futurama" exhibit that spoke in breathtaking terms about "the world of tomorrow," a world of ice-making fridges, TVs, washing machines, two-month vacations, and superhighways. If their fears were proven true, America would have a very different future from the one envisioned by the exhibits at the world's fair.

Wigner and Szilard's momentous trip got off to an inauspicious start. In their effort to save the world from the threat of a Nazi atomic bomb they forgot one small detail: directions to Moore's cottage. They got confused by the name of the town and drove to Patchogue on the south shore. "Perhaps I misunderstood the name Patchogue on the telephone," Wigner remarked. "Let's see if we can find some similar name on the map." "Could it be Peconic?" asked Szilard. "Yes, that was it," said Wigner. "Now I remember." The two then drove to Peconic. Although they knew the name of the street where Einstein was staying, they did not know how to find it. During the summer, the town was overrun with tourists and visitors who could offer little help with directions. After asking numerous bathing-suit-clad beachgoers for directions to "Dr. Moore's cottage," Szilard grew impatient and despondent. "Let's give up and go home, perhaps fate intended it," he said. Wigner replied, "But it's our duty to take this step." He suggested that they ask a child for directions. "After all," he said, "every child knows him." The two scientists then saw a seven-year-old boy standing at a corner carrying a fishing rod. Szilard leaned out the window and asked, "Do you know where Einstein lives?" The boy replied, "Of course I do," and pointed the way out to them.

By the time the physicists arrived at Dr. Moore's two-story white cottage, they were hot, tired, and cranky from the drive.

Einstein was in better spirits, having spent the morning sailing. They found Einstein wearing an old shirt and wrinkled pants, looking, according to Wigner's recollection, "perfectly content to be thinking only of physics." Einstein bowed courteously as he greeted his former students, inviting them to join him on the screened porch overlooking a green lawn. Once settled, Einstein served the men iced tea and they began to speak in German about the reason for the visit. Szilard and Wigner provided Einstein with a short primer on the latest fission research and explained that uranium bombarded by neutrons can split. They went on to explain that the splitting of the atom could lead to a chain reaction and an atomic bomb.

Szilard later recalled that "almost as soon as I began to tell him about it he realized what the consequences might be and immediately signified his readiness to help us and if necessary 'stick his neck out,' as the saying goes." Prior to his meeting with Wigner and Szilard, Einstein had thought fission was only a theoretical possibility and that he would not live to see it "in my time." For the past few years, Einstein had been devoting most of his energy to developing a unified theory of the universe. He had not worked in the field of nuclear research for many years, and he had not kept up with the scientific literature. He had published his famous equation ($E = mc^2$) in 1905, but only now were the true and, in the context of impending world war, horrifying ramifications of the equation becoming clear. According to Wigner's later memoirs, "Einstein also realized the political and military meaning of nuclear fission: that it could yield explosives strong enough to make the Nazis invincible. And Einstein was just as horrified as I was by that prospect. He volunteered to do whatever he could to prevent it."

Einstein decided it was better to direct the letter to the Belgian ambassador than the royal family. That afternoon, the three men sat around the dining room table as Einstein dictated a letter in German. Wigner wrote it down longhand. They thought it prudent to send a copy of the letter to the State Department as well so Washington would not think they were meddling behind the scenes in military matters. That afternoon, Wigner and Szilard drove back to Manhattan, and Einstein decided to take advantage of a good breeze and a clear sky to go sailing again. Little did he know that his actions that day would set in motion a series of events that would change world history.

Within days Szilard's plan became much more far-reaching, for he discussed the matter with economist Alexander Sachs, a friend and unofficial adviser to President Franklin Roosevelt. If Einstein wrote a letter to Roosevelt, Sachs promised to hand-deliver it. Einstein again agreed and asked Szilard to come back to his house so they could draft a second letter. Szilard arrived at Einstein's Long Island home on Sunday, July 30, in a 1935 Plymouth driven by fellow Hungarian physicist Edward Teller, who later remarked, "I entered history as Szilard's chauffeur." Einstein dictated a short draft in German that Szilard took down. Over the next few days, Szilard translated Einstein's dictation, going through draft after draft. In the end, he prepared both a short and a long version. On August 2, he mailed them to Einstein, who signed both versions, but indicated that he preferred the longer version.

One biographer called the letter "one of the most important in world history." "Some recent work . . . leads me to expect that the element uranium may be turned into a new and important source of energy in the immediate future," Einstein wrote, warning ominously that Hitler had stopped exports of uranium from occupied Czechoslovakia. "This new phenomenon would also lead to the production of bombs, and it is conceivable that extremely powerful bombs of a new type may be constructed." Then came the warning: "Some of the American work on uranium is now being repeated in the Kaiser Wilhelm Institute in Berlin."

The task of alerting FDR to the dangers of atomic weapons was now squarely in the lap of Alexander Sachs. However, history intervened to prevent the timely delivery of the letter. On September 1, 1939, Hitler unleashed his fire and steel on the Polish. In a brilliant display of military skill and power, the Germans conducted a blitzkrieg (lightning war), sending 1.5 million men pouring over the Polish border. "Close your hearts to pity," Hitler told his generals. "Act brutally." Two days later, honoring their commitments to Poland, Britain and France declared war on Germany. World War II in Europe had begun.

With Roosevelt consumed with the growing war in Europe and fighting a powerful peace movement at home, he had little time for meetings about future problems. Despite numerous calls to the president's secretary, Sachs could not get into the Oval Office. By October, Szilard and Einstein were losing patience with Sachs and discussed the possibility of starting over and finding a new emissary. Szilard told Einstein that Sachs "[had] spoken repeatedly with Roosevelt's secretary and [had] the impression that Roosevelt is so overburdened that it would be wiser to see him at a later date." Szilard decided to give Sachs another ten days to deliver the letter; if he could not do so, he would have to find another way to alert FDR to the nuclear threat.

Just as the physicists were losing patience, Sachs finally secured an hour of FDR's time on Wednesday, October 11, 1939. "Alex, what are you up to?" FDR asked. Instead of reading the letter, Sachs tried to summarize the views of Einstein and Szilard, but Roosevelt seemed distracted and impatient. Sachs walked out of the Oval Office unsure of his effort and fearful that he would not get a second chance to do a better job. He went back to his room at the Carlton Hotel and "didn't sleep a wink." He paced back and forth in his hotel room before going to a small park across the street and sitting on a park bench. "What could I say to get the president on our side in this affair, which was already beginning to look practically hopeless? Quite suddenly, like an inspiration, the right idea came to me. I returned to the hotel, took a shower, and shortly afterwards called once more at the White House."

At their second meeting, FDR seemed to be in a better mood and more receptive to Sachs's attempts to brief him on atomic fission and the dangers of atomic weapons. FDR asked Sachs, "What bright idea have you got now?" Then, "How much time would you like?" Sachs replied, "All I want to do is to tell you a story. During the Napoleonic Wars a young American inventor came to the French emperor and offered to build a fleet of steamships that Napoleon could, in spite of the uncertain weather, land in England." Napoleon refused to accept the idea that ships could be built without sails and sent the inventor away. It proved to be a critical turning point in the war. "England was saved by the shortsightedness of the adversary," Sachs said, quoting the British historian Lord Acton. "Had Napoleon shown more imagination and humility at that time, the history of the nineteenth century would have taken a very different course."

The president sat and thought for few minutes. He then took a pen and paper, wrote a short note, and handed it to the orderly standing nearby. The orderly left and returned in a few moments with a package that FDR handed to Sachs. It contained a bottle of brandy dating to the time of Napoleon. Roosevelt instructed the orderly to open the bottle and pour two drinks.

Roosevelt raised his glass to Sachs. "Alex, what you are after is to see that the Nazis don't blow us up?"

"Precisely," Sachs replied.

FDR then got on his intercom and signaled his secretary, Edwin "Pa" Watson, to come into the office. When Watson entered, FDR told him, "Pa, this requires action."

Despite the presidential imperative, initial work on atomic research was slow and disorganized. Watson proposed the creation of an Advisory Committee on Uranium headed by Dr. Lyman J. Briggs, head of the Bureau of Standards. Project S-1, the initial name given to the project, struggled with inadequate funding and bureaucratic indifference. The reason was simple: in 1939 the United States was a second-rate military power. During the 1930s, disillusion with World War I and concern about jobs at home had intensified America's instinctive isolationism. By 1937, 60 percent of Americans believed that U.S. involvement in World War I had been a mistake, and they were determined not to repeat the same mistake again in the 1930s. Congress reflected the isolationist sentiment by passing restrictive neutrality legislation. It passed three major neutrality acts that limited Roosevelt's ability to respond to the growing crisis in Europe. The underfunded American military, equipped with vintage World War I rifles and tanks, was ranked seventeenth in the world. There was simply no peacetime precedent for the type of intensive scientific-military cooperation that was necessary to produce a nuclear weapon.

Eventually, Hitler's war machine forced the nation to confront the reality of war. On December 7, 1941, Japan attacked the American Pacific fleet in Pearl Harbor. On December 11, Hitler declared war on the United States and Congress quickly returned the favor. Six months later, Roosevelt accelerated the program to build the bomb. He assigned the project to the military, which code-named the nationwide network of research labs, factories, and military bases the Manhattan Engineer District. Shortly afterward, the project was placed in the hands of General Leslie Groves. He recruited a thirty-eight-year-old physicist named J. Robert Oppenheimer, who set up his top-secret lab at the Los Alamos Ranch School for boys in the Jemez Mountains of New Mexico. While the army converted the school into makeshift laboratories and apartments, Oppenheimer traveled around the country recruiting a team of scientists whom Groves called "the greatest collection of eggheads ever."

Einstein was not permitted to work on the Manhattan Project because the FBI considered him a security risk and Groves refused to clear him. Einstein realized that once the Manhattan Project got under way, that "virtually all nuclear physicists [in the United States], as well as countless scientists from other disciplines, had vanished, their addresses unknown." He was never contacted, in large part because FBI director J. Edgar Hoover believed that a Jewish pacifist, who also supported many liberal political causes, could not be trusted with such an important project. Einstein's FBI file noted that "it seems unlikely that a man of his background could . . . become a loyal American citizen." Hoover's suspicions kept the most brilliant scientist of the century from working directly on the most important scientific project in modern times. "I wish very much that I could place the whole thing before him," Vannevar Bush, chief of the Office of Scientific Research and Development wrote, "but this is utterly impossible in view of the attitude of people here in Washington who have studied his whole history."

The new Manhattan Project created whole cities almost overnight in places like Hanford, Washington; Oak Ridge, Tennessee; and Los Alamos, New Mexico. The size of the project, at its peak, rivaled that of the entire American automotive industry. But officially the new Manhattan Project towns did not exist, and the entire operation was shrouded in secrecy. At Los Alamos, for example, armed guards patrolled a ten-foot-high barbed-wire fence, an elaborate alarm system identified any activity near the fence, and powerful searchlights kept the area lit at night. The military, worried the Germans might try to kidnap one of the scientists, assigned bodyguards to accompany them into town. All outgoing mail was censored. The government told people living in the area that the facility was a hospital for pregnant army wives.

Once the fission research program proposal became a reality, it quickly left the direct control of the men who originally proposed it to FDR. Teamwork and discipline now replaced independence and creativity as the key qualities the government was looking for in its scientists. Groves stated, "Sure, we would never have had an atom-bomb if Szilard had not shown such determination during the first years of the war. But as soon as we got going, so far as I was concerned he might just as well have walked the plank!" A new class of scientists emerged to usher the project to its eventual fruition.

By late 1944, military victories on the ground had made the original purpose of the Manhattan Project moot. Following the long-delayed invasion of Normandy in June, Allied armies pushed inland, reaching Strasbourg in November. American intelligence believed the town housed the Nazi atom bomb project, which they feared was near completion. Instead, they found documents revealing that the Germans were at least two years behind the Americans in developing the bomb. Hitler had never devoted as many resources to developing a bomb as Szilard and others feared. Instead, he poured money into developing weapons that could be produced and used on the battlefield in months, not years.

By March 1945, Szilard, now working at the University of Chicago's Met Lab, had developed strong reservations about using the bomb. Appropriately, Szilard spent many hours walking up and down the Midway, the location of the Chicago World's Fair, contemplating how this new weapon would change the future. He was convinced it would be a mistake to use the bomb against the Japanese and he was again determined to get a message directly to Roosevelt. Once again he turned to Einstein for a letter of introduction. Since Einstein lacked the proper security clearance, Szilard was not allowed to talk with him about the content of his letter, and instead simply asked for a cover letter of introduction to FDR. "He told his old friend simply that there was trouble ahead and asked for a letter of introduction to the President," observed the historian Richard Rhodes.

The letter got him an appointment with First Lady Eleanor Roosevelt, which was scheduled for May 8, 1945. On April 12, however, Roosevelt died of a cerebral hemorrhage, elevating Harry Truman to the presidency. By this point the atom bomb project had developed a momentum of its own. Truman did not learn about the Manhattan Project until he was briefed by Secretary of War Henry L. Stimson on April 25, thirteen days after Roosevelt's death. The new president knew little about the bomb's origin and probably was unaware of Einstein's role in convincing Roosevelt to launch a program to build it. But now he understood its potential power. "Within four months," Stimson told him, "we shall in all probability have completed the most terrible weapon ever known in human history, one bomb of which could destroy a whole city."

Stimson's estimate was off by one month. In July, project scientists exploded the world's first atomic device at Alamogordo, New Mexico. The bomb weighed five tons. At its core was a package of uranium 235 about the size of a football. Within nine seconds the temperature at ground zero equaled that on the surface of the sun. An awed Dr. Oppenheimer, witnessing the enormous fireball created by the explosion, was reminded of a passage from Hindu scriptures: "I am become Death, destroyer of worlds."

Military planners, scientists, and politicians engaged in heated secret meetings about whether to use the new weapon, and if so, how? Was the bomb just another weapon of war, or did its destructive power make its use immoral? The United States had already killed hundreds of thousands of Japanese civilians after Pearl Harbor through a deadly campaign of fire-bombing major population centers. A March raid involved 334 B-29 bombers that dropped 1,700 tons of bombs, destroyed 16 square miles, and killed as many as 100,000 civilians. Was it any more immoral to drop a single bomb that would produce similar results? Should the military offer a public demonstration of the destructive power of the new weapon by detonating it on a deserted island, in the hope it would intimidate the Japanese into pulling out of the war?

Szilard believed the atom bomb was different from any other weapon, and he wanted the opportunity to make his case directly to President Truman. He located a scientist from Truman's hometown of Kansas City who had the necessary connections to get him into the White House for a meeting with presidential aide Jimmy Byrnes. Szilard argued that the bomb was going to change the balance of power because it would make obsolete the advantage that traditional industrial power had provided. The United States was by far the strongest industrial power in the world, he argued. Ironically, that industrial might, which allowed the United States to develop the bomb in the first place, would be rendered moot when other nations developed nuclear weapons—which he was certain they would do within a few years. "Perhaps the greatest immediate danger which faces us," he warned prophetically, "is the probability that our demonstration of atomic bombs will precipitate a race in the production of these devices between the United States and Russia."

Byrnes was not swayed by Szilard's argument. If nothing else, he argued, the United States needed to use the bomb to justify the huge expenditures made during the war to build it. "How would you get Congress to appropriate money for atomic energy research if you do not show results for the money which has been spent already?" he said. Byrnes was not worried about the Russians or the threat of an arms race, since the Soviets at that time did not possess large quantities of uranium or high-grade ore. In reality, American scientists had shown that even low-grade ore, widely available in the Soviet Union, could be used to make bombs.

For Truman, the decision to use the atomic bomb was not about science or morality, but about power and politics. Although Hitler's army surrendered in May, thousands of American soldiers were being killed in a series of bloody island-hopping campaigns in the Pacific. Nearly 10 percent of the 70,000 American troops who invaded Iwo Jima in March were killed; another 3,500 died taking Saipan the following July. Still, the military was planning a massive invasion of the main islands in the fall and warned the president that American casualties could top 250,000. In May, a secret Interim Committee made up of scientists and politicians recommended that the administration use the bomb, without prior warning, ideally against a civilian population. The "most desirable target," they concluded, "would be a vital war plant employing a large number of workers and closely surrounded by workers' houses." The goal was "to make a profound psychological impression on as many inhabitants as possible." The bomb offered an added benefit: it could keep the Soviets out of the Pacific war and tame their postwar ambitions in Europe.

On August 6, 1945, Einstein was vacationing at Saranac Lake in New York when he heard the news that the atom bomb had been dropped on Hiroshima. His only recorded reaction was "Oh, Weh [Oh my God]."

* * *

Surely scientists would have eventually cracked the secrets of the atom bomb if Einstein had never written his famous letter to FDR. But it was the combination of Szilard's persistence and Einstein's fame that focused Roosevelt's attention, and the crisis atmosphere of World War II that allowed the government to marshal unprecedented resources behind the Manhattan Project. Einstein later regretted the role he had played in the bomb's development. He had hoped that atom bombs would make wars obsolete, lessen world tensions, and free leaders to focus their limited resources on providing a higher standard of living for their citizens. Instead it produced a nuclear arms race and increased international tensions. "I made one great mistake in my life," he wrote in 1954, just five months before his death, "when I signed the letter to President Roosevelt recommending that atom bombs be made."

It was this "great mistake" that would impact every aspect of American society and culture in the postwar era. Since 1945, the nation has struggled to balance nuclear hopes with nuclear fears. The bomb, which President Truman hailed as "the greatest achievement of organized science in history," also possessed the power to destroy the world. "Seldom, if ever, has a war ended leaving the victors with such a sense of uncertainty and fear," said CBS radio journalist Edward R. Murrow five days after Hiroshima, "with such a realization that the future is obscure and that survival is not assured." A few weeks later the *Washington Post* editorial-ized that the life expectancy of the human race had "dwindled im-measurably."

The bomb transformed America's relationship with the outside world. Since George Washington first warned against "entangling alliances" with Europe, the United States had maintained a healthy distance from the affairs of other nations, especially dur-ing peacetime. That all changed after the Soviets, as Szilard had warned, developed their own bomb in 1949. The threat of nuclear annihilation permanently altered America's role in the world, forcing the nation to abandon its instinctive isolationism and as-sume the responsibilities of a global superpower. In the words of one diplomat, we were forever "deisolated."

The new weapon ignited a heated cold war between the United States and the Soviet Union and set off a costly arms race. The Brookings Institution estimated that the United States alone spent more than $4 trillion (in 1996 dollars) between 1940 and 1995 on its nuclear weapons program. At its peak of production, the United States was making 25 nuclear bombs a day. At any given moment, the president could unleash 3,423 nuclear warheads against targets in the Soviet Union, Eastern Europe, and China. Together these weapons would produce 7,847 megatons of explo-sive force—the equivalent of 600,000 Hiroshimas. The Soviet nu-clear arsenal was just as deadly, if less accurate.

The destructive power of the bomb did force the world's super-powers to deal with their rivalry by peaceful means. The United States and the Soviet Union emerged from World War II with fundamentally opposed world views and strategic goals, but in-stead of producing a new world war, they engaged in a cold peace. Between 1500 and 1945, Europe was the most war-ravaged area on Earth, accounting for nearly two-thirds of all war-related deaths.

After 1945 it was one of the most peaceful. The horrible images of Hiroshima, which deterred the Americans and the Soviets from using what Truman called the "energy of the sun" to settle their differences, helped maintain that peace.

The threat of "mutually assured destruction" (MAD) may have prevented the two superpowers from fighting in Europe, but it did produce a succession of bloody proxy wars in Korea and Vietnam. At home, fears of Communist subversion, skillfully manipulated by demagogues like Wisconsin senator Joseph McCarthy, produced public hysteria and shifted American politics to the right. Cold war anxiety also led to a dramatic increase in government spending. Fears of a Soviet missile landing on an American city convinced the fiscally minded President Eisenhower to approve the largest public works project in American history—the interstate highway program—which, he claimed, was necessary to "permit quick evacuation of target areas." "The ideal" city in the nuclear age, noted a group of scientists, "was a depopulated urban core surrounded by satellite cities and low-density suburbs." Later, President Kennedy used the cold war to justify support for civil rights legislation. How, he asked, could the United States be a beacon of hope for people around the world if we denied basic civil rights to our own citizens?

Although many of the scientists who worked on the Manhattan Project regretted their roles in promoting the arms race, the public hailed them as heroes. Their invention fused science and government in ways unthinkable a few years earlier, turning research scientists into popular icons. By 1964, physicists were held in such high regard that only Supreme Court justices and doctors enjoyed more status among the public. The Manhattan Project also gave birth to a new age of "Big Science": the unprecedented fusing of scientific knowledge, government power, and private money. In Washington, the lesson of the Manhattan Project was simple: bring enough scientists and enough money together, and any problem can be solved. The days of the independent scientist working alone in his private laboratory was gone, replaced by a team of scientists working on multimillion-dollar, government-sponsored research projects. In the 1930s, many prominent scientists refused federal funding because they believed that it would limit scientific freedom. But after World War II, government money flowed freely into private labs and university campuses.

With the coffers overflowing with federal dollars, Big Science took aim at new projects that would transform American life after the war. Scientists launched the first phase of the computer revolution in 1946 when they flipped the switch to start up the mammoth Electronic Numerical Integrator and Computer (ENIAC). This mainframe computer weighed 30 tons, filled an enormous room at the University of Pennsylvania, consumed 150,000 watts of power, and used 18,000 vacuum tubes. The machine required so much power it was rumored that when the scientists turned it on the lights in the city of Philadelphia dimmed. The Defense Department sponsored the creation of this computer for one purpose: to calculate missile trajectories. Over the next twenty years, however, business adopted mainframe computers to handle basic tasks such as automating payroll, billing, and inventory controls. In the 1960s, Defense Department scientists working to develop a decentralized communications system that could survive a nuclear war created the Internet.

The fusing of science, security, and politics raised a myriad of new questions about the health of American democratic institutions. In many ways, the demands of modern science, with its emphasis on expertise, specialized knowledge, and secrecy, are often at odds with the needs of democracy, which requires openness and citizen participation. In his January 1961 farewell address, President Eisenhower gave eloquent expression to those concerns. He worried that cold war fears had produced a "military-industrial complex" that distorted our priorities and transferred decision-making power from the people to "a scientific-technological elite." While his successor, John F. Kennedy, was promising to increase defense spending and escalate the arms race, Eisenhower, the general-turned-statesman, spelled out the hidden domestic costs of the cold war:

> Every gun that is made, every warship launched, every rocket fired signifies, in the final sense, a theft from those who hunger and are not fed, those who are cold and are not clothed. This world in arms is not spending money alone. It is spending the sweat of its laborers, the genius of its scientists, the hopes of its children. The cost of one modern heavy bomber is this: a modern brick school in more than 30 cities. It is two electric power plants, each serving a town with a population of 60,000. It is two fine, fully equipped hospitals. It is some 50 miles of concrete highway. We pay for a single fighter with a half million bushels of wheat. We pay for a single destroyer with new homes that could have housed more than 8,000 people. This, I repeat, is the best way of life to be found on the road the world has been taking. This is not a way of life at all, in any true sense. Under the cloud of threatening war, it is humanity hanging from a cross of iron.

Nowhere has the impact of the atom bomb been greater, and more painful, than in the Japanese city of Hiroshima. On August 6, 2005, Hiroshima marked the sixtieth anniversary of the dropping of the bomb. More than fifty thousand people observed a moment of silence at Peace Memorial Park. The town's mayor issued a "Peace Declaration," calling for the abolition of all nuclear weapons. For residents of this city, the anniversary marked a tragic turn in world history. Yet for many American soldiers who at the time were preparing for the invasion of Japan, and whose lives may have been saved by Truman's decision, the bomb represented a necessary evil. All parties agree that the bomb changed history, but they will continue to debate its ultimate legacy.

For Further Reading

Michio Kaku offers the most readable account of Einstein and his influence in *Einstein's Cosmos* (2005). Fred Jerome reveals J. Edgar Hoover's obsession with Einstein in *The Einstein File* (2002). Many of the scientists who worked with Einstein have either written memoirs or are the subject of excellent biographies. See William Lanouette with Bela Szilard, *Genius in the Shadows* (1997); Eugene Wigner, *The Recollections of Eugene P. Wigner* (1992); Peter Goodchild, *Edward Teller: The Real Dr. Strangelove* (2004).

The starting point for any discussion of the Manhattan Project is Richard Rhodes's masterful *The Making of the Atom Bomb* (1986). Also useful is Robert Jungk, *Brighter Than a Thousand Suns* (1970). On the decision to use the bomb, see Dennis D. Wainstock's *The Decision to Drop the Atomic Bomb* (1996). John Hersey's *Hiroshima* (2nd ed., 1985) remains a powerful telling of the aftermath of the bombing. Paul Boyer's *By the Bomb's Early Light* (1985) investigates the intellectual culture behind the development of the bomb. On the rise of Big Science, see Jessica Wang, *American Science in an Age of Anxiety* (1999).

9

September 9, 1956

When America Was Rocked

E d Sullivan hosted the most popular variety show of the time on television, *The Toast of the Town*, airing at 8 P.M. on Sunday night. Most of the early spots on television went to popular radio personalities—people like Jack Benny and Arthur Godfrey. Sullivan was a forty-six-year-old sports-turned-gossip columnist who wrote a regular piece for the New York *Daily News* called "Little Old New York." His column gave him contacts in the emerging world of television, and CBS executives decided to let him host their new variety show. Sullivan was an odd choice. He lacked the natural good looks common among television personalities—one writer described him as "cod-eyed and cement-faced." His thick neck made him appear perpetually hunched over. Since he suffered from ulcers he often gulped down the pain medication belladonna before going on the air. The medication soothed his ulcers but dilated his pupils, making it difficult for him to read his cue cards, which helps explain why he seemed terminally tongue-tied and often flubbed his introductions. Sergio

Franchi became "Sergio Freako" and he once read "World War II" off a cue card as "World War One One."

Yet Sullivan was a fixture on CBS from June 20, 1948, when he hosted his first "Rilly Big Shew," until he went off the air on June 6, 1971. His first big show featured two young comedians, Dean Martin and Jerry Lewis, who were paid $100 each for their appearance. The program quickly developed a reputation for showcasing the hottest acts. Sullivan featured just about every possible form of entertainment—ventriloquists, bullfighters, puppets (the Italian puppet mouse Topo Gigio set the all-time record for appearances with fifty), along with big-name stars such as Bob Hope, Dinah Shore, and Walt Disney.

Sullivan had one cardinal rule: the acts had to be appropriate for the "family hour." Whether they sang, danced, spun plates, or cracked jokes, all the guests on his show had to be suitable for both adults and children. Thus Sullivan acted as the gatekeeper, the national arbiter of taste, at a time when American culture was going through a period of extraordinary change. *Life* once called him television's "only institution," and David Halberstam gave him the title of "unofficial Minister of Culture in America."

Like many other self-proclaimed guardians of American culture, Sullivan was determined to project an idealized image of American life. The variety show itself, a direct descendant of vaudeville, was based on the idea of a shared national culture—the notion, widely accepted in the 1950s, that Americans were becoming more alike. Whether black or white, male or female, young or old, we were all consumers at heart, and a growing economy promised to make everyone a member of the solid middle class. Between 1940 and 1960, the gross national product (GNP) more than doubled, from $227 billion to $488 billion. The median family income rose from $3,083 to $5,657, and real wages rose by almost

30 percent. Since everyone would enjoy the benefits of a booming economy, no one would have the time or the desire to protest or to challenge the status quo. Surveys showing that 75 percent of Americans considered themselves part of the middle class contributed to the growing sense that the nation was evolving toward a classless society. "Never had so many people, anywhere, been so well off," the satisfied editors of *U.S. News & World Report* concluded in 1957, reaffirming the belief that the American experiment was a model for the rest of the world.

Prosperity and the desire for a better life inspired millions of Americans to move to Levittown, New York—inspired suburbs where all houses looked identical: one story high, with a twelve-by-sixteen-foot living room, a kitchen, two bedrooms, and a tiled bathroom. They were also filling their homes with the same new gadgets. By 1960, 96 percent of the nation's families owned refrigerators, 87 percent their own TV set, and 75 percent their own washing machine. In metropolitan areas across the country, small mom-and-pop stores gave way to mammoth shopping malls on the edges of the cities, which housed national retail chains. Interchangeable motels and fast-food chains materialized nearby. In 1955 an ambitious salesman, Ray Kroc, established a chain of burger joints called McDonald's, which would become the symbol of the fast-food industry. Perhaps more than anything else, Americans were all watching the same television shows with their glossy image of middle-class suburban life where supportive wives spent their days minding the household and the clean-cut kids while their faithful husbands provided for the family and solved the crisis of the day.

The omnipresent shadow of both the cold war and the atomic bomb contributed to the emphasis on conformity. The cold war sharpened the contrast between capitalism and Communism, reinforcing the belief that America stood as a beacon of hope in a troubled world. Church membership and professions of faith became popular methods of affirming "the American way of life" during the cold war. Sales of Bibles reached an all-time high. In 1954 Congress added the phrase "under God" to the Pledge of Allegiance and the next year mandated "In God We Trust" on all U.S. currency. The return to religion found expression in religious songs like "I Believe," and movies like *The Robe* and *The Ten Commandments.*

Despite the efforts to emphasize conformity and consensus, signs of change were everywhere. Between 1940 and 1960, the number of women in the workforce doubled. By 1952, 2 million more women were at work than during World War II. Evidence of changing sexual behavior also challenged the celebration of traditional family life. Alfred Kinsey, an Indiana University zoologist who had previously studied bees, decided to turn his attention to human sexuality. His studies, *Sexual Behavior in the Human Male* (1948) and *Sexual Behavior in the Human Female* (1953), concluded that premarital sex was common and that married couples frequently engaged in extramarital affairs.

Nowhere was the contradiction between ideals and reality more striking than in the lives of African Americans. The South's racially segregated schools formed only one piece in a vast mosaic of institutionalized racism. Wherever one looked in early postwar America, blacks were treated as second-class citizens. In August 1955, Emmett Till, a fourteen-year-old black youth from Chicago visiting relatives near Greenwood, Mississippi, was killed, his mutilated body dumped in the Tallahatchie River, because he allegedly whistled at a white woman. Till's mother insisted on an open casket at the funeral so that, in her words, "all the world can see what they did to my boy." The battered face of Emmett Till was fresh in people's minds when, on December 1, 1955, civil rights activist Rosa Parks intentionally violated Alabama law by refusing to give up her seat to a white person on a city bus in Montgomery. Then twenty-six-year-old Martin Luther King Jr., pastor of the Dexter Avenue Baptist Church, agreed to head the Montgomery Improvement Association (MIA), created to promote and support a boycott of the Montgomery buses. It would be the first of an escalating series of protests that would shatter the walls of segregation in the South.

The most potent change was coming from young people. Because of an unprecedented postwar baby boom, there were more young people in America than at any previous time in history. It was after World War II that the word *teenager* entered the American language for the first time. Postwar prosperity provided America's 13 million teenagers with more money than ever before. American teens now had the purchasing power to taste the fruits of abundance, and to do so without having to seek parental approval. In 1956, teenage income from allowances and part-time jobs reached $7 billion a year. The average teenager had $10 a week to spend in 1958 compared with $2.50 in 1944, and teens spent more than $10 billion a year on products. Teenage girls spent $20 million on lipstick, $25 million on deodorant, and $9 million on permanents. Male teenagers owned 2 million electric razors. Together they spent about $75 million on pop records.

The expansion of public education also contributed to the development of a teenage culture. In 1930, only 50 percent of children aged fourteen to seventeen were students. By 1950, the ratio had increased to 73 percent. In response to the enormous new demand for space, school districts rushed to open new schools and build new classrooms. During the 1950s, California opened one school every week. A high school education was supposed to inculcate middle-class values. But by segregating young people with many others of the same age, universal education gave teenagers the opportunity to develop their own values. "Adolescents today are cut off, probably more than ever before, from the adult society," observed James Coleman in *The Adolescent Society*. "They are dumped into a society of their peers, whose habitats are the halls and classrooms of their schools, the teen-age canteens, the corner drugstore, the automobile."

Writers, directors, and advertisers appealed directly to teenagers' sense of alienation from the adult world. The publication of J. D. Salinger's *Catcher in the Rye* (1951) marked the beginning of the youth culture. The novel traced the thoughts and actions of sixteen-year-old Holden Caulfield, who roams around New York City recording his rejection of the phoniness and corruption of the adult world. In movies like *Rebel Without a Cause,* teen idol James Dean abandons the middle-class values of his parents for the excitement of a lower-class car culture. For many adults a more troubling sign of the emergence of a separate youth culture was the dramatic rise in juvenile delinquency. Between 1948 and 1953, the number of teenagers charged with crimes increased by 45 percent. As early as 1953, the federal government's Children's Bureau predicted that the exploding teenage population would soon produce an increase of 24 percent in car thefts, 19 percent in burglaries, and 7 percent in rapes. The New York *Daily News* reported in 1954 that "rowdyism, riot, and revolt" were the new three *R*s in New York public schools.

That youth culture found its most powerful expression in popular music. A mix of rhythm and blues, country, and white gospel music, this new genre gained enormous popularity among African Americans in the late forties. Because of its association with blacks and its strong sexual overtones, most whites dismissed the new sound as "race music." At the beginning of the decade, it was being recorded only by small record companies and played only on African American radio stations. Pressed by growing teenage demand, major record companies produced white versions of songs originally recorded by black singers. Most white audiences never heard LaVerne Baker's original version of "Tweedle Dee" or "Dance with Me Henry"; instead, they listened to the more acceptable "white versions" by Georgia Gibbs. The genre grew more and more popular every year. In 1955, twelve of the year's top fifty songs were rock and roll, including "Rock Around the Clock," written by two white songwriters and recorded by an all-white group, Bill Haley and His Comets. By the end of the 1960s it had sold 15 million copies and become one of the best-selling singles in history. It was the first rock-and-roll song to gain mass popularity among teens.

In 1951 a white disc jockey named Alan Freed began playing "race music" by Fats Domino and Chuck Berry on his popular Cleveland radio station, renaming it "rock and roll," an urban euphemism for dancing and sex. "How y'all, everybody. This is Alan Freed, king of the Moondoggers . . . Y'all ready to rock 'n' roll?" His white teen audiences loved it and, for the first time, started demanding the original black versions of songs. By bringing "race music" to a white teenage audience, Freed shattered musical barriers and helped begin a national music craze.

Meanwhile, in segregated Memphis, Tennessee, Sam Phillips, owner of tiny Sun Records, was listening to the new genre and hearing the sound of cash registers. "If I could find a white man with the Negro sound and the Negro feel, I would make $1 billion," he said. In the summer of 1953 a nineteen-year-old truck driver named Elvis Aron Presley walked into Sun Records to make a record and changed the course of American pop culture.

Elvis was born in rural Tupelo, Mississippi, on January 8, 1935. He was born thirty-five minutes after his stillborn twin brother, Jesse Garon. They lived in what was called a shotgun shack—so named because theoretically someone could stand at the front door, fire a shotgun, and the pellets would go straight through the back door. His mother had worked a rare factory job before her marriage, and his father—so poorly educated that he sometimes misspelled his name, Vernon, as Vernin—did odd jobs. When Elvis was two, Vernon spent time in jail for trying to doctor a check for a little extra cash. As a child Elvis consumed comic books and found special inspiration in Captain Marvel, with his glistening hair and long sideburns. For his eleventh birthday, his mother gave him a $13 guitar. "I remember Elvis used to carry that ol' gi-tar around," recalled his cousin. "It didn't have but three strings most of the time but he could beat the dickens outta it."

Although he grew up in the segregated South, Elvis was surrounded by black music. In 1948, the Presleys moved to Memphis, where Vernon thought he could secure more steady work. It was there in the urban slums and projects where he lived with poor whites and blacks that Elvis found himself immersed in the music of delta blues, country, and white gospel. In Memphis, WDIA, a fifty-thousand-watt station, broadcast a combination of gospel, blues, and jazz—black artists—to a mixture of black and white homes. Gospel quartets were also popular in Memphis, and Elvis and his then girlfriend had been huge fans of one in particular called The Statesmen. Led by tenor Harvie Lister, the group was sometimes denounced for being too "black-sounding." By his junior year in high school Elvis was wearing a ducktail, applying rose oil tonic and Vaseline to his hair, and growing his sideburns long. He bought his clothes at Lansky's, a store more often frequented by flashy black men. Most of his classmates at Humes

High School found him odd. One recalled that Elvis "had no personality, if you know what I mean. Just acted kind of goofy, sitting in the back of class, playing his guitar. No one knew that he was ever going to be *anything*." After graduating in 1953 he started working at the Precision Tool Company, but he spent his evenings playing music with friends from the local housing project.

Popular myth reports that Elvis Presley went to Sun Records in the summer of 1953 to record a personal record as a birthday present for his mother. It is more likely, though, that Elvis was recording for himself—his mother was born in the spring. Sam Phillips recalled seeing Elvis's Crown Electric Company truck parked outside the studio a number of days before he finally worked up the courage to walk in.

Regardless, he recorded two Ink Spot numbers—"My Happiness" and "That's When Your Heartaches Begin"—for a price of $3.98 plus tax. Marion Keisker, who was working at the studio that day, wrote "Good ballad singer. Hold." next to Elvis's name. "He had a style about him," Phillips recalled about his first impressions of Elvis. "Physically, he had the long sideburns, which was unusual then, and the hair oil that was unconventional." What impressed Phillips most of all, however, "were his eyes, which were very pure." In May or June 1954, Marion Keisker placed a call to the Presley family asking Elvis if he would like to try a new song—"Without You"—that Phillips had picked out for him. Elvis ran the few blocks from his home at 462 Alabama Street to the studio, arriving, as Keisker recalled, "before I had hardly put the phone down." Soon Presley's face was a common sight at the studio.

Sam teamed Elvis up with guitarist Scotty Moore and bassist Bill Black (who were to become his regular band). Together they suffered though Elvis's painful attempts to croon "Without You," and later, "Harbor Lights" and "I Love You Because." The group broke for coffee and "all of a sudden," remembered Scotty Moore, "Elvis started singing a song, jumping around, acting the fool, and then Bill picked up his bass and started acting the fool too, and I started playing with 'em. Sam had the door to the control booth open. . . . He was either editing some tape or something, and he stuck his head out and said, 'What're you doing?' We said, 'We don't know.' 'Well, back it up,' he said, 'try to find a place to start and do it again.'" Elvis, Moore, and Black were performing "That's All Right, Mama," which had been recorded seven years before by Arthur "Big Boy" Crudup. "This song popped into my mind that I had heard years ago," Elvis later remembered, "and I started kidding around with it."

In July, Sun Records released "That's All Right, Mama" with "Blue Moon of Kentucky," a bluegrass waltz that Elvis turned into pop music, on the B side. Phillips distributed them to important Memphis DJs, including "Sleepy-Eyed" John Lepley at WHHM, Bob Neal at WMPS, and Dewey Phillips of WHBQ. "Get yasself a wheelbarrow load of mad hogs, run 'em through the front door, and tell 'em Phillips sentcha," shouted Dewey. "This is Red Hot and Blue comin' atcha from the magazine floor of the Hotel Chisca. And now we got somethin' new gonna cut lost, DEE-GAWWWW! Cut LOOSE! Good people, this is Elvis Presley. . . ."

The stations were flooded with calls from excited teenagers wanting to hear the song, and the single sold several thousand copies in the first few weeks. Phillips was pleased with the reception the music was getting, but realized that he had to cultivate Elvis Presley as a star, too. He wrangled a spot on the program as the warm-up attraction for a Slim Whitman package show on the afternoon and evening of July 30, 1954. The afternoon show went poorly, with Elvis singing only ballads that his then-very-limited fan base had never heard. That evening, however, Elvis performed on the balls of his feet, his lip twisted in a snarl, his legs shaking like an R&B singer. "Everyone was screaming and everything," Elvis remembered in 1956, "and my manager told me they was hollering because I was wiggling." It wasn't that "the Pelvis" had created a completely new way of moving his body—the gyrations for which Elvis is known were common to black clubs, lower-class bars, and strip joints—it was that for the first time, he did it before mainstream audiences.

Though Elvis had achieved celebrity status in Memphis, he was virtually unknown elsewhere. In October he was invited to perform at the Grand Ole Opry. "We don't use nigger music at the Grand Ole Opry," he was told. Presley broke into tears and swore he would never perform again. He quickly recovered and started at the Opry's rival, Louisiana Hayride, which offered him a year-long contract, earning eighteen dollars per show. Elvis quit his day job and began appearing in stage shows in addition to his radio appearances.

In 1955, Sam Phillips sold Elvis's contract to "Colonel" Tom Parker for a record $40,000. Parker, once a carnival barker who promoted dancing chickens, gambled what seemed like a lot of money at the time, but the risk soon made Parker a very wealthy man. Parker arranged Elvis's switch from Sun Records to RCA just as his career started to soar. He broke through completely in 1956 with his hit single "Heartbreak Hotel," which made him a nationwide sensation. In April 1956 he already owned six of RCA's all-time top twenty-five records and was selling $75,000 worth of records a day. Between 1956 and 1958, Presley had ten number-one hit records, including "Heartbreak Hotel," "Hound Dog," "All Shook Up," and "Jailhouse Rock."

Why did Elvis emerge as such a huge star in the mid-1950s? Raw talent alone cannot explain his success. His voice was not unique, his guitar playing was mediocre, and he could not even read music. It was the synthesis of black blues and white country music, the mixing of a white face and poor black music, that made him so unique and so threatening. "Presley is a potent new chanter who can sock over a tune for either country or R&B markets," observed the influential *Billboard* magazine, calling Presley "a strong new talent." What made Elvis truly unique, Phillips believed, was that he was a white man who possessed "the Negro sound and the Negro feel."

Elvis's recording of "That's All Right, Mama" came on the heels of a landmark moment in the history of race in the South—exactly forty-nine days after the *Brown v. Board of Education of Topeka* decision. The *Brown* decision declared segregation in public schools to be illegal, claiming that "in the field of public education the doctrine of 'separate but equal' has no place." The historic decision triggered massive resistance to ending Jim Crow among state and local politicians in the South. Nineteen southern senators and seventy-seven representatives signed a manifesto in 1956 that bound them to "use all lawful means to bring about a reversal of this decision which is contrary to the Court and to prevent the use of force in its implementation." Perhaps stung by the backlash, the court refused to demand an immediate end to segregation. Instead, the following year it required local authorities to show "good faith" and to move with "all deliberate speed" toward desegregation of all public schools.

Ironically, rock was undermining the cultural pillars of segregation at the same time that the courts were attacking its legal underpinnings. In the South, blacks and whites drank from separate water fountains, attended segregated schools, and were even buried in different cemeteries. Only in the music they listened to were they becoming equal. Rock, in other words, promoted a cultural intermingling at a time when social mixing was still illegal. "He was white but he sang black," said Chet Atkins, who helped produce Elvis's early RCA records. "It wasn't socially acceptable for white kids to buy black records at the time. Elvis filled a void." Teens who rushed to the record store to buy Elvis's records were not necessarily trying to make a statement about racial equality, but they were endorsing a new cultural sensibility created by black Americans. Not surprisingly, the White Citizens Council of Alabama saw the link between cultural and political change. It claimed that rock and roll—"Negro music"—was "designed to force 'Negro culture' on the South."

In addition to challenging racial stereotypes at a critical time in the nation's history, Elvis tapped in to the spirit of rebellion among the army of American teens. "Without my left leg, Ah'd be dead," he drawled in 1956. Elvis acted out onstage the hostilities and confusion felt by most teenagers. Under the tutelage of Colonel Parker, he carefully cultivated the image of the sexy rock-and-roll rebel who challenged the sexual and social conventions of the time. He was everything parents feared their children would become—cocky, brash, tough, and, most of all, sexual. Elvis radiated sexual rebellion—from the tight pants, pink silk shirts, eye shadow, ingratiating curling lip, slick hair, and long sideburns to the provocative hip thrusts.

Elvis's rise to prominence coincided with a national panic about juvenile delinquency. The fears led to the creation of a high-profile Senate subcommittee on juvenile delinquency chaired by presidential hopeful Estes Kefauver of Tennessee. One worried parent wrote the committee that Presley's "strip-tease antics threaten to 'rock 'n' roll' the juvenile world into open revolt against society. The gangster of tomorrow is the Elvis Presley type of today."

The more parents objected to rock music, the more young people embraced it as their own. "What is this thing called rock 'n' roll?" wondered the *New York Times*. "What is it that makes teenagers throw their inhibitions as though at a revival meeting? Is this generation of teenagers going to hell?" *Look* magazine asked whether rock was "music or madness?" "Smash the records you possess which present a pagan culture and a pagan concept of life," advised *Contacts*, the Catholic Youth Center newspaper. Summing up the prevailing view at the time was Frank Sinatra, who was quoted as saying that rock 'n' roll was "sung, played and written for the most part by cretinous goons, and by means of its almost imbecile reiteration and sly, lewd, in plain fact dirty, lyrics it manages to be the martial music of every side-burned delinquent on the face of the earth."

For the guardians of public morality, Elvis was even more threatening and dangerous because his challenge was so covert. He did not smoke or drink, he was both religious and patriotic, and always respectful to his parents. He was always "yes-ma'aming" and "no-siring" everybody. Elvis was a polite revolutionary whose coupling of southern gentility with rebellious music forged a safe middle ground between hedonism and holiness.

* * *

It was only appropriate that Presley would use television to bring his message of rebellion to the masses. Although television had been invented in the 1920s, it did not gain widespread acceptance until the 1950s. Mass production and technological advances in the 1950s allowed most American families to own a set. The size of the screen expanded from twelve inches to nineteen and twenty-one inches; even as color was introduced in 1953, the cost of the sets declined from $700 in the late 1940s to as little as $200 by 1955. In 1946, about one of every eighteen thousand people owned a TV set. By 1960, nine out of every ten American homes had a TV.

Television worked hard to reinforce an idealized image of American life. Most shows avoided controversy and celebrated traditional American values. Families were intact, men worked during the day, women stayed at home. No one was ever sick. No one was poor. African Americans were absent from TV's fictions. "We never had any blacks on television," said a casting director for CBS. Shows like *Ozzie and Harriet, Father Knows Best,* and *Leave It to Beaver* presented glossy images of middle-class suburban life. Millions gathered around the television set each week to watch as Superman, a comic book hero turned television star, fought for "truth, justice, and the American way."

In January 1956 Elvis made his television debut on Tommy and Jimmy Dorsey's *Stage Show,* a family-oriented program produced by comedian Jackie Gleason for CBS-TV to draw viewers to his sitcom *The Honeymooners.* "He's a guitar-playing Marlon Brando," Gleason said of Presley. Elvis followed the June Taylor Dancers, who opened *Stage Show* every week, and cautiously made his way through "Shake, Rattle and Roll" and "I Got a Woman," while members of the audience either screamed or applauded. Overall, he seemed anxious and uncomfortable in his first television appearance. While he gave the show a ratings boost, *The Perry Como Show* still won in the ratings that night. Elvis would make six more appearances on *Stage Show* over the next seven weeks, each performance generating more excitement and in turn a larger audience. By his fifth appearance, Presley was more comfortable with the camera and with the screaming audience, dancing seductively through the whole performance of "Heartbreak Hotel."

After the Dorsey brothers threatened to walk off if Elvis was invited back to *Stage Show*, the Colonel arranged for him to appear on *The Milton Berle Show*. So on June 5, 1956, Elvis opened with "Hound Dog" in a pale checked jacket, dark pants, polo shirt, and white socks. He straddled the microphone and swayed seductively while his audience screamed. As Presley slowed the tempo to sing the chorus for the last time, he turned sideways so the audience saw him in profile, rested his hand near his crotch, and thrust his pelvis. It was hardly subtle. "If he did that on the street," one L.A. policeman observed, "we'd arrest him." The show was so successful that Milton beat out *The Phil Silvers Show*, a competitor in its time slot, for the first time that season.

The appearance on *The Milton Berle Show* produced high ratings, but it further outraged many critics. Ben Gross of the New York *Daily News* claimed that "[popular music] has reached its lowest depths in the 'grunt and groin' antics of one Elvis Presley." *Time* was no kinder, observing that Elvis's body "takes on a frantic quiver, as if he had swallowed a jackhammer." *TV Scandals* sputtered, "What's most appalling is the fans' unbridled obscenity, their gleeful wallowing in smut." *America,* the Catholic weekly, minced no words with an article titled "Beware Elvis Presley." "If the agencies (TV and other) would stop handling such nauseating stuff," the paper continued, "all the Presleys of our land would soon be swallowed up in the oblivion they deserve."

However, it was becoming clear that despite the complaints of parents and critics, Elvis Presley was the ticket to higher ratings and greater advertising dollars. In June 1955, NBC launched a new variety show hosted by Steve Allen to compete directly with Ed Sullivan. Initially, Allen hoped to capitalize on Presley's popularity, booking him to appear on July 1 for $7,500. But he started to equivocate when Elvis's popularity seemed overshadowed by notoriety. "There has been a demand that I cancel him from our show," Allen told his audience in June. "As of now he is still booked for July 1, but I have not come to a final decision on his appearance. If he does appear, you can rest assured that I will not allow him to do anything that will offend anyone." An NBC spokesman assured viewers that "we think this lad has a great future, but we won't stand for any bad taste under any circumstances."

On the night of the July broadcast Allen awkwardly introduced Elvis to his audience. "Well, you know," he said, "a couple of weeks ago on *The Milton Berle Show*, our next guest, Elvis Presley, received a great deal of attention, which some people seem to interpret one way and some viewers interpret it another. Naturally, it's our intention to do nothing but a good show. . . . We want to do a show the whole family can watch and enjoy, and we always do, and tonight we're presenting Elvis Presley in his, heh heh, what you might call his first comeback." In reality, Allen wanted Elvis for the ratings but he did not want any of the controversy, so he removed any hint of sexuality or rebellion from Elvis's performance. Elvis walked onstage wearing a top hat and white gloves and looking very uncomfortable. "Elvis, I must say you look absolutely wonderful," Allen said. "You really do. And I think your millions of fans are really going to get kind of a kick seeing a different side of your personality tonight."

The opening number, "I Want You, I Need You, I Love You," went well enough but "Hound Dog" proved embarrassing for performer and audience alike. Allen had Elvis sing to a hound dog dressed in an identical tuxedo. Elvis played along as best as he could, circling the microphone around when the dog looked away, picking her up when she trembled, and doing his best to be a good sport about it all, but this was not the Elvis that teenagers loved.

The Monday after this performance, Ed Sullivan called his friend Mary Smith at the Trendex rating service. "Presley's done you in," she told him. "He racked up 20.2. You had 14.8." Publicly Sullivan continued to assert that Elvis is "not my cup of tea." When a reporter called to get his reaction to Allen's ratings victory, Sullivan insisted that one Sunday did not make an entire season, and he continued to assert that Presley was unsuitable for family viewing. He would not compromise his high standards for a few ratings points. A few hours later, however, Sullivan was on the phone with Colonel Parker negotiating the biggest deal in the history of his show. Unable to stem the tide of demand and fascination with this emerging megastar, Sullivan signed Elvis to an unprecedented three-appearance deal for $50,000. He explained his change of heart by saying that after watching a tape of Presley perform, he had come to the belated realization that the singer was not really undermining public morality. In reality, competition had forced his hand. "Presley is the hottest thing in television right now," Sullivan admitted. "I guarantee we'll have the biggest audience in our eight years of experience when he comes on."

Elvis's first appearance on Sullivan's show, scheduled for September 9, was one of the most hotly anticipated events in the brief history of the new medium of television. *TV Guide* marked the occasion by placing Elvis on its cover wearing a gray striped blazer and a white collared shirt, singing into a boom microphone, a lock of his hair falling in his face. The "controversial rock 'n' roll singer who is presently the idol of the teenage world, headlines tonight's show," it announced.

Sullivan was recovering from an automobile accident on September 9 when Elvis Presley made his first appearance, so he good-naturedly sent Sullivan a get-well card and a picture autographed to "Mr. Ed Sullivan." Oscar-winning actor Charles Laughton filled in for Sullivan. Since Elvis was in Hollywood making a movie, *Love Me Tender,* he taped his performance at the CBS studio in Los Angeles. The other networks all expected Elvis to garner huge ratings. NBC simply conceded that CBS was going to win in ratings that evening and showed a movie.

Laughton introduced Presley to the national audience as "Elvin Presley." Standing alone onstage wearing a loud plaid jacket, Elvis opened with a subdued version of his hit "Don't Be Cruel." Then Elvis introduced a brand-new song, which would be "completely different from anything we've ever done. This is the title of our brand-new Twentieth Century Fox movie and also my newest RCA Victor escape—er, release." Shrugging at the audience's laughter, Elvis launched into "Love Me Tender." All was pretty tame until he started rocking to Little Richard's "Ready Teddy," which Elvis ended with two verses of "Hound Dog." The studio audience of teenage girls screamed at every pelvic gyration, but the audience at home never saw Elvis dance: the camera pushed away just as he started to move. The *Philadelphia Inquirer* would later joke that Sullivan got only half what he paid for.

The show lived up to everybody's expectations, reaching 82.6 percent of the television audience. Estimates suggest that four out of five television sets were tuned in to Elvis's first performance on *The Ed Sullivan Show,* garnering the highest ratings in television history—a record toppled only when the Beatles appeared on the show in 1964. Disc jockeys all over the country taped the show and played "Love Me Tender" on the air, forcing Elvis to rush the release of the single three weeks later.

The response was predictable: record sales soared and critics pounced. "Mr. Presley has no discernible singing ability," wrote legendary *New York Times* critic Jack Gould. "His specialty is rhythm songs which he renders in an undistinguishable whine; his phrasing, if it can be called that, consists of stereotyped variations that go with a beginner's aria in a bath tub. For the ear he is an unutterable bore, not nearly so talented as Frank Sinatra back in the latter's rather hysterical days at the Paramount Theater." The Reverend William Shannon wrote in the *Catholic Sun* that "Presley and his voodoo of frustration and defiance have become symbols in our country, and we are sorry to come upon Ed Sullivan in the role of promoter." A disc jockey in Ann Arbor, Michigan, started an "I Hate Elvis!" Club, which included membership cards with the inscription "He makes me feel surgical—like cutting my throat." *Rolling Stone* was closer to the truth when it observed in its history of rock and roll: "The night Elvis appeared on 'Toast of the Town,' civilization threw in the towel."

* * *

Elvis Presley's performance that night on *The Ed Sullivan Show* lasted only a few minutes, but it symbolized the emergence of a new youth culture that would transform American culture and politics in the postwar era. Elvis Presley was the Trojan horse of that new youth culture. At the beginning of the decade, there was a limited range of cultural options for young people. They were encouraged to wear the same style clothing, watch the same television shows, listen to the same music, and admire the same people—General MacArthur, Joe DiMaggio—as their parents did. Elvis helped forge a wider range of cultural options by creating a musical style that appealed directly to the taste and sensibility of young people. Now, while their older brothers and sisters were still swooning over Doris Day and Perry Como, rebellious teens were twisting their hips to the beat of "Jailhouse Rock."

Ironically, Ed Sullivan, the gatekeeper of traditional values, would give legitimacy to the youth revolt by placing his seal of approval on Presley and, later, the Beatles. "I just want to say to you and the nation that this is one decent, fine boy," he told his audience following Elvis's final performance on January 6, 1957. By the end of 1956, 68 percent of music played by disc jockeys was rock and roll, an increase of two-thirds over the previous year.

Elvis's shrewd manager, Colonel Parker, successfully exploited the power of television to turn Elvis into more than just a music idol. Merchandisers scrambled to put Presley's picture on every conceivable product intended for the teen and preteen market. By the end of 1957, seventy-eight Elvis Presley–related items had brought in $55 million. Elvis made personal appearances in department stores to sell fluorescent portraits, shoes, skirts, blouses, T-shirts, sweaters, charm bracelets, handkerchiefs, purses, pencils, soft drinks, Bermuda shorts, blue jeans, toreador pants, pajamas, and pillows.

Elvis's appearance on *The Ed Sullivan Show* opened other venues for rock and roll to reach mainstream culture. In August 1957, *Bandstand* made its debut on 67 stations as a daily national afternoon dance party program. The show premiered locally on Philadelphia's WFIL in 1952 and was hosted by DJ Bob Horn. In 1956, Horn was fired after being arrested for drunk driving. His replacement was the young, clean-cut Dick Clark, whose only previous experience was reading Tootsie Roll commercials on Paul Whiteman's *TV Teen Club*. Within a month, *Bandstand* was America's top-ranked daytime show and the only place where viewers could watch popular rock and roll, week after week. "In those days, you had Ed Sullivan and Steve Allen doing variety shows and they had no room for a Bill Haley or the Penguins singing 'Earth Angel,'" noted Clark. Before it came to an end thirty-seven years later, Clark had hosted 650,000 dancing teens, 10,000 lip-synching musical guests, and reached millions of mostly female viewers. *American Bandstand* would have more influence over rock and roll than any other source.

Elvis obscured the old distinctions between high and low culture and instead created a new democratic culture—much to the dismay of established authorities. At the beginning of the decade, a few popular singers like Perry Como and Frank Sinatra held broad appeal, but most radio stations played to the musical tastes of a specific segment of the market. Educated whites tuned in to classical stations; rural whites listened to country and western music; middle-class whites kept to pop; blacks to jazz or rhythm and blues. Elvis played the key role in breaking down these self-imposed musical barriers. By the end of the decade, white audiences were rushing to record stores to buy the original black versions of songs. *Billboard* magazine noted that "race music" was "no longer identified as the music of a specific group, but can now enjoy a healthy following among all people, regardless of race and color." Radio stations and record companies now featured black artists. Little Richard sang, shouted, danced, gyrated, and sweated profusely through "Tutti Frutti." Antoine "Fats" Domino, less threatening to whites than Little Richard, belted out songs such as "Blueberry Hill" (1956) and "Whole Lotta Loving" (1958). Chuck Berry, who was known for his famous "duck walk" across the stage, hit the charts with "Roll Over Beethoven" (1956) and "Johnny B. Goode" (1958).

Americans voted for the new culture of democracy at their local record stores. In 1950, Americans purchased 189 million records; by the end of the decade that number had soared to more than 600 million. Teenagers accounted for nearly 70 percent of all record sales. In 1956 alone, Elvis Presley sold more than 3.75 million albums. The development of the transistor radio, which sold for as little as $25, helped boost record sales by allowing the new music to penetrate deep into teen culture. The Elvis Presley model sold for $47.95—teens could put down $1 and then pay $1 a week. By the end of the decade, American companies were selling 10 million transistor radios a year. This radio ran on regular flashlight batteries and was small enough to fit in a woman's handbag.

Not everyone embraced the new culture of democracy. Critics viewed it as an assault on traditional standards that would inevitably lead to a "dumbing down" of American culture. In 1957 the editor of the *Richmond News Leader* wrote sarcastically, "If so many like something, it must be good. . . . To which we say, Humbug." A democratic spirit was fine for politics, where everyone should have an equal voice, but culturally some forms of expression were clearly superior to others and rock blurred those distinctions. He went on to complain that "one of the chief disadvantages of democracy is that in order to insure political equality, it is forced to go along with the myth of intellectual and cultural equality. They are in no way related. The virtues of the one do not extend over the other."

Much to the dismay of the *Richmond News Leader*, technology, especially television, had obliterated the barrier separating politics and culture. Music played a critical role in that process. The cultural mixing of black and white helped break down racial barriers and lay the foundation for the political success of the civil rights movement of the 1960s. "In a real sense you have paved the way for social and political change by creating a powerful, cultural bridge between black and white," Martin Luther King told a gathering of black DJs in 1967. "You introduced youth to that music and created a language of soul and promoted the dances which now sweep across race, class and nation."

Once he started making movies in the late 1950s, Elvis seldom challenged the conventions of his own stardom. He created a musical genre that soon surpassed him, leaving him behind in B movies and an increasingly isolated cultural bubble until his premature death in 1977 at the age of forty-two. In the years since his death Elvis has been transformed into a cultural myth. His Graceland mansion, which opened to visitors in 1982, is the second most visited home in the country. Only the White House receives more visitors. Even now, more than two decades after his death, there are thirty-five thousand registered Elvis impersonators in the United States and his record sales have topped 1 billion globally. The official Elvis postage stamp is the best-selling commemorative stamp issued by the U.S. Postal Service.

But his legacy is secure. Elvis did more than sell records—he defined an era. He gave voice to a youth revolt that touched off a social revolution in the 1960s and 1970s. The generation that came of age in the 1950s—the Elvis generation—loosened social mores about sex and drugs and challenged all forms of authority. In the 1950s, teens made American culture more democratic; in the 1960s they would turn their attention to making the nation's political institutions more responsive to their needs. These same questioning, skeptical, and self-aware teenagers swelled college campuses, transforming the 1960s into a decade of social experimentation and government activism. In the late sixties, American composer and conductor Leonard Bernstein would call Elvis Presley "the greatest cultural force in the twentieth century." Elvis "introduced the beat to everything and he changed everything—music, language, clothes, it's a whole new social revolution—the

Sixties comes from it. Because of him a man like me barely knows his musical grammar anymore." John Lennon once observed, "Before Elvis there was nothing."

For Further Reading

Peter Guralnick's two-volume biography of Elvis offers the most thoughtful and detailed analysis of the rock star's rise and fall: *Last Train to Memphis: The Rise of Elvis Presley* (1994) and *Careless Love: The Unmaking of Elvis Presley* (1999). Albert Goldman provides a controversial look at the darker side in *Elvis* (1984). David Halberstam provides an insightful portrait of Elvis in his entertaining *The Fifties* (1993). The history of rock and roll is examined in Craig Werner, *A Change Is Gonna Come: Music, Race, and the Soul of America* (1998) and James Miller's *Flowers in the Dustbin* (1999). *Rolling Stone* magazine's *Rock of Ages* is probably the best one-volume study of the history of rock.

On the role of teens in the cold war era, see Grace Palladino's *Teenagers* (1996) and Thomas Hine's *The Rise and Fall of the American Teenager* (2000). Lynn Spigel's *Make Room for TV* (1992) considers the transformation wrought by television on family life, as does Karal Ann Marling's *As Seen on TV* (1994). Steve Gillon examines the long-term impact of the generation in *Boomer Nation* (2004).

10 June 21, 1964
Freedom Summer

One morning my son Andrew kissed me good-by and went off to fight for freedom," wrote Mrs. Robert Goodman. "I never saw him alive again. As any mother who has lost a son in battle knows, this is a terrible thing to bear." Mrs. Goodman's son, Andrew, was a twenty-year-old Queens College anthropology major when he died on June 21, 1964. He did not fall on foreign soil and he was not killed by enemy fire. Andrew was murdered by members of the Ku Klux Klan on an isolated road in rural Mississippi. His death, along with those of his two companions, Michael Schwerner and James Earl Chaney, would help change the future of race relations in America.

America's national self-image has always rested on the assumption that it is a democratic nation. We all learned that the thousands of soldiers who died in the carnage at Gettysburg in 1863 fell so that government "of the people, by the people, and for the people" would not perish. Most Americans certainly would have agreed with the influential political writer Herbert Croly, who wrote in 1909 that the United States was a "Land of Democracy," a nation "committed to the realization of the democratic ideal." But perhaps the most striking example of the gap between American ideals and social realities is the fact that, when Croly made his statement, fewer than half of all Americans possessed the right to vote. The nation took a big step toward narrowing that gap in 1920 when, after a seventy-year campaign by suffrage supporters, Congress passed and the states approved the Nineteenth Amendment to the Constitution, granting women the right to vote. That amendment nearly doubled the size of the electorate.

There was one group that was systematically barred from participating in the American ritual of voting: African Americans. Following World War II a combination of forces began undermining the pillars of racial segregation in the South. In 1954 the Supreme Court overturned the legal justification for one of the principal pillars of white supremacy in *Brown v. Board of Education of Topeka, Kansas*. The following year, a forty-two-year-old civil rights advocate named Rosa Parks challenged Alabama's segregation laws when she refused to give up her seat on a city bus to a white person. Her simple act of courage sparked the Montgomery Bus Boycott, which demonstrated that intimidation could no longer repress black aspirations.

Younger blacks, impatient with the slow pace of change and convinced that more aggressive tactics could force the government to take bolder action to redress existing wrongs, set the tempo of change in the 1960s. Late in the afternoon on Monday, February 1, 1960, four well-dressed black students sat down at a segregated lunch counter at a Woolworth's department store in Greensboro, North Carolina, and ordered a cup of coffee. The next day, twenty-seven black students occupied the Woolworth's lunch counter; on Wednesday, sixty-three. By Friday, more than three hundred protesters jammed the store and the nearby Kress's five-and-dime. As news of the sit-ins reached other cities, the protest spread "like a fever." By the end of 1960, more than seventy thousand people in more than 150 southern cities and towns had participated in protests. In April 1960, these younger, more militant protesters formed the Student Nonviolent Coordinating Committee (SNCC).

At the same time members of the Congress of Racial Equality (CORE) challenged racial segregation in interstate transit. By 1960 the Supreme Court had barred racial segregation in bus and train stations, airport terminals, and other facilities related to interstate transit. But southerners widely ignored these decisions. In May 1961 seven black and six white "freedom riders" left Washington on two buses headed for Alabama and Mississippi. "Our intention," declared CORE national director James Farmer, "was to provoke the southern authorities into arresting us and thereby prod the Justice Department into enforcing the law of the land." Over the next few months more than three hundred Freedom Riders were arrested.

Many black leaders believed that racism would never be overcome until blacks exercised political power. In 1964, only two million of the South's five million voting-age blacks were registered to vote. The Fifteenth Amendment, passed almost a century earlier, had guaranteed the right to vote, but Washington let the states decide the qualifications for voting. In the South, states developed sophisticated and effective measures to deny voting privileges to blacks. Seven states used literacy tests, which allowed registrars to deny blacks the ballot if they misspelled a word in their application. Five states employed a "poll tax," which effectively disenfranchised poor blacks and poor whites. Alabama required blacks to be accompanied to the polls by white citizens who would "vouch" for their character. When laws failed to keep blacks off the rolls, whites often resorted to physical violence and economic intimidation.

Mississippi had been especially clever in developing methods to disenfranchise blacks. In 1955, the legislature abolished the practice of satellite registration, which allowed blacks to register in their local precincts. Now they needed to travel, often long distances, to register at the county courthouse—the symbol of white "justice" in the South. The small number of blacks who had managed to register before 1955 had to "reregister" under the new rules. Instead of a literacy test, the state developed a more difficult "understanding test," which often required black applicants to answer questions about obscure state regulations. Mississippi's poll tax of $2 was among the highest in the South.

This was a state frozen in time. Relations between the races had changed little since the end of the Civil War. After a brief window of opportunity during Reconstruction, the state's white leadership rewrote the constitution in 1890, denying blacks all rights of citizenship. While most of the South had turned to mechanized forms of cotton production, Mississippi still relied on cheap black labor. For that reason, blacks in Mississippi tended to be more rural and more disenfranchised than anywhere else in the South. Black family income in Mississippi in 1960 was the lowest in the nation: Nearly 86 percent of black families lived below the poverty line. Neither education nor politics offered a way out. Only 7 percent of blacks had completed high school and even fewer were registered to vote. The state had five counties where blacks made up a majority of residents. The five counties combined did not have a single registered black voter.

The state's political leadership was determined to keep things that way, and was willing to use violence to keep blacks in their place. Many of the state's leading politicians were Klan members or sympathizers; others were simply demagogues. Governor Paul Johnson Jr. referred to the National Association for the Advancement of Colored People as "Niggers, Alligators, Apes, Coons and Possums." Not surprisingly, it was also the most violent southern state. Blacks who had the audacity to register to vote often found their names on Klan death lists. "Violence and police brutality still have the upper hand in Mississippi," lamented Medgar Evers, a civil rights organizer who was later murdered by a white supremacist.

In 1964, SNCC organized a voting rights campaign in Mississippi, where only 5 percent of blacks were registered to vote. The campaign was the brainchild of Robert Moses, a Harvard-educated philosophy student who traveled to Mississippi to organize local blacks to overthrow the repressive system of Jim Crow. Moses was born and raised in a poor family in Harlem. "We struggled to make ends meet," he reflected, "but we also had a very strong family life." After graduating from Stuyvesant High School, he attended Hamilton College, a small liberal arts college in upstate New York. After graduating in 1956, he went to Harvard to earn a graduate degree in philosophy. But two years into graduate school a family crisis interrupted his studies. His mother died and his father had an emotional breakdown. Moses dropped out of school, returned home, and supported himself by teaching mathematics at a prep school. He was "mesmerized" by the pictures of young blacks challenging the white supremacy of the South that appeared on the front page of the *New York Times*. During his spring break from teaching Moses decided to go to the South to see the sit-ins firsthand. He called his uncle, an architect living in Virginia, and asked if he could come down and observe the sit-ins taking place at Newport News. "I joined their picket lines and discovered a genuine feeling of release," he reflected.

In 1961, he joined SNCC and traveled to Mississippi for the first time. The experience changed his life. At the end of the next school year he returned to Mississippi to head SNCC's voting rights campaign. He was a man of contradiction within SNCC: an adult surrounded by young people; a quiet, contemplative man surrounded by activists; a philosopher leading a political movement. In his quiet, unassuming way he would emerge as one of the most inspirational figures in a movement filled with inspired leaders. "There was something about him, the manner in which he carried himself, that seemed to draw all of us to him," reflected fellow activist Cleveland Sellers. "He had been where we were going. And more important, he had emerged as the kind of person we wanted to be."

Most of the major civil rights organizations in the South were headquartered in Atlanta and sent volunteers into urban areas. Moses saw a need for civil rights organizing in rural areas where many of the poorest blacks lived, so he set up an office in McComb, Mississippi. Under an umbrella organization, the Council of Federated Organizations (COFO), SNCC teamed up with CORE and the NAACP to launch its voting rights campaign. SNCC workers endured repeated beatings and murders, but had little success getting the attention of either the White House or the national media for their efforts to gain the vote for blacks. In two years, SNCC managed to add only four thousand names to the voting rolls in Mississippi.

Deadlocked, Moses proposed that the group invite well-connected white students from the North to join the struggle. If they suffered the same brutal treatment as blacks, he reasoned, the nation would take notice. "These students bring the rest of the country with them," he told fellow members of SNCC. "They're from good schools and their parents are influential. The interest of the country is awakened and when that happens, the government responds to that issue." According to Mary King, inviting northern white students was, unfortunately, the only way to get the nation to focus on their plight. "With that double standard and racism of the news media that found whites more newsworthy than blacks—we hoped to attract human and material resources and bring the case of black people living in a vestigial system of slavery to the attention of the nation and the world."

Not everyone agreed with the strategy. Many black activists feared that liberal whites would be unable to develop the trust of rural blacks and that interracial teams would only antagonize local whites and produce more violence. They also worried that well-educated northern students would try to assume leadership positions in the organization. Moses, however, insisted that the drive for voter registration should be an integrated effort and the participation of white students was essential for their success. In the spring of 1964, COFO set up recruiting centers at Yale, Harvard, the University of Illinois, Oberlin College, the University of Oregon, Stanford University, and the University of North Carolina.

*   *   *

Andrew Goodman fit the profile of the typical application for the "Freedom Summer" program. Like the nearly nine hundred other applicants, he was an idealistic, liberal white student who was wealthy enough to forgo a summer of paid employment. This was not his first involvement in liberal causes. In 1958, he had attended a Youth March for Integrated Schools in Washington, D.C., organized by Bayard Rustin and CORE. In December of his senior year of high school, Goodman and a friend took a Greyhound bus to study poverty in Appalachia. After high school he tried his hand at theater and originally enrolled in the theater arts program at local Queens College. Like much of the nation, however, he watched the images of blacks demanding equal access to the American dream being assaulted by fire hoses and billy clubs. "This is terrible," he told his mother, reflecting the youthful idealism of the time. "We're living in what is supposed to be a democracy, and they're not allowed to vote."

In June, Andrew traveled to a SNCC orientation session for 750 summer volunteers at the Western College for Women in Oxford, Ohio. Andrew arrived on the campus late on the night of June 13. Like the other volunteers he was photographed and handed forms to fill out. The training sessions consisted of small gatherings where volunteers learned details about their assignment and general assemblies where they were given instructions on how to protect vital organs when attacked and how to develop relationships with the local black community. "Don't come to Mississippi this summer to save the Mississippi Negro," Moses warned the volunteers. "Only come if you understand, really understand, that his freedom and yours are one." A civil rights attorney gave the volunteers some practical advice. "If you're riding down somewhere and a cop stops you and starts to put you under arrest even though you haven't committed any crime— go on to jail," he advised. "Mississippi is not the place to start conducting constitutional law classes for policemen, many of whom don't have a fifth-grade education." At one of the assemblies, John Doar, a sympathetic representative of Robert Kennedy's Justice Department, informed them of the limits of federalism. "There is no federal police force," he said. "The responsibility for protection is that of the local police. We can only investigate." After the speech, many students complained that the federal government was abdicating its responsibility to provide protection. Later, in the privacy of their rooms, some cried.

Among those leading the training session were veteran SNCC field workers from Mississippi, known as "jungle fighters." Andrew quickly developed a friendship with two of the veterans. Michael Schwerner, twenty-four, was a stocky, goateed social worker from lower Manhattan known by the local Mississippi Klan as "the Jew boy." He and his wife, Rita, had been active in the civil rights movement in the North, participating in protests in Baltimore and New York City. The 1963 bombing of the Sixteenth Street Baptist Church in Burmingham, Alabama, that claimed four young lives convinced the couple to devote themselves completely to the civil rights movement—and that meant going south. In January 1964 they gave away their cocker spaniel, Gandhi, sublet their apartment, and made the long trip from Brooklyn to Mississippi. Because of Michael's background and training, Moses gave him the responsibility to build a community center in Meridian, where he would teach blacks to read and register to vote. Schwerner scored his first victory when he organized a boycott to force Bill's Dollar Store, where large numbers of blacks shopped, to hire a black woman who had been trained at the center.

Working in Meridian, the Schwerners quickly became friends with a twenty-one-year-old local black man, James Earl Chaney, who traveled with them to the orientation session in Ohio. An oldest child, James, or J. E., as his family called him, had his first experience in the civil rights movement in 1959 when, at the age of sixteen, he started a campaign to wear yellow NAACP buttons to his local high school. When he refused the principal's request to remove them, the school suspended him for a week. The following year, he was expelled after being accused of starting a fight in gym class. The principal told him he was "no good" and "would never amount to anything." Rejected by the army because of asthma, James bounced around in odd jobs until a former schoolmate introduced him to CORE, where he worked briefly as a volunteer. "Mama, I believe I done found an organization that I can be in and do something for myself and somebody else, too," he said. In April, Rita and Mike made Chaney a full-time staff member. "We believe that since he long ago accepted the responsibilities of a CORE staff person, he should be given now the rights and privileges which go along with the job." In June, the couple invited Chaney to accompany them to Ohio to attend the training sessions.

During the training sessions in Ohio, Schwerner spent time with Andrew Goodman and was immediately struck by his maturity and commitment—two of the qualities he needed in his community. "We were impressed with what a decent, bright, and self-controlled person he was, and how he didn't have to fall all over himself to prove how much he loved Negroes," said Rita. Schwerner invited Andy to work with him on his project in Meridian. Initially, Andy said no, claiming that he was already committed to working on a project in Canton, Mississippi. A few days before leaving for his assignment, however, word reached Ohio that the Klan had pistol-whipped an aging parishioner and then burned down the Mount Zion Methodist Church in Neshoba County, Mississippi. Just a few weeks earlier, Schwerner and Chaney had visited the church, and the all-black congregation had invited them to set up a community center. The burning was clearly an act of retaliation—a common Klan tactic. In 1964 alone, twenty black churches in Mississippi were firebombed. Realizing there was a greater need for his services in Meridian, Goodman changed his assignment. He would be going back to Mississippi with Schwerner and Chaney.

On Saturday, June 20, Goodman, Chaney, and Schwerner, along with four others, piled into a blue station wagon for the sixteen-hour drive to Meridian, Mississippi. They left at 3:30 A.M. to avoid driving in Mississippi in the dark. Goodman had no idea what was waiting for him.

Many Mississippi whites viewed the Freedom Summer of 1964 as a foreign invasion. The *Clarion Ledger*, Jackson's segregationist crier, blamed "Communist forces," claiming "the ultimate aim, we believe, is a black revolution." The mayor of Jackson purchased shotguns and ordered a thirteen-thousand-pound armored personnel carrier to fend off the invaders. The city police force was expanded from 200 to 390. The Klan used white fear of Freedom Summer to recruit dozens of new members, including many local law enforcement officials. Even before the arrival of the students, the Justice Department reported Klan violence in Mississippi at "alarming proportions." Because of internal fighting over money and power, the Klan in Mississippi divided into two groups: the United Klan with about seventy-six klaverns and the White Knights with another fifty-two. Early in the morning of June 7, 1964, members of the White Knights met in the long-abandoned Boykin Methodist Church. "Fellow klansmen, you know why we are here," declared Sam Bowers Jr., a local businessman and the first imperial wizard of the White Knights. "We are here to discuss what we are going to do about COFO's nigger-communist invasion of Mississippi which will begin within a few days."

Schwerner, Goodman, and Chaney arrived in Meridian late on Saturday night and slept for a few hours before leaving early the next morning to inspect the damage at the Mount Zion church, interview witnesses, and reassure local blacks. Before leaving, Schwerner explained to the volunteers in the office what precautions were required whenever anyone traveled to Neshoba County. "There's an immutable rule here: 'no-one is to remain in Neshoba [County] after four P.M.' If for any reason we aren't back by four P.M., you should alert [the COFO office in] Jackson and begin checking every city jail, county jail, sheriff's office, police station and hospital between Meridian and Neshoba."

On Sunday, June 21—Father's Day—the three men made the forty-five-minute drive to Meridian, arriving early in the afternoon at the home of Ernest Kirkland, a local supporter who agreed to help identify possible witnesses. Kirkland got into the back of the station wagon and drove with the men to the burned-out church. There was not much left—the metal bell, some charred hymnals, and twisted steel from what had once been the roof. The group then went to secure affidavits from some of the eyewitnesses before returning to Kirkland's house later that afternoon. Mrs. Kirkland offered Chaney a piece of homemade chocolate cake. After about thirty minutes, Schwerner said, "Now we've got to get back to Meridian."

There were two routes home. They had driven that morning on Highway 491. Going home, they decided to drive to Philadelphia, Mississippi, and pick up Highway 19. It added about twenty minutes to the drive, but with the Klan so active in the area, the men knew not to travel the same road twice in the same day. Also, Highway 491 was a narrow clay road that could easily be blocked while Highway 19 was a paved two-lane road with wide shoulders. With Chaney at the wheel, they started the drive around 3 P.M., which would get them home in time for their self-imposed curfew.

While driving back to Meridian they were stopped for "speeding" by Philadelphia's deputy sheriff, Cecil Price. The sheriff immediately recognized the goateed Schwerner, who was on a Klan death list. Instead of giving the men a ticket, Price escorted them to the local jail. Price told them that Justice of the Peace Leonard Warren would have to set the speeding fine and they would stay locked up until he could find the judge. Price was stalling for time: There was a list of fines for speeding and other traffic violations posted in the jail. He used the extra time to contact the leader of the Neshoba County Klan, Edgar Ray Killen, who doubled as a preacher. Price held the men in jail long enough for Killen to organize a posse of Klan members at the Longhorn Café. Among the members of the posse was Wayne Roberts, a burly ex-Marine, dishonorably discharged for fighting and drunkenness. He had been calling for Schwerner's murder for months. Now he would have his chance.

Around 10 P.M. Price told the three workers they could go. All they needed to do was post a $20 cash bond. They put up the money and a little after 10:30 P.M. the three young men left Philadelphia thinking they were finally out of danger. What happened next is told primarily through the dry testimony of FBI informants, which fails to capture the horror the men must have experienced on that hot and humid night.

After being released, they were recaptured after a hundred-mile-per-hour chase by Deputy Sheriff Price and two carloads of armed Klansmen. The Klansmen ambushed the car and took the three to an isolated spot on Rock Cut Road. "Are you that nigger lover?" Wayne Roberts is said to have demanded of Schwerner. "Sir, I know just how you feel," Schwerner replied. With that, Roberts shot him in the heart. Next, Roberts shot Goodman, execution style, with a single .38-caliber bullet through the head.

"Save one for me!" shouted Klansman James Jordan, running over to Chaney and shooting him in the stomach. Roberts then fired into Chaney's back and head. They also brutally beat him. A doctor said that in his twenty-five years he had "never witnessed bones so severely shattered." "Ashes to ashes, dust to dust," the Klan chanted as they carried out the executions. "If you'd stayed where you belonged, you wouldn't be here with us."

The three bodies were then tossed into the station wagon and driven along dirt roads to a farm about six miles southwest of Philadelphia, where a local businessman was digging a cattle pond. This seemed like the perfect place to bury bodies so they could never be discovered. The first step in building a pond is to create an earthen dam by digging a ditch thirty feet wide, five or six feet deep, and a hundred or more feet long. The ditch is then filled with packed red clay, which hardens and prevents water from seeping out. Once the clay base is in place, dirt is piled on top until it reaches the necessary height. On the night of the murders, the red clay had been packed into place but no dirt had been laid on top. The three men were tossed into the ditch, facedown, lying side by side. Goodman and Schwerner were lying head to head; Chaney was in the opposite position. One of the killers used a bulldozer to cover the bodies with about two feet of dirt. Over the next few weeks more dirt was added until the dam stood at more than eighteen feet.

To confuse investigators, the murderers left the burned-out station wagon fifteen miles northeast of Philadelphia on the edge of Bogue Chitto Swamp, forcing authorities to begin their search by dredging the swamp. The bodies were buried six miles southwest of Philadelphia, nearly twenty-one miles from where they left the car. The hope was that by the time authorities had wasted weeks searching the rivers and swamps, the earthen dam would be covered with grass and the bodies would never be found. Dredging the swamps in summertime was difficult and dangerous work. "It tickles the hell out of me," one of the murderers said, "just to think of old J. Edgar's boys sweatin' out there in that swamp, with all them chiggers, water moccasins and skeeters." The Klansmen then went home, certain that proof of their crime would never be found.

Back in Meridian, the local SNCC workers grew worried when they did not hear from the three workers. Mary King began telephoning every jail and detention center in the counties surrounding Philadelphia. Using a pseudonym of Margaret Fuller of the *Atlanta Constitution*, she telephoned every police headquarters, each sheriff's office, and the mayors of smaller towns in the six-county area, to ask if they were holding the three men. She hoped that by pretending to be a reporter she could provide some protection to the workers. One of the first calls was to Deputy Sheriff Cecil Price, who denied having the three in his custody.

By the next morning, veterans of the Freedom Summer project feared the worst—Schwerner, Chaney, and Goodman had become the first martyrs of the movement. And tragically, Moses's strategy was working. These civil rights workers were not like others who had been killed—two of them were white. Washington politicians and New York journalists suddenly cared a great deal about the missing civil rights workers. The parents of the missing children were able to bring pressure on Washington. They arranged private meetings with both President Johnson and Attorney General Robert Kennedy. No president ever had to worry about appearing insensitive to the grieving parents of black children in the South. Privately, Johnson complained that meeting with the parents of the civil rights workers would establish a dangerous precedent: "I'm afraid that if I start house-mothering each kid that's gone down there and that doesn't show up, that we'll have this White House full of people every day asking for sympathy," the president told his deputy attorney general in a secretly taped phone call.

Now, pressured by intense media attention, Johnson not only met privately with the grief-stricken parents, he personally provided them with regular updates about the investigation, and rushed before the cameras to assure the nation that the government would use every resource at its disposal to solve the mystery. A White House official even assured Mrs. Goodman that her son's death was "a turning point in the battle over civil rights."

The day after the three workers went missing, Attorney General Robert Kennedy authorized the FBI to get involved in the search, sending 140 agents to Philadelphia. The FBI justified involvement in the search under the so-called Lindbergh law of 1934, which made it a federal crime to take a kidnapped person across a state line. The law assumed that anyone missing twenty-four hours after a suspected kidnapping had been taken across state lines. A few days later, a hundred sailors from the nearby Meridian naval air station arrived, joined a few days later by another hundred.

Many local blacks looked at the massive dragnet with a mix of anger and amazement. African Americans had been going missing for more than a century in the South and the federal government had looked the other way. FBI director J. Edgar Hoover had never shown much enthusiasm for investigating white violence against local blacks, but now that two of the victims were from well-connected white families, he was pulling out all the stops in finding the murderers. While the search for the bodies and the killers would unite the nation in support of greater civil rights protections, it increased racial tension within the southern civil rights movement and marked the beginning of the end of the integrated effort to end Jim Crow. It underscored a painful reality for many blacks living in the South: The press and public cared only when a white person was killed. "We all know that this search with hundreds of sailors is because Andrew Goodman and my husband are white," said Rita Schwerner. "If only Chaney were involved, nothing would've been done."

Searchers found the station wagon two days later at Bogue Chitto Swamp, the tires burned off, the windows blown out. But there were no bodies. Over the next forty-four days, hundreds of FBI agents swarmed over the area and journalists from around the world suddenly discovered the reality of southern "justice." While searching for the three workers, FBI agents came across other bodies they weren't seeking, including a four-year-old boy, never identified, wearing a CORE T-shirt, and two men—all black and all apparently victims of Klan justice.

The search focused worldwide attention on segregation—just as Moses had hoped. Polls showed a majority of the public wanted the government to send troops to Mississippi. A number of newspapers, including the *New York Times,* black newspapers like the *Baltimore Afro-American* and the *Atlanta Daily World,* and even southern moderate papers like the *Atlanta Constitution* and the *Arkansas Gazette,* favored federal intervention to protect the rights of southern blacks. Despite the pressure, the Johnson administration was unwilling to ask Congress for a voting rights bill. The last thing the president wanted to do was to alienate the white southern base of the Democratic Party in an election year. His opponent, Arizona senator Barry Goldwater, was already picking up white votes with his strong states'-rights rhetoric. Johnson wanted to get civil rights demonstrations out of the news until after the election. If he could win an electoral landslide and bring with him large majorities in both houses of Congress, he would consider the bill. But first things first; and for Johnson that meant winning the election.

If the Klan's goal in killing these men was to frighten or intimidate students from coming to Mississippi that summer, they failed. The *New York Times* reported that the murders had not dissuaded the four hundred students attending the second week of COFO training sessions. "I expected things like that to happen," said a volunteer from New Jersey, "but this makes it real, knowing those young people were here last week."

"I'm more determined to go ahead," said an Indiana student. "This proves something needs to be done." On Monday, June 29, the *New York Times* reported that some 300 student volunteers, undeterred by the horror of the Schwerner-Chaney-Goodman murders, had entered Mississippi, joining the 145 already there. Before summer's end, the paper reported, another 300 would arrive.

But without the bodies, the state's arch-segregationist senator James O. Eastland dismissed the whole incident as a "publicity stunt," speculating at one point that the three workers were vacationing in Cuba with their comrade Fidel Castro. In a secretly recorded phone call he assured the president that no harm could have come to them. "There's not a Ku Klux Klan in that area; there's not a Citizen's Council in that area; there's no organized White man in that area, so that's why I think it's a publicity stunt," he declared in his thick Mississippi Delta accent. His views reflected popular opinion in the Deep South. "You just don't know how those people operate," said the editor of the local *Neshoba Democrat*. "They'll do anything to raise money. This is just the kind of hoax they'll pull on us and then we get all the publicity for it." Americans for the Preservation of the White Race (APWR) circulated a bulletin in Philadelphia repeating the hoax claim, and urging whites not to cooperate with the FBI investigation: "The racial agitators and governmental communists have now launched their summer offensive in Mississippi. After failing to be able to generate any large scale street riots due to the quick-thinking, alert Mississippi Law Enforcement Officials and the cooperation of citizens, special deputies and auxiliary police, they have shifted their tactics." APWR called the tactic the "persecution hoax." They accused the civil rights activists of killing their own members, or arranging for their "disappearance" in order to justify federal intervention. "If these National Police were sincere Americans they would insist that something be done about the treason in Washington, rather than the communist directed incidents in Mississippi," they concluded.

A break in the case finally came on July 31 when a paid informant, whose identity was so secret the FBI refused to reveal his identity to the attorney general, told investigators that the missing men were buried under an earthen dam on Olen Burrage's farm. FBI agents obtained a search warrant, secured heavy earth-moving equipment, and began tearing down the dam. On Tuesday, August 4, they found the decaying bodies of Michael Schwerner, James Chaney, and Andrew Goodman beneath fifteen feet of dirt. Goodman had a ball of clay squeezed tightly in his hand, suggesting that he was still alive when he was buried in the makeshift grave.

During the summer of 1964 perhaps only the presidential campaign received more coverage than the search for the bodies of the three civil rights workers. The day after the bodies were discovered, however, the story was pushed off the front pages by word of a Vietnamese attack on American destroyers in the Gulf of Tonkin.

Before the summer ended, opponents of Freedom Summer had burned or bombed thirty-five houses, churches, and other buildings. "It was the longest nightmare I have ever had," recalled one organizer. Despite daily beatings and arrests, the volunteers expanded their program to challenge the state's lily-white Democratic organization. They formed their own Mississippi Freedom Democratic Party (MFDP) and elected a separate slate of delegates to the 1964 Democratic National Convention. To underscore both their outrage and their commitment to change, Freedom Summer veterans stood outside the convention hall in Atlantic City, New Jersey, with placards reading: CHANEY, SCHWERNER, GOODMAN. They were determined to make sure that the rest of the nation knew why it was necessary for the Democratic Party to abandon its segregationist past and embrace an integrationist future.

On August 22, the convention's credentials committee listened to the MFDP's emotional appeal: "Is this America, the land of the free and the home of the brave, where we are threatened daily because we want to live as decent human beings?" asked Fannie Lou Hamer, the daughter of sharecroppers who had lost her job and been evicted from her home because of her organizing efforts. When the regular all-white delegation threatened to walk out if the convention seated the protesters, Johnson feared the controversy would hurt his election in the South. "If you seat those black buggers," Texas governor John Connally warned, "the whole South will walk out." In response, the president offered the dissidents two at-large seats and agreed to bar from future conventions any state delegation that practiced discrimination. The Freedom Democrats rejected the compromise. "We didn't come all this way for no two seats," protested Hamer, but in the end, Johnson and his liberal allies prevailed and the convention voted to accept the compromise.

The "compromise" at Atlantic City angered many blacks who

no longer felt they could achieve justice through the system, pushing many toward more militant politics. The radical Stokely Carmichael believed that the defeat of the MFDP challenge indicated the need for racial power. The experience showed "not merely that the national conscience was generally unreliable but that, very specifically, black people in Mississippi and throughout this country could not rely on their so-called allies."

"Things could never be the same," SNCC's Cleveland Sellers wrote. "Never again were we lulled into believing that our task was exposing injustices so that the 'good' people of America could eliminate them. We left Atlantic City with the knowledge that the movement had turned into something else. After Atlantic City, our struggle was not for civil rights, but for liberation."

In many ways, Freedom Summer marks the dividing line between the hope and idealism of the early 1960s and the discord and dissent that followed. Freedom Summer can be seen as a breeding ground for the social turmoil that would consume the nation for the rest of the decade. The murders of the three civil rights workers confirmed the wisdom of Moses's strategy, but it also angered many African Americans who resented that the nation paid attention to Mississippi only when white people were killed. After 1964, whites were no longer welcome to participate in the local struggle. Two days after the bodies were found, Congress passed the Gulf of Tonkin Resolution, giving President Johnson a blank check to wage war in Vietnam. No longer welcomed in the South, the army of radicalized, liberal students returned to their northern college campuses with a new cause to fight.

*   *   *

There is little doubt that the intense media attention during the summer of 1964 helped change the state of Mississippi. According to one SNCC member, "After '64, Mississippi became a part of America." Curtis Wilkie, a *Boston Globe* columnist who started his career as a reporter at the *Clarksdale Press Register* in Mississippi, noted that the murders "served as the catalyst for an awakening and a long, redemptive process that is still at work in Mississippi." When Martin Luther King visited Philadelphia in 1966, he called it "a terrible town, the worst I've seen." Four years later, Philadelphia's schools were integrated. Blacks, whites, and Choctaw Indians then ate together in Philadelphia's restaurants and sat next to one another at the Ellis Theater, the town's only cinema.

Highlighting the brutality of southern racism, these murders set the stage for America's "Second Reconstruction." Southern whites had always used violence to suppress their black population, but now television cameras projected into the homes of millions of Americans disturbing images of police dogs mauling elderly black women and fire hoses knocking innocent children to the ground. Since 1955, when blacks boycotted the Montgomery bus system to protest segregation in public transportation, television worked to undermine public support for the southern power structure. Martin Luther King's brilliant strategy of nonviolent confrontation highlighted the compelling moral contrast between peaceful blacks demanding basic American rights and a violent white political leadership determined to deny them those rights. The daily news coverage of the three murders in the summer of 1964 focused public outrage like never before, adding momentum to the relentless drive for civil rights legislation.

Two months later, Lyndon Johnson signed the Civil Rights Act of 1964, the most far-reaching law of its kind since Reconstruction. At its heart was a section guaranteeing equal access to public accommodations. It also strengthened existing machinery

for preventing employment discrimination by government con-
tractors and empowered the government to file school desegregation suits and cut off funds wherever racial discrimination was
practiced in the application of federal programs.

The following year, after his landslide victory against Barry
Goldwater in the presidential election, Johnson demonstrated in
dramatic fashion that Chaney, Goodman, and Schwerner had not
died in vain. On March 7, 1965, black leaders organized a fifty-
four-mile march from Selma, Alabama, to Montgomery to petition Governor Wallace for protection of blacks registering to vote.
On the other side of the Edmund Pettus Bridge, which crosses the
Alabama River, a phalanx of sixty state policemen wearing hel-
mets and gas masks awaited the marchers. After a few tense minutes, the patrolmen moved on the protesters, swinging bullwhips
and rubber tubing wrapped in barbed wire. The marchers stumbled
over one another in retreat. The images, shown on the evening
news, horrified the nation and finally pushed the administration
to support a powerful new voting rights bill.

On August 6, 1965, in the President's Room of the Capitol,
where 104 years earlier Lincoln had signed a bill freeing slaves impressed into the service of the Confederacy, Johnson signed into
law the Voting Rights Act of 1965. With a statue of Lincoln to his
right, Johnson reflected on when blacks first came to Jamestown
in 1619. "They came in darkness and chains. Today we strike away
the last major shackles of those fierce and ancient bonds." Johnson
closed by invoking the words of the civil rights movement itself,
telling the hushed chamber and a television audience of 70 million
that "it is really all of us, who must overcome the crippling legacy
of bigotry and injustice. And we *shall* overcome."

The Voting Rights Act, which authorized federal examiners to
register voters and banned the use of literacy tests, permanently

changed race relations in the South. Not surprisingly, the most dramatic result was in Mississippi. In 1965, just 28,500 blacks, a mere 7 percent of the voting-age population, had been registered; three years later, 250,770 blacks were registered. Between 1964 and 1969, the number of black adults registered to vote increased from 19.3 percent to 61.3 percent in Alabama and from 27.4 percent to 60.4 percent in Georgia.

The killings also forced the FBI to take an aggressive stand against racial violence in the South. After initially moving slowly to respond to the crisis, the FBI soon switched gears and initiated a campaign to eradicate the Klan. FBI director J. Edgar Hoover declared war on the Klan, using the same techniques he had used so successfully against the Communist Party in the 1940s and 1950s, and would also use later against antiwar protesters. He ordered implementation of the Counterintelligence Program (COINTEL-PRO) to "expose, disrupt and otherwise neutralize the activities of the various Klans and hate organizations, [and] their leadership adherents." The program infiltrated groups, developed informants, spread false rumors about financial indiscretions, and employed a range of other measures to disrupt Klan organizations. By 1965, nearly 70 percent of all new members joining the Klan were FBI informants. By the end of that year, the FBI made up 15 percent of Klan membership in the state, including many high offices in the organization. Across the South, the FBI had nearly two thousand informants inside the Klan. But despite the FBI's vigorous campaign to stamp out the Klan, small cells continued to terrorize the South. In 1967 a synagogue and a rabbi's home in Jackson were bombed, and the following year, seven black churches and a synagogue in Meridian were bombed. By 1968, the public had grown tired of the violence, robbing the Klan of the local support and sympathy that it needed to survive. Combined with the active federal campaign to stamp them out, Klan membership dropped from its peak of between five and six thousand to fewer than five hundred.

That "redemptive process" also included bringing justice to the killers. On Friday, December 4, 1964, the FBI arrested twenty-one men for the murders. The government charged nineteen under a Reconstruction-era federal law (U.S. Code, Title 18, Section 241) with conspiring to violate the constitutional rights of the three civil rights workers, which carried a maximum penalty of a $5,000 fine and a ten-year imprisonment. The other two men were charged with refusing to disclose information about the crime.

In 1967, the defendants stood trial in Mississippi before an all-white, working-class federal jury. The government's case rested primarily on the testimony of FBI informants who had identified nine of the defendants as Klan members and stated that Edgar Ray "Preacher" Killen had bragged about killing the three civil rights workers. Justice Department attorney John Doar, who once warned volunteers that Washington could not protect them, summed up the government's case, arguing that "a secret organization was formed, the White Knights of the Ku Klux Klan," to kill Schwerner, who "was hated and despised." To return a not guilty verdict, Doar said, was "to say that there was no night-time release from jail by Cecil Price; there were no White Knights; there are no young men dead; there was no murder. If you find that these men are not guilty, you will declare the law of Neshoba County to be the law of the State of Mississippi." Defense attorney H. C. Watkins played on the local sympathy of the jury, claiming that "Mississippians rightfully resent some hairy beatnik from another state visiting our state with hate and defying our people. It is my opinion that the so-called workers were not workers at all, but low-class riffraff."

In October 1967 the jury delivered its verdict. Seven defendants were convicted, receiving sentences of between four and ten years. Eight were acquitted. Killen and two others had mistrials because one member of the jury refused to convict "a man of the cloth." None faced murder charges and none served prison terms of more than six years. But the judge was satisfied that the punishment fit the crime. "They killed one nigger, one Jew and a white man—I gave them all what I thought they deserved," he said. Although far short of justice, the verdicts did represent an important step forward. The convictions were the first ever in Mississippi for the killing of civil rights workers. The *New York Times* called the verdict "a measure of the quiet revolution that is taking place in southern attitudes." Goodman's mother pronounced the verdict "a landmark decision. This reflects the changes that have occurred in the south," she said.

In the long run, a new generation of political leaders, prosecutors, and activists have come of age determined to overturn the wrongs of the past. One of those leaders is the journalist Jerry Mitchell, whom the *Atlanta Constitution* dubbed a "red-headed, Southern-fried Columbo." After graduating from college Mitchell started working at small newspapers in Texas and Arkansas. Motivated by a deep Christian faith and a strong sense of social justice, he decided to turn his investigative skills to investigate civil rights. "It says in Psalms, 'God loves justice,'" he said. "It's a part of who we Christians are. I don't think God ever intended for someone to walk away from a murder."

Oddly enough, Hollywood helped ignite Mitchell's interest in the murder of the three civil rights workers. In 1989, he watched the movie *Mississippi Burning*. The popular and controversial movie starred Gene Hackman and Willem Defoe as FBI agents tracking down the murderers. Critics complained that the movie glorified the role of the FBI, but it put the case back on the radar screen. "There's a scene in the movie where the black kids are marching and holding American flags in their hands and the sheriff runs into the crowd and starts snatching them out of their hands," Mitchell recalled. He asked Bill Minor, a local reporter who covered Mississippi during those years, whether that scene was accurate. "And Bill Minor said, 'That really happened, but it happened right after Medgar Evers was killed.' That was the beginning of an education for me."

After seeing the movie, Mitchell devoted himself to examining the unsolved cases of the period. His major breakthrough came when he stumbled on the once-secret files of the Mississippi State Sovereignty Commission. Founded in 1956, the agency spied on anyone involved in efforts to integrate the state. The files contained some eighty-seven thousand names and details of many of the Klan killings of the era. The agency existed until 1977, when it was finally disbanded, and its files were sealed until 1998. Mitchell managed to get access starting in 1989.

Over the next few years, using materials from the files, Mitchell wrote a series of exposés that forced local authorities to take a closer look at some of the unsolved murders from the tumultuous 1960s. In 1989, the state reopened the investigation into the 1963 murder of NAACP official Medgar Evers. In 1994, a jury convicted former Klansman Byron De La Beckwith. In 1998, another Klan leader, Sam Bowers, was convicted for ordering the 1966 firebombing that killed NAACP leader Vernon Dahmer in Hattiesburg, Mississippi. In 2002, Bobby Frank Cherry was convicted for the 1963 bombing of a Birmingham, Alabama, church that killed four little girls.

In the course of his investigation, Mitchell discovered that Sam Bowers had bragged in an interview with a Mississippi state archivist that the Klan member responsible for the murder of the three civil rights workers had never been caught. "Everybody knows who I'm talking about," Bowers said. Mitchell later determined that that man was Edgar Ray Killen. In 2005, the new investigation resulted in the seventy-nine-year-old preacher being tried for murder, proving that, as William Faulkner once wrote, "The past is never dead. It's not even past." A balding, frail man, Killen spent most of the trial hooked up to a breathing tube. But prosecutors reminded the racially mixed jury of his terrorist past, claiming that he had arranged for the three men to be picked up by police and then handed over to a Klan posse.

Forty-one years to the day that the three men went missing, the jury found Killen guilty and the judge sentenced him to three consecutive twenty-year prison terms, one for each victim. "Each life has value," the judge said, "and each life is equal to other lives. There are three lives involved in this case, and three lives should be respected." Rita Schwerner Bender, Schwerner's widow, sat in the front row for the entire trial. "Mississippi has taken one small step for mankind," she said after the verdict. Chaney's younger brother, Ben Chaney, hugged Bender after the verdicts were read. "When I was growing up in Meridian, there was a lot of laughter in our house. But for forty-four days in 1964, we didn't laugh. We only cried," Chaney said. "Now my mother feels like she's happy. The life of her son has some value."

Carolyn Goodman, Andrew's eighty-nine-year-old mother, often studied a painting of her son that hangs in her Manhattan apartment. "It was Andy in the morning of his life," she says. "I still think of him that way." In June she traveled from New York to Mississippi to be in the courtroom, to face Killen, but also to keep her son's memory, and his idealism, alive. Andrew, James Chaney, and Michael Schwerner were reluctant martyrs in the nation's ongoing struggle to realize the full promise of American democracy. "Andy's grandfather always told him to be a doer," she told reporters after the verdict. "Andy was that kind of person. He believed in the Constitution and that people had rights."

Those rights have expanded dramatically since the early days of the republic. Passage of the Voting Rights Act in 1965 effectively extended the franchise to all groups in America. In 1971, the Twenty-Sixth Amendment to the Constitution lowered the voting age from twenty-one to eighteen. The gradual expansion of the franchise from white men of property, to all white men, to women, and finally to African Americans, came about through years of hard work and sacrifice. Those who fought to gain the right to vote often risked their lives and their livelihood to force the nation to live up to its democratic ideals. The plaque that hangs just inside the door of the rebuilt Mount Zion Church in Mississippi offers an appropriate epitaph to those three civil rights workers, and to the countless, and often nameless, others who gave their lives expanding and strengthening the foundation of American democracy:

OUT OF ONE BLOOD GOD HATH MADE ALL MEN
THIS PLAQUE IS DEDICATED TO THE MEMORY OF

MICHAEL SCHWERNER
JAMES CHANEY
ANDREW GOODMAN

* * *

WHOSE CONCERN FOR OTHERS, AND MORE PARTICULARLY
THOSE OF THIS COMMUNITY, LED TO THEIR EARLY
MARTYRDOM. THEIR DEATH QUICKENED MEN'S
CONSCIENCES AND MORE FIRMLY ESTABLISHED JUSTICE,
LIBERTY AND BROTHERHOOD IN OUR LAND

For Further Reading

The best treatments of the murders can be found in William Bradford Huie's *Three Lives for Mississippi* (1965) and in Seth Cagin and Philip Dray's *We Are Not Afraid* (1988). John Dittmer's history of the civil rights movement in Mississippi, *Local People* (1994), reveals the commitment and grit of ordinary people that sustained an extraordinary social movement. Doug McAdam's *Freedom Summer* (1988) studies the impact of SNCC's watershed moment on a generation of activists. Clayborne Carson's *In Struggle* (1981) offers the definitive history of SNCC.

For an excellent overview of the civil rights movement, see Robert Weisbrot's *Freedom Bound* (1991). Len Holt's *The Summer That Didn't End* (1965) describes the racial awakening of Mississippi's black population during Freedom Summer. Mary Aickin Rothschild's *A Case of Black and White* (1982) looks at the motivations of the white volunteers who went south in 1964. David Garrow offers the best account of Selma and its impact in *Protest at Selma* (1978). The Miller Center at the University of Virginia has assembled a number of primary sources, including the recordings of private phone conversations between President Johnson and many of the participants. See http://www.whitehousetapes.org/exhibits/miss_burning/text.

Epilogue

A s each of these days reveals, the fabric of our national past is rich, diverse, and full of surprising twists and turns. A pacifist scientist, Albert Einstein, was instrumental in the creation of the world's most destructive weapon—a nuclear bomb. In a misguided effort to preserve the "southern way of life," a group of white racists murdered three civil rights workers, but their actions focused the national spotlight on the brutality of southern racism and forced federal intervention. Secular thinkers like Clarence Darrow celebrated their symbolic victory over Christian fundamentalism in the Scopes trial, but their actions actually made the movement stronger, determined to fight another day. Workers at Homestead seized the Carnegie steel mill in order to preserve workers' rights, but their defeat signaled the triumph of business and set back organized labor for a generation. In perhaps the most tragic irony, English settlers destroyed native cultures in order to create a nation devoted to liberty, individual rights, and democracy.

In one way or another, each of the days chronicled in this book and in the series on The History Channel underscores our nation's ongoing struggle to live up to the ideals of the American Creed—that abstract constellation of shared beliefs in individual rights, equality, and democracy. The days marked important changes in our nation's history. In some cases that change was immediate and tangible. Daniel Shays' rebellion led directly to calls to create a new constitution. The discovery of gold in California resulted in the largest mass migration in American history. The bloody battle at Antietam altered the course of the Civil War, and the assassination of William McKinley elevated Theodore Roosevelt to the presidency. Einstein's letter set in motion a chain of events that led directly to the American effort to build a nuclear bomb. In other cases, however, the impact, though real, was more symbolic. In retrospect, the Puritan victory at Mystic marks an important moment in the transfer of power in North America from native peoples to European settlers. The crushing defeat of workers at Homestead symbolizes the emergence of industrial power in America, while Elvis's appearance on *The Ed Sullivan Show* represented the emergence of a new youth movement in the 1960s.

Whether real or symbolic, these days changed the nation but they did not resolve the fundamental tensions at the heart of American democracy. Daniel Shays inspired the constitutional framework that has governed the nation for more than two centuries, but his revolt failed to resolve basic questions about the scope of government's power. The Civil War battle at Antietam saved the Union and allowed Lincoln to issue his Emancipation Proclamation, but it left unresolved the fate of the former slaves. The assassination of William McKinley allowed Teddy Roosevelt to assume the presidency at a critical time in the nation's history.

But while he established the United States as a great military power, Roosevelt provided little practical guidance on how the nation should use its new strength and influence.

Now, in our modern era, the issues facing our country have changed, but we are still struggling with many of the same questions. The sacrifice of Civil War soldiers, the campaigns of suffrage advocates, and the determination of civil rights workers helped guarantee basic freedoms, like the right to vote, for all Americans. But today, apathy and cynicism keep many people from exercising that right. The continuing debate over affirmative action suggests that the clash between minority rights and majority rule remains unresolved. Since the first contact with native peoples in the seventeenth century, the nation has struggled to incorporate racial and ethnic minorities into the mainstream of American society, and in many ways continued the practice of marginalizing Native Americans. The massive wave of immigrants that flooded American cities after 1965 has raised new questions about the nation's racial and ethnic identity and intensified debate about who really deserves to be called an "American." The recent controversies in many states including Kansas and Pennsylvania about adding "intelligent design" to classroom teachings about the origins of life reveals that the Scopes trial did not end the debate over the proper role of religion in American society. An earlier generation of parents who watched Elvis on *The Ed Sullivan Show* were shocked by the decline of community standards. Many of the screaming teens of the 1950s, who once rebelled against their parents' authority, are now parents themselves and fret about their children being exposed to images of sex and violence on television and on the ubiquitous Internet.

There have been many turning points in our country's past, and some events are considered more historically significant than the days discussed here. While the signing of the Declaration of Independence, the assassination of Abraham Lincoln, and the attack on Pearl Harbor changed the nation in numerous and important ways, they also did not resolve the tensions at the heart of our great democratic experiment. After all, being an American is not about resolving questions or conflict; it's about engaging in the constant struggle to live up to the lofty but unfulfilled ideals the founders set for the nation. "The idea of the search is what holds us together," noted historian Daniel Boorstin. "The quest is the enduring American experiment. The meaning is in the seeking."

Acknowledgments

I could not have completed this book without the help of a talented team of research assistants: Tash Smith, Mike Barnett, George Milne, Anna Bostwick, and Sterling Fluharty from the University of Oklahoma, and Steve Sachs of the University of Florida. I am indebted to University of Oklahoma president David Boren, provost Nancy Mergler, deans Robert Griswold and R. C. Davis-Undiano, and associate dean Carolyn Morgan, for giving me the freedom to work on this book. My agent, Esther Newberg, helped find the project an appropriate home at Crown, where Carrie Thornton provided valuable editorial assistance.

At The History Channel, I am indebted to Carrie Trimmer for her patience in sorting through the sometimes complicated licensing agreements, and to executive producer Susan Werbe, who skillfully balanced the demands of producers, historians, and network executives. As always, I am grateful to Abbe Raven for her friendship, encouragement, and support. Abbe has been a mentor to me, and she has been the driving force behind the success of The History Channel and the recent revitalization of A&E. Projects as big as this require the input and hard work of far too many people to list here, but I would like to mention a few: Lynn Gardner, Mike Mohamad, Tim Nolan, John Verhoff, Anthony Giacchino, Anne Atkinson, and Charlie Maday.

A special word of thanks to The History Channel president-USA, Dan Davids, who gave me the opportunity to write this book. There are few people who care more about The History Channel, or have devoted more effort and energy to its success, than Dan Davids. I appreciate the confidence that he has shown in me and the many opportunities he has made possible. I have promised to give him the very first copy of this book. Hopefully, that will allow him to bury an old bone.

All of us at The History Channel and A&E have been privileged to work for Nick Davatzes, who retired as CEO of A&E Television Networks (AETN) in 2004 after twenty-one years at the helm. It is appropriate that a book about American identity would be dedicated to Nick, who embodies the finest qualities of the American character. He is a successful businessman who has never lost touch with his humble roots. A tough ex-marine who talks about tolerance and compassion. A man of conservative temperament who welcomes change and embraces diversity. Nick not only helped create both A&E and The History Channel, he set an example of principled leadership and personal integrity that will shape the company for years to come.

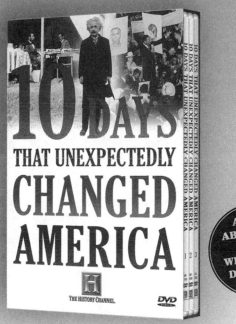

Shays' Rebellion. Antietam. The Scopes Trial.
Experience these events through THE HISTORY CHANNEL® presentation
of *10 Days That Unexpectedly Changed America*, collected on 3 DVDs.

Offering a fresh perspective on the American experience,
10 award-winning documentary filmmakers present 10 pivotal moments
in US history and the often unexpected changes they triggered.

FEATURING THE WORK OF ACCLAIMED DIRECTORS

Joe Berlinger
R.J. Cutler
Kate Davis & David Heilbroner
Michael Epstein
Rob Epstein & Jeffrey Friedman
Barak Goodman & John Maggio
Rory Kennedy
James Moll
Bruce Sinofsky
Marco Williams

THE HISTORY CHANNEL.

ALL PRODUCTIONS IN ASSOCIATION WITH FOR THE HISTORY CHANNEL®
SUPERVISING PRODUCERS FOR @RADICAL.MEDIA GREG SCHULTZ & SIDNEY BEAMONT
EXECUTIVE PRODUCER FOR THE HISTORY CHANNEL SUSAN WERBE   CO-EXECUTIVE PRODUCER JOE BERLINGER